Why Theatre Education Matters

Understanding Its Cognitive, Social, and Emotional Benefits

Thalia R. Goldstein

Foreword by Ellen Winner

TEACHERS COLLEGE PRESS
TEACHERS COLLEGE | COLUMBIA UNIVERSITY
NEW YORK AND LONDON

Published by Teachers College Press,® 1234 Amsterdam Avenue, New York, NY 10027

Front cover light image by Matthew Jungling via Unsplash; curtain by Florin Capilnean via Pexels.

This work was partially funded by several grants from the National Endowment for the Arts to the author (1910339-38-22; 1881377-38-20; 1844329-38-C-18; 17-3800-7003). All information herein is the opinion of the author and not reflective of the opinions of the National Endowment for the Arts.

Library of Congress Cataloging-in-Publication Data

Names: Goldstein, Thalia R., author. | Winner, Ellen, writer of foreword.
Title: Why theatre education matters : understanding its cognitive, social, and emotional benefits / Thalia R. Goldstein ; foreword by Ellen Winner.
Description: New York, NY : Teachers College Press, 2024. | Includes bibliographical references and index.
Identifiers: LCCN 2024005590 (print) | LCCN 2024005591 (ebook) | ISBN 9780807769980 (paperback ; acid-free paper) | ISBN 9780807769997 (hardcover ; acid-free paper) | ISBN 9780807782538 (epub) | ISBN 9780807782538 (epub)
Subjects: LCSH: Acting—Study and teaching—Psychological aspects. | Acting—Psychological aspects.
Classification: LCC PN2075 .G65 2024 (print) | LCC PN2075 (ebook) | DDC 792.02/8019—dc23/eng/20240314
LC record available at https://lccn.loc.gov/2024005590
LC ebook record available at https://lccn.loc.gov/2024005591

ISBN 978-0-8077-6998-0 (paper)
ISBN 978-0-8077-6999-7 (hardcover)
ISBN 978-0-8077-8253-8 (ebook)

Printed on acid-free paper
Manufactured in the United States of America

Praise for *Why Theatre Education Matters*

"Brilliant! In *Why Theater Education Matters*, author, actor, and scientist Thalia Goldstein leaps from pages in a book into high school drama classes. She compellingly illustrates why theatre is central and *not* peripheral to a 21st-century education. At last, a deep dive, research-based treatise explains how acting supports students as they learn a suite of skills that crosscut academic domains: collaboration, communication, critical thinking, and creative innovation, among others. An easy read and a helpful tool, this book deserves a standing ovation."

—Kathy Hirsh-Pasek, professor of psychology, Temple University

"*Why Theatre Education Matters* is an essential resource for theatre educators and advocates. Through rigorous analysis of data from field research in actual acting classes, Goldstein illuminates the essential and intrinsic value of theatre education, offering a strong case for its inclusion in curricula nationwide."

—Matt Omasta, professor and chair,
Department of Theatre, Miami University

"What if there were one activity that develops traits such as mindfulness, emotion regulation, and social understanding? In this landmark work, psychologist Thalia Goldstein shows that theatre education does that, and much more. The book is simultaneously eye-opening, inspirational, accessible, and pragmatic. It offers researchers and theatre practitioners alike an evidence-based analysis of the psychological foundation of acting, and an invaluable conceptual framework for the mental orientations that grow from acting classes, the 'Acting Habits of Mind.' As well as being of immense importance to those who advocate for theatre's value in education and society, it is a fascinating read for anyone who has ever wondered 'what do actors do?'"

—Richard J. Kemp, professor and head of acting and directing,
Indiana University of Pennsylvania, author of *Embodied Acting: What Neuroscience Tells Us About Performance*

"*Why Theatre Education Matters* brings rigorous, psychological research to the pedagogical study of how theatre training benefits young people. This timely, accessible book offers a comprehensive rationale for, and introduction to, Goldstein's groundbreaking framework, the Acting Habits of Mind. Her rich bridging of psychological theory, acting exercises, and case study examples offers a roadmap and invitation for theatre educators to teach for more effective learning. I'm certain this book will have a significant impact in the field of theatre education, research, and practice for years to come."

—Kathryn M. Dawson, associate professor of theatre,
The University of Texas at Austin

For Ms. Bilik, Dr. Bogar, Ms. Tracey Huffman,
Dr. Cole, Dr. Levitt, Dr. (Dr.) Professor Feldshuh,
and Mr. Larry Arancio.

For the teachers.

Thank you.

Contents

Foreword

Why are classes in the arts treated as an add-on in nearly all of our schools—nice if we have the time and money for them, but easily cut when budgets get tight?

Some might say that is because studying the arts will not get you a job. But then again, will studying math get you a job as a mathematician? Unlikely. And anyway, is education reducible to job training? Should it be—especially when the work landscape is changing so fast that we have no idea what the jobs of the future will be?

Others might say that the fragile position of the arts in schools is because they do not train "serious" cognitive skills like reading, writing, calculating, and now coding. Alas, in response to this view, educators grasp on to claims that the arts actually make students better in reading, writing, and arithmetic. Really? Actually, the research evidence for this is even flimsier than the position of the arts in our schools.

So, what are arts education advocates to do?

Psychologist Thalia Goldstein has peered into one important kind of arts class: the teaching of acting. Proceeding carefully and rigorously, she has sought (1) to uncover the kinds of learning that actually goes on in acting classes, and (2) to show that this learning connects to qualities of mind that psychologists, educators, and, indeed, thoughtful individuals everywhere firmly believe are important—ways of thinking and behaving that not only are important for participation in the arts but can also be used in other kinds of school subjects and in areas of life outside of school.

If you were asked what students are meant to learn in an acting class, you might reply that such classes teach students to memorize, to project their voices clearly, and to gain in self-confidence by overcoming stage fright. And if you were asked what actually goes on in an acting class, you might guess that, having memorized their lines at home, students come to class to practice their roles. These answers are not wrong, but, as revealed by Thalia Goldstein's careful analyses, they only tell us a small part of what is really going on.

A more complex picture comes into focus when you read this book, which is to my knowledge, the first book on acting that does not just theorize about how acting should be taught, but instead shows what actually *is* taught in high schools that value the arts. Thalia Goldstein takes you to acting classes in urban, suburban, and rural high schools across the United States. She describes moments in acting classes where students are provoked to develop thinking dispositions (the Acting Habits of Mind) that may well be best learned in acting class, but that are important outside of acting class as well.

Consider two powerful examples. *Body Awareness and Control* is one of the dispositions stressed in acting class. Goldstein shows the many ways in which this habit is developed, from exercises in breath awareness to careful analysis of how a character's physicality expresses the character's identity. She then goes on to reveal scientific findings showing the importance of bodily awareness for our well-being. Being in touch with the feelings in our body is essential for emotion understanding, emotion regulation, and decision-making, among other things.

Consider Others, another Acting Habit of Mind, involves awareness of other people's inner mental life. Acting students have to think about the emotions, thoughts, beliefs, and motivations not only of the character whom they are enacting but also of all of the other characters in a scene. When we read a novel, we get to know people we would never meet in our daily lives. And when we act, we have to *become* these people. Our understanding of human nature is surely expanded, and, as Goldstein shows, our empathy is also enlarged.

This book is a gift to theatre educators. To begin with, it provides theatre educators explicit language with which to describe the "hidden curriculum" of theatre education—what is really going on underneath the surface. While strong theatre educators may already be teaching in the ways described in this book, they will now have a framework to describe the outcomes their methods can achieve.

Second, this book provides theatre educators with a rich set of tools for provoking the Acting Habit of Minds. In the chapter on *body awareness*, for example, there is an exercise in which students are asked to verbalize the nonsense word *jabberwocky* in a way that expresses a specific emotion using gestures and posture. In the chapter on *consider others*, student A describes a character to student B who must then interpret what A has in mind and then generate that character, showing how that character would act under various circumstances (running late, having forgotten something, trying to persuade someone of something, and so on).

In the large, this book constitutes an advocacy tool for theatre educators to show those outside the field why studying acting is important for developing big, broad habits of mind that we know are also deployed when we leave the stage and approach everyday life—in school, in work, in the broader community. Relatedly, this book will prove illuminating for researchers who want to design further investigations of the sticky transfer question: When students acquire these habits of mind in acting class, do these habits generalize to other areas of school and life, and if so, where? And so, readers, open the pages of this most unusual book and enter into the world onstage. To tweak Shakespeare, the stage can be all the world.

—*Ellen Winner*
Professor Emerita,
Department of Psychology and Neuroscience,
Boston College
Senior Research Associate, Project Zero,
Harvard Graduate School of Education

of positive outcomes across type of student, level of class, context, and population. Theatre has been theorized for centuries to bring people together, form collaborative community, and meet people where they are. But first, we have to know what it is.

Acknowledgments

A study that takes places in five states, across five school districts, does not happen with one person or even a few dedicated people. Many, many people helped in reflection, discussion, support, and editing for this project. Thank you in particular to Leah Adams, Jennifer Drake, Craig Fisher, Aimee Forte, Katie LaCelle, Olga Kornienko, Scott Knowles, Joanne Seelig Lamparter, Jayme Moran, Kateri McRae, Mara Moreland, Sasha Newman, Matt Omasta, Ed Roggenkamp, Finn Roggenkamp, Kim Sheridan, Elizabeth Steele, Stacy Young, Martin Weiner, and Ellen Winner. Many members of my lab, including graduate students, undergraduate research assistants, and summer interns helped with data collection, cleaning, and coding. Thank you to Anna Sofia Caruso, Karlan Cruz, Denisse LaVigna-Cuellar, Harley Dodson, Jackson Gress, Kaylee Heslin, Leyla Kates, Tiffany Morina, Haley Mundy, Caroline Stephens, Megan Stutesman, Brittany Thompson, Russell Thomas, Ruby Trujillo, Sumukhi Vaid, and DaSean Young.

I am grateful for the continuing support of the National Endowment for the Arts, without whose grants and research support this project could not have occurred. Thank you, too, to the team at Teachers College Press, particularly Sarah Jubar, who answered every email and whose enthusiasm for this project gave me confidence.

A special thank you to the school districts, theatre teachers, students, parents, and schools who participated. Thank you to Boston Arts Academy, Eureka High School, Humboldt County Office of Education, Imagination Stage, and The Madeira School for giving me access to your schools and letting my team lurk in your classrooms for a bit. Finally, my deepest gratitude to the teachers. Jean Bazemore, Nikki Kaplan, Kelsey Mickeljohn, Steve Nostrum, Jewel Orem, Juanita Rodriguez, Justin Scheuer, Maura Tinghe, Nanette Voss, and Melanie Zapper. Thank you. I hope I have done the extraordinary work you do proud.

Introduction

The question of why schools and communities should spend time and valuable resources on the arts is debated continually in K–12 and university settings, in teacher training programs, on school boards, and at the national policy level. Practitioners and educators in the arts are constantly in the position of having to defend themselves from defunding and a lack of support for students at all levels of education—from preschool through high school and college (Holcomb, 2007). Nationally and internationally, the arts are often subsumed by learning areas considered "more important" (Winner et al., 2013); in classrooms, the arts are often used in service of other academic areas, rather than for their own inherent value (Davis, 2008). In interdisciplinary/multidisciplinary work, the arts often "dress up" other art forms, used simply for aesthetics post hoc, rather than for learning through authentic processes (Guyotte et al., 2014).

As a result, many arts organizations and educators over the past 50 years have turned to the idea of *transfer* as a reason to keep arts in schools; if research can show engaging in the arts transfers to help students in more "traditional" or "academic" areas, then perhaps the arts can garner more support. However, transfer from arts to non-arts domains is difficult to investigate and even more difficult to prove (Diamond & Ling, 2016; Sala & Gobet, 2017). Evidence for transfer from the arts has a long and conflicted history of support. When studies of transfer from arts to non-arts skills are positive, they garner publicity and promotion. But they are often oversold, causing doubts about accuracy (Mehr 2015; Winner et al., 2013). Theatre education has managed to steer clear of major headlines and controversies (e.g., the overhyped "music makes you better at math"), but the questions still remain.

These transfer claims are known as *instrumental claims* for the value of the arts—for example, that theatre should be taught only because it positively affects English SAT scores or social–emotional learning. Research does provide evidence for positive gains as a result of engaging in theatre (see Table I.1), and there are a set of papers any researcher should look at before starting their own project (see our companion website at TheatreEdMatters.com). However, this evidence is mixed in terms of outcome, scientific rigor, age of participants, and context of the theatrical activity. In addition, there

Table I.1. A Selection of Findings From Acting Classes for Adolescents (Ages 13–18), Across Various Types of Psychological Outcomes

Citation	Outcomes	Methods	Type of Acting
Goldstein et al. (2013)	Emotion suppression (lowering)	Quasi-experimental (art control group)	Acting major at high school for the arts
Goldstein & Winner (2012)	Theory of mind and empathy	Quasi-experimental (art control group)	Acting major at high school for the arts
Stutesman et al. (2022)	21st-century skills: creativity, collaboration, communication, problem solving, initiative	Quasi-experimental, mixed methods (no control group)	Conservatory style classes
Trayes et al., (2011)	Positive emotions, sense of togetherness, integrity	Quasi-experimental (no control group)	5-month after-school theatre competition group
Alfonso-Benlliure et al. (2021)	Flexibility, creative self-concept, originality	Correlational	2+ years engagement in drama activities
Goldstein et al. (2009)	Theory of mind (positive) and empathy (null)	Correlational	Acting classes
McLauchlan (2010)	Social and personal growth, enjoyment, teamwork	Qualitative, descriptive	School drama classes
Hughes & Wilson (2004)	Initiative, risk taking, confidence, friendship, exploration and expression of feelings	Qualitative, descriptive	Youth theatre organizations and classes
McCammon et al. (2012)	Social skills, self-confidence, enjoyment	Qualitative, descriptive	Adults reflecting on high school theatre/speech classes
Yassa (1999)	Social interactions, self-confidence, enjoyment	Qualitative	Drama involvement
Larson & Brown (2007)	Emotional regulation, emotion knowledge, enjoyment	Qualitative	Rehearsal for a school musical production

***For a larger set of resources on preschool, elementary school, college, and professional acting classes, and their findings—including meta-analyses—please see our online resource: TheatreEdMatters.com.*

is almost no empirical research theorizing or showing *which activities* within the theatre classroom affect *which outcomes*.

Looking only to instrumental claims as a reason to do theatre will always fail to give weight and strength to the deeper purpose of theatre for students and the ways in which it works. And while teachers and students should not have to do theatre to benefit other academic domains, an understanding of the psychological foundation of learning to act will help build an argument for theatre as beneficial both for its own sake and for what it can teach students about their lives and their worlds. Theatre can and does teach outcomes that other academic domains can not or are not as well-suited to teach. It also teaches an artistic practice, valuable in its own right. It is from this perspective that I developed and conducted the study reported in this book.

WHAT, PSYCHOLOGICALLY, IS AN ACTING CLASS?

The *Thinking On Stage* study collected data from 2017–2020 in a nationally representative (urban, suburban, and rural; magnet, conservatory, and general education; public and private) sample of school-based acting classes for grades 9–12. Through careful, systematic, rigorous study of these acting classes, with a purposeful eye toward their psychological content, the study's report in this book provides an answer to the question "What, psychologically, is an acting class?"

To note, I studied acting classes, but theatrical activities can be called many things, including theatre education, acting training, drama-based pedagogy or technique, integrated drama, improv, psychodrama, and on and on. Theatre forms also vary by age. In younger ages (preschool and early elementary school), children engage in socio-dramatic play, creative play, dramatic play, or pretend play. For older children and adults, there are clubs and teams that engage in theatre-adjacent activities such as debate or rhetoric, which often include acting out characters and scenes. There are plays put on in schools across the world, mostly licensed from professional sources, but sometimes also written in-house by teachers or students.

While none of these activities were directly studied in the reported research, all are related and have strong overlaps with the study's findings (see Chapter 13 for a discussion of theatre adjacent activities). Here, I focused on high school acting classes, which are more formalized than acting classes for younger children and more general than professional-level classes. I looked at the range of classes students can take while in grades 9–12 in the United States, focused on theatre and drama for its own sake. My primary sampling characteristic was looking for technique classes that provided students an education in how to perform characters—scripted and improvised—for audiences.

Through a focused lens on what an acting class is, I asked what it requires from its students and its practitioners at a cognitive, social, and emotional level. By looking from the perspective of the classes themselves, I saw the ways in which skills are used, integrated, called upon, and fostered through engagement in acting classes. This is a first step before beginning to theorize the kinds of skills acting classes build that could spill over (i.e., transfer) from the acting classroom to opportunities in other domains and everyday life. Only after understanding what an acting class actually is can we make reasonable, testable hypotheses about how learning in an acting class may transfer into other areas.

By taking this naturalistic and foundational approach, I allowed for the considerable variety of acting classes as they happen in real schools, with real students. Scholars and teachers of theatre have often theorized about the best way to act onstage, how to build acting skills, shape talent, and train a passable or good actor to be great. But it is the teachers on the ground, responsive to the needs of their immediate students in their immediate classroom, with all their outside influences, individual contexts, and curricular demands, who are putting theory into practice. Teachers are the ones creating opportunities for students to learn psychological abilities through their engagement with acting activities. Hence, collecting data from classes as they exist today will allow us to build theory for best practices and outcomes moving forward.

A note: While I was able to work with a broad range of schools, including significant numbers of students from under-resourced areas and those who may hold stigmatized social identities, all classes were for adolescents who are typically developing. Neurodivergent students may experience different kinds of theatre activities and acting exercises, and therefore different outcomes from drama training (e.g., Corbett et al., 2014; Guli et al., 2013).

STANDARD EXERCISES AND APPROACHES FOR ACTING CLASSES

In the United States and elsewhere in Western educational systems, there are a set of nationally and locally determined standards, and often, set curricula that teachers must abide by when deciding what to do in their classrooms with their students. The Every Student Succeeds Act (i.e., the governing national education law) was active during the time of data collection for this book. All findings occur within these standards, and thus classes should link directly back to different goals within the National Core Arts Standards for Theatre. Theatre standards explicitly shape what is taught in theatre classrooms, and the findings of this study must be contextualized *within* the requirements of the national and local communities in which these schools are situated, and therefore may not be generalizable to all schools and all communities outside of the United States. Theatre both benefits from and is constricted by these standards.

Yet even within set curricular standards, teachers in different locations with students from various backgrounds use individualized versions of standard exercises and approaches. It is critical to keep in mind who sets the standards, and the historical ideas of the supremacy of a White, male, European canon of authors and theorists. These ideas restrict teachers and students from beginning from a perspective of culturally responsive and culturally relative work. Here, I looked across a variety of schools, where students hold a diversity of social, racial, cultural, and class identities. While I found foundational similarities across these schools for both the breakdown of how teachers use their time with the students and the Acting Habits of Mind they are teaching, it is unknowable right now where these teachers could stretch with their students if not bound by a canon that is still Eurocentric and tied to a historically exclusive paradigm. In this book I show over and over how theatre is a flexible tool kit, meaning its many exercises, components, and pieces can be used across contexts with different skills levels and populations in order to be of best benefit. Letting teachers use this tool kit to its fullest will support all students.

The flexibility in building from this foundation is key. It is what allows theatre to be both a place of healing and hold the possibility of harm. Great teachers (like the ones we worked with here) meet students where they are and push them to explore and express themselves without constraint. They use and teach with psychological foundations that are clear, achievable, and have the capacity to build students' habits across domains and topics. However, there is also the possibility that acting teachers can use theatre to manipulate or silence the emotions of their students. Care and training are necessary to prevent passive and active harm.

HABITS OF MIND

Before this work, there was no published book-length work that, with systematic empirical evidence, showed the psychological foundations of acting classes. There is a high demand for this information because while teachers see effects of theatre education in their own daily lives and with their individual students, they also need a well-informed, researched, expert perspective that is more broadly based than personal experience. This book, I hope, will be such a resource, taking a larger view than just the immediate classes, context, and neighborhood of each teacher, to build knowledge of acting's effects and expected psychological outcomes. This book is necessary as teachers, policymakers, and students continue to advocate for their art form. It is my hope this study will allow researchers, practitioners, teachers, actors, and policymakers to understand the reasons why theatre should be not only as common as music and visual arts in schools, but as common as algebra and American literature.

For the last 19 years (since leaving my time as an auditioning and working actor and dancer in New York City and on tour), I have conducted studies that investigate connections between acting classes and cognitive, social, and emotional skills across childhood, adolescence, and adulthood. Through my doctoral studies, postdoctoral fellowship, and now running my own research group, my labs and students have worked with preschoolers doing creative dramatics play, children taking their first acting classes, teens in rigorous and exclusive magnet boarding schools for the arts, college theatre majors, acting teachers, and professional actors. For each group studied, we have asked similar questions on whether and how theatre causes psychological change. Specifically, we have asked if enrollment in acting classes is associated with higher levels of empathy, emotional control, understanding others, positive self-concept, and/or prosocial behaviors than enrollment in other kinds of arts courses or business as usual in schools. For the most part, the answer has been "yes, but . . ." (which is unfortunately not as good as "yes, and . . ."). Often, we found positive effects, but sometimes we see no effects, sometimes effects only for some kids and not others, and sometimes, even a negative finding or two.

So, after many years of this work, the question lingered: where are differences coming from? The type of theatre? The type of student? The timeline? The outcome? The measurement strategy? Eventually, it became apparent that the best course of action would be to go back to the source: acting classes and acting teachers.

Happily, there was already a model: the *Studio Thinking* books (Hetland et al., 2007; 2013; Sheridan et al., 2022), which looked in-depth at visual arts classes, taking into consideration the Habits of Mind taught through arts classes. I explain what Habits of Mind are more completely in the Part II Introduction, but they are basically thinking strategies that cut across psychological ability and skill to be put to use for problem solving and learning. The Habits of Mind approach to arts classes works well as a way to break down arts classes for what they actual are—training grounds for young people to learn the skills necessary to engage in their particular art form. It takes each art form as it is, not as we *wish* it would be or how it *could* be for other purposes.

By approaching theatre from a Habits of Mind perspective, we can allow theatre to be the always complex, sometimes messy, ultimately adaptable art form and training it has long been advertised as by theatre professionals and educators. I hypothesized the Acting Habits of Mind would be psychological skills so ingrained into how theatre works and how it is taught they would be found across locations and contexts, from professional training schools to basic general elective courses. It was this foundation that I sought, and this foundation I believe I found.

STRUCTURE OF THIS BOOK

In Part I, What Is an Acting Class?, I walk through, briefly, the study that discovered these Acting Habits of Mind. All the details about the method of school selection, data collection, coding, and analyses are available to the reader in the appendix, but Chapter 1 provides an overview. Chapter 2 discusses the structure of acting classes found in every single class and every single location—the four elements/activity types within acting classes from which the Acting Habits of Mind are integrated and practiced.

In Part II, The Eight Habits of Mind Taught in Acting Class, I lay out the eight Acting Habits of Mind, giving real-world examples of how each are used in single moments in classrooms or as the centerpiece of a long exercise. I show how each is tied to psychological skills and adolescent development, discussing related psychological abilities where we have extensive research outside of the acting classroom. In each chapter, I give the definition, vignettes across all levels and class types we filmed and analyzed, quotes from teacher interviews, and repeating exemplars.

Then in Part III, Connections, I bring it all back together again, taking on the intricacies of scene study, the complex ways in which acting teachers use the same exercises for different groups of students, how teachers integrate multiple Acting Habits of Mind in one exercise, and general developmental and level trends in acting classes. I discuss how theatre can be applied across the academic curriculum and for social, emotional, and creative development in its students. I show where acting is already being useful, and where it could be used going forward.

Finally, given everything I found in this study, I lay out a roadmap for future work in the science of acting classes, the development and curriculum that acting classes can work in, the future of research in the psychology of theatre, and note the importance of play, community, and joy. On this book's companion website (TheatreEdMatters.com), you will find a growing and up-to-date list of additional resources on acting and its effects across age groups; an executive summary to share with administrators, policymakers, and advocates; and a set of exercises (with short video exemplars) that are specifically focused on each Acting Habit of Mind.

Throughout, I focus not on what should be done in acting classes, nor the best practice of an acting classroom, but instead what is actually being done in acting classes today—decisions teachers make on daily curriculum, whether or not they are aware of the Acting Habits of Mind their teaching fosters. This book provides a theoretically and empirically supported foundation from which future tests of the effects of theatre education can be built, studies relevant to policy and practice of arts education can be constructed, and interventions that use techniques and theories from theatre education can be developed.

By the end of this book, the reader should have a stronger understanding of what acting classes for high school students are, what kinds of psychological skills they recruit and integrate, and, therefore, where future research and practice should go next (calls for future research are set apart in boxes in each chapter). However, it is not just my hope that this book will be read once through and then put on a shelf with other theoretical tomes about acting and theatre. Instead, this book is meant to be a living report and document of exercises, emphases, and techniques from acting classes across a variety of contexts. I hope it can serve as inspiration for the many and varied ways acting can be used to practice and integrate skills, and turned to again and again to show how acting and theatre are not just one thing, but a set of tools to be used by teachers appropriate to context, population, and goal. I hope the integrated discussion of related scientific findings can be pointed to as research in theatre progresses. I hope, too, research psychologists will come away with a host of new ideas for exploring the ties between theatre classes and measurable psychological skills and abilities.

What students are learning, pragmatically and practically, is how to act. But what they are taking away is deeper, psychological, and possibly transferrable when they leave the theater. From Shakespeare to devised works, formal performances to site-specific improv games, the Acting Habits of Mind underlying training open doors to bigger and better thinking for all who choose to walk through.

Part I

WHAT IS AN ACTING CLASS? AN EMPIRICAL INVESTIGATION

theatre, etc.). Thus, any useful study of acting classes has to take that into account. While individual analyses and contextual implications are always valuable and necessary, my goal with this study was to discover findings and thus provide information that is broad and flexible enough to be used and understood no matter what kind of teacher, administrator, or student is reading this book, whether in a private conservatory with only a handful of dedicated students or a first-year general education class where the students are experiencing improvisational exercises for the very first time.

THE SCHOOLS

Our schools were chosen with the goal of including variety and diversity, not just across racial or ethnic groups of students, but also location, other student demographics, socioeconomic status of the surrounding neighborhood, whether the school required audition for entry, the amount of time students spent in acting classes over the course of their weeks, and the general requirements of the school itself. While I could not, of course, vary every single school-based variable for measurement, I believe there is a good range. Details on all the schools can be found in the appendix, but Table 1.1 provides a summary of school, location, filming times, and teachers.

THE CLASSES

To be included in our study, a class had to be classified as an "acting," "drama," or "directing" class, but the activities of the filmed classes (confirmed by the teacher) were focused on "acting," meaning they focused on the performance of characters for an audience. Even this restriction, however, allowed for a broad range, including classes focused on script analysis, discussion of sets and props, improvisational exercises, choosing materials for auditions, acting for camera, rehearsal, and preparation for performance. What we did not include in filming or analyses were classes where students were learning the technical aspects of theatre (such as lighting, scene design, and costuming) or classes that were focused on drama as a literary form (typically in English departments). We also included only formal classes that students took for credit (or paid for), and not extracurricular activities, rehearsals, or clubs, even though students also learn how to act in those contexts. Not every school had the option to take a straight "acting" class—often the teaching of acting was included in drama classes, directing classes, or theatre arts classes. However, we planned our filming and visits to schools on days in which the teachers were teaching acting.

Table 1.1. Summary of Acting Class Filming Locations

School Name	Urbanicity	Public or Private	Magnet, Conservatory, or Neighborhood	Hours Filmed	Types of Classes Filmed	Number of Classes Filmed	Teacher Names
Imagination Stage	Suburban	Private	Conservatory Afterschool	16 hr, 32 min	2	8	Jewel, Nikki
The Madeira School	Suburban	Private	Boarding General	10 hr, 6 min	1	8	Kelsey
Boston Arts Academy	Urban	Public	Magnet	16 hr, 34 min	4	10	Juanita, Maura
Humboldt County	Rural	Public	Neighborhood	6 hr, 37 min	5	7	Steve, Nanette, Melanie, Jean
Eureka, St. Louis, MO	Suburban	Public	Neighborhood	6 hr, 37 min	2	7	Justin
Total	3 Suburban, 1 Urban, 1 Rural	2 Private, 3 Public	1 Conservatory, 1 Magnet, 1 Boarding, 2 Neighborhood	56 hr, 26 min	14	40	10 teachers

THE ANALYSES

We treated these films and interviews in two different ways: first, looking at the *content* of the classes, how they were structured, organized, and set up. Second, looking at the *discourse* of the classes, and how teachers were introducing concepts and habits—what were they saying to get students to integrate and recruit various Acting Habits of Mind?

For the content, we were interested in what types of activities teachers were using in their classrooms, and whether these activities could be categorized in a structured way for particular goals or strategies. We discovered that every activity in a class can be categorized into one of four types, explained fully in Chapter 2:

Preparation
Generation
Interpretation
Reflection

These activity types engage students in distinct ways and recruit a variety of Acting Habits of Mind and technical skills students will need to act. Each activity type organizes the space, time, and student interactions in different ways, and serves a different purpose for student development. The segments of class flow back and forth, without breaking up the progression of the day. There is no one type of activity particularly emphasized over any other, and importantly, all of these different kinds of activities were found in all different class types.

Not every class had ever type of segment every day (see the class breakdown for the flow of each of the 40 classes in Figure 2.1), but over the course of just a few classes, every activity type was covered, regardless of level or focus of class. Some classes focused more heavily on one type of segment than others, some moved rapidly across them. Across classes, every single exercise and task we saw across location and type of acting class fell into one of these four categories; there were no moments of class that were not part of this categorization. These four activity types also match scientific findings on the creative process in a variety of ways, as explained more in Chapter 13.

Simultaneously to this analysis, I looked at the instructional discourse of the classes, the words teachers used throughout the classes to set up activities, give instruction, lecture, and offer feedback, and what intention was underlying those words. My team and I focused on what information teachers were getting across when they instructed and responded to students: What were they trying to say? What were the ways in which teachers helped and coached students? What was the introduced content in the activities allowing students to solve problems and complete goals?

Figure 1.1. The Eight Acting Habits of Mind, With Short Definitions

Habit	Definition
Body Awareness and Control	Understand and control your physicality.
Release Inhibitions and Be Playful	Perform fully and without self-judgment.
Imagine and Envision	Create and think beyond perception.
Consider Others	Think about others' minds, emotions, and perspectives.
Think Collaboratively	Actively and purposefully communicate and work with others.
Be Flexible	Be open to new ideas and changing ideas.
Commit to Choices	Make firm, bold, and definitive decisions.
Reflect and Think Metacognitively	Thoughtfully consider your own and others' actions.

The overarching goal of the study was to discover generalities of acting classes consistent across urbanicity, class type, location, type of school, and context that could be considered foundational to the way acting is taught and practiced. I was not interested in a study on theoretical perspectives on the best way to act, but a practical perspective on what is actually happening in adolescent acting classes across the United States. What are students being taught, and how? What are they experiencing, and in what way? From this analysis, we developed our list of the eight Acting Habits of Mind (see Figure 1.1; more on the development of these terms in the appendix).

As readers will see as they go through the rest of the book, these Acting Habits of Mind and the content sections of classes flow together and inform one another, and by taking this perspective across acting classes, we can begin to think about how the elements of acting inform curriculum outside of theatre, interventions that could use theatre, and ultimately, the reasons why theatre is a deep, motivating, and flexible activity that can be used across student groups and pedagogical perspectives.

But first, it is important to understand the types of activities that make up an acting class. This allows us to then see how the Acting Habits of Mind are adaptably used and applied for maximum practice across acting strategies and tasks.

CHAPTER 2

The Content and Structure of Acting Classes

Before we can investigate the Acting Habits of Mind recruited, fostered, and integrated into acting classes, we first have to know what an acting class actually is. What are the activities and elements of a class that set up students to engage with various Acting Habits of Mind? How do teachers frame activities and get students to engage with interest?

Popularly, acting classes are viewed in one of two ways. They are either a sort of mini rehearsal for performance, where students work with a script, learn their lines, and perform for an audience. Or they are a series of improvisational games, where students have to move around hooting like monkeys or pretending to be ice cream cones (as popularized by *A Chorus Line*). The truth is actually much deeper and more interesting than either of those options.

Over the course of any one particular class, teachers use various exercises, structures, and activity types with modifications scaffolded for the class depending on the level and time of year. Through our systematic analysis, we discovered all observed activities and exercises in acting class can be classified into one of four types:

1. *Preparation* activities, involving getting ready.
2. *Generation* activities, involving the creation of new material.
3. *Interpretation* activities, involving working with pre-written scripts and characters.
4. *Reflection* activities, involving formal thinking about what just happened.

Each of these segments of class can integrate, recruit, and foster each of the eight Acting Habits of Mind, but with different emphasis. They generally occurred in order from Preparation to Generation to Interpretation to Reflection during classes, although there are some notable variations and a lot of individual differences. See Figure 2.1, at the end of this chapter, for a visual representation of the ordering and pacing of these segments in each of our 40 classes.

As noted in the appendix, what we saw in these classes was necessarily in response to the requirements of the standards and curriculum set up by the states the schools were located in (California, Missouri, Virginia, Massachusetts, Maryland) and the school districts they did (or did not) have to answer to. Interestingly, teachers never (not in a single post-class interview) pointed to the theatre standards or curricular requirements when discussing their pedagogical goals for a day, structure of the class, or why they picked an exercise. While they were undoubtably influenced, it was not front of their minds while teaching.

In addition, Imagination Stage is a private conservatory after-school program and The Madeira School is an independent high school, so they may be less bound by national core arts standards and curricular requirements than our other three public schools. Yet we did not see significant differences in the four activity types or Acting Habits of Mind found in these schools compared to the others.

CALL FOR FUTURE RESEARCH

How curriculum standards affect the acting choices and the psychological skills being trained across acting classes, and what a classroom not bound by the requirement of these standards might look like is open for future research in education to determine. For now, state and federal curricular requirements are part of the background, and not the foreground, of my findings.

Following, I give a brief introduction to each activity type and an example where that activity type was foregrounded in a classroom.

PREPARATION: GETTING THE BODY, VOICE, MIND, AND SPACE READY FOR THE WORK OF ACTING

Acting classes almost always begin with a warm-up—the preparation of the body and mind for participation in acting. This warm-up is not just physical, but also vocal and mental. There is sometimes a technical aspect to preparation (e.g., setting up a camera to record scenes), or a short discussion (e.g., of professionalism or how to comport yourself in classes). Teachers occasionally lead a theoretical discussion of the exercise or materials to be worked with in class that day, or a discussion of expectations for students to focus on for any particular class (e.g., listening carefully to each other). Some teachers combine different types of warm-ups (e.g., vocal warm-ups with movements), others work through each separately. But there is always a formal moment to begin class.

Physical preparation for acting can look like a PE class, with jogging, sit-ups, push-ups, and stretching, asking students to get their bodies active and warm. Sometimes physical preparation for acting looks like a dance class, with music and movement to the beat. There is often a level of silliness to it; students are encouraged to move around and loosen their bodies without thinking about what they look like. Or they are purposefully told to make awkward or ridiculous sounds and movements without self-judgment (see Chapter 4 for a discussion of the related Acting Habit of Mind *release inhibitions*). These types of physical preparations are centered on letting go of the observational self and self-judgment and focusing on the movement of the body and voice (see Chapter 3 for a discussion of the related Acting Habit of Mind *body awareness and control*). In addition to the physical, vocal preparation can range from singing exercises to vocalizations paired with movement. Preparation also can involve discussion and engagement in the technical aspects of performance, such as voice volume, how to think about vocal cords and breathing while making noise, and lowering center of balance while moving, giving more physical stability.

Many classrooms include a moment of mental preparation, involving neutral breathing or meditation. Students are taught short mindfulness practices or relaxation practices, discussed as bringing the body in concert with the mind. Students are taught to be aware of a sense of self and what they are feeling in the present moment. This mental warm-up often involves leaving the outside world behind and coming into the acting space as a blank slate, prepared to learn and be open to direction and instruction.

Occasionally, teachers will lay out the plan for the day during Preparation activities, discussing professional expectations and the ways in which the class will run. Sometimes this is while the students are warming up physically, and sometimes this is more traditionally pedagogical. In higher level classes (e.g., for juniors and seniors in our conservatory and magnet schools), students run their own physical, vocal, and mental warm-ups, picking their own exercises, or following a student leader for the day. The Preparation segment of class in these cases is a routine, the same each day, or involves a small set of rotating exercises students pick from and put together to prepare body and mind. Often teachers point out that students should use these Preparation activities any time they have to perform, and when in professional performance settings they should have a personal suite of activities to choose from to prepare physically, vocally, and mentally.

These Preparation activities separate the students from their other classes and activities of their day, adjust their minds and bodies to engage in character and performance work, and show students that acting classes are different than other types of classes. Preparation activities accounted for, on average, 24.6% of class time, with a range of 2–48% of class time.

While these physical and mental warm-ups are not acting themselves, they engage the body and voice, the main instruments of the actor, to be ready for engagement in acting exercises and performance. This points to the technical aspects of acting—the ways in which students are learning specialized, purposeful methods of moving their bodies to portray characters. The body in acting is an instrument (see Chapter 3, *body awareness and control*), similar to how students in other arts classes must use the technical aspects of watercolors or a violin to create their art. In acting classes, the art comes through the body and voice.

In students' days, there may be other classes that use parts of the body—art (to paint) and music (to play), physical education (for sport), or dance (for movement). But the majority of classes in schools—math, English language, and science—require not just no use of the body, but active suppression of bodily needs and movement. In these classes, stillness and quiet rule the day. Theatre classrooms turn that perspective on education on its head, asking students to focus on their body and voice and the ways in which it will be called on to serve them. Preparation activities are often framed as ways to "wake up" the body from its stillness in other parts of the academic day and reorient the mind to the needs of acting performance. Preparation activities center the student as agents, rather than passive experiencers of the tasks in class. Preparation activities require a sense of self-awareness, of understanding the limits of the body, voice, and mind, and of learning how the body and mind can change with purposeful focus.

Preparation Example Class

As an example, Class 13 for juniors at Boston Arts Academy incorporated every kind of Preparation activity, including physical, mental, and verbal warm-ups, group play, and a brief reflection with corrections, all in one segment of class. This class was exemplary for the ways Preparation activities were used throughout the time.

In this 87-minute class, these Preparation activities lasted 31 minutes, more than a third of the class time. For the first 10 minutes of class, Juanita, the teacher, talked about the previous night's homework and the organization of the class for the day. She had individual conversations and a sense of closeness with the students, asking about their family situations, including setting up an appointment to discuss a personal issue at a later time. Then, she passed the running of the class to a student volunteer to lead a vocal warm-up. This involved saying phrases and words in louder and softer voices, with a call-and-response. The class then moved into tongue twisters, including a standard we saw in several classrooms, "To sit in solemn silence" from Gilbert and Sullivan's operetta *The Mikado*. When pronunciation was not correct, Juanita interjected with corrections on the crispness of consonants and ordering of several similarly sounding sentences. However, for the most part, this part of class was self-led by students. Juanita also reminded students during the vocal warm-up they had to practice and do homework on pronunciation and warm-up exercises as part of their character study at home.

After the vocal warm-up (approximately 7 minutes), students moved into a physical group game where they had to bounce a beach ball in the air 100 times without letting it hit the ground. However, they first had to space themselves out around the room and were not allowed to move from their positions. Instead, they had to figure out how to reach out and get the ball toward classmates from where they placed themselves. This Preparation activity not only engaged their bodies, ready to hit the ball, but also their communication and work with others (see Chapter 7 for a discussion of the related Acting Habit of Mind, *think collaboratively*). Students were asked to engage almost as a volleyball team, deciding and communicating in the moment who would be next to hit the ball, making sure they passed it around the room, and counting together. They had to explicitly inform each other about the next move, and implicitly read each other's body and facial expressions to make adjustments to their own movements. It took a few tries to get to 100 ball hits in a row, and the tension grew as they got closer to their goal number each time. In fact, they found out later in the Reflection on this activity that tension was the point. After 5 minutes of trying, the students made 100 hits without dropping the ball, and the room erupted into cheers and joyful jumping up and down.

After this successful completion of the passing the ball exercise, Juanita came forward into the circle and led a brief Reflection on why and how this warm-up exercise worked. The discussion led to the point that audience members react positively to performances that are not just playing at authenticity but are actually authentic—where performers are experiencing real hope, real tension, and a true objective. Performance works, Juanita noted, when actors are able to communicate all actions and emotions to an audience in its authenticity. She connected this back to Stanford Meisner's theories of acting—the acting theory under study and practice in the current week. Meisner, of course, proposed that when truth, built tension, and ultimate diffusion of tension was happening for the actors, it also was happening for the audience. Juanita quoted for the class: "Your body becomes automatically engaged and you live truthfully under imaginary circumstances."

She was clear that investment from the students would be reflected in investment from audience members. The Preparation exercise was meant to be transferred to more complicated scenes involving characterization, memorized lines, rehearsed movements, and broader narratives, all of which are harder to perform simultaneously than during an exercise with a single goal. The class discussed how the students should not pretend or act invested in a goal, but actually be invested. Students discussed how they should take the commitment they were feeling during the group warm-up time and transfer it to the commitment they could feel as their characters and when performing their actions. Finally, after these 31 minutes of Preparation, the class moved into a Generation segment, in which they improvised scenes with each other based on the emotional arcs of characters they were playing.

On other days, we observed this same class and others at Boston Arts Academy doing sit-ups, push-ups, and basic yoga exercises. Across our schools, teachers discussed how to transfer Preparation moments into other segments of class. Preparation activities were referred to as useful both for their own sake, and for their ability to teach skills and ideas used across the spectrum of other activities students engage in, both in the classroom and in later acting experiences. At Imagination Stage, for example, the teacher Nikki noted how warm-up would eventually become something student actors would be required to do for themselves before they began a rehearsal, and how they would be expected to show up to a theater ready to work, fully prepared. Preparation was framed not just for class to begin or as an introduction to something else. It is a part of acting.

GENERATION: CREATING NEW MATERIAL AND IMPROVISED PERFORMANCE

Typically, after students finish their physical, vocal, and mental Preparation activities, classes involve a set of activities where students improvise or create new material from a prompt. This segment is Generation, the on-the-spot creative thinking and behaving part of class. In our sample, sometimes a Generation part of class also came after some Reflection, or occasionally the students would engage in some Interpretation, such as a discussion of a script, and then begin an exercise in which they generated material from reading and thinking about characters. While acting classes are not often framed in terms of creative output or divergent thinking, this segment of class is the very definition of these skills (see Chapter 12 for a discussion on creativity).

Across all classes, students were taught to respond to prompts, follow their instincts, and think of something new each and every time they engage in a Generation activity. Prompts could be specific (e.g., you are an animal who needs to find something to eat) or broad (e.g., walk around using the whole space). They involved character types (e.g., pretend to be an alien) or the self (e.g., say a made-up word using different emotional expressions). Generation activities occurred in a variety of ways: individually or in a group setting, in character or as the self, with words, movement, or the combination of physicality and wording. Individual improvisations required students to come up with answers to prompts quickly and make firm decisions on how to explore and communicate their choices, while group improvisations required students to place their impulses in line with their group as a whole. Group improvisations also required students to build off each other and keep a close watch and understanding on what their fellow ensemble mates were doing. These activities are often team building (called by several teachers "ensemble building") exercises, asking students to trust and feel comfortable with each other, and to pay close attention to each other.

Generation activities can be based on character prompts, single word prompts, or physical goals. They can be based on material from full scripts or single words. Students are sometimes asked to improvise as a character they are working on (e.g., as Juliet) or as a character made for the improv itself. Generation activities ask students to go beyond what is in front of them and create something new. These can be physical games that have only nonsense sounds attached to them, or word games with no physical movement, but often the Generation section builds on the Preparation by having students combine mind and body once again to create a new scene or action. Just as in many Preparation activities, students here too are asked to let go of self-judgment and behave in a way they may consider silly or embarrassing, and to commit to that behavior fully and without limitation. Teachers described trying to loosen the students up and get them to stop being self-conscious, linked directly to the Acting Habit of Mind of *release inhibitions and be playful* (Chapter 4). A lack of self-judgment and a positive view of the self is needed to perform actions in front of other people that students might never otherwise do.

There are endless improvisational exercises and games that can be taught in an acting class, both individualistic and group-based, and these are used broadly and thoroughly throughout the theatre world. They have even bled into the corporate team-building world, medical training, and school exercises in other subjects (see TheatreEdMatters.com for books on acting improvisational exercises). The level and types of prompts, complexity of rules, and expectations for Generation activities vary depending on how much time the class spends on these activities and how long the students have been working together and on these skills. However, what makes Generation activities different from scene study or rehearsal is that students are asked to create movement and words just as themselves, and to express themselves through the exercises.

While in other types of academic classes, students are often asked to come up with their own responses to prompts, rarely is creating material as central to class time as Generation activities for acting class. Most other academic domains require a lot of baseline knowledge before students can go out on their own to create something new. While acting classes require skill-building, learning a corpus of materials and characters, and theories of acting performance, classes are only rarely pedagogical lectures where students sit and listen to learn. Instead, students are tasked every day with thinking about and acting out material. This active engagement and learning, when properly applied, has been shown across domains to be one of the best ways to get students to learn, and acting class puts that to the test (Clark & Mayer, 2008; Freeman et al., 2014). In Generation segments of class, students are trying new ideas, ways of moving and performing, connecting with their fellow classmates to collaborate on suggestions, and making a whole picture from an initial point. While Generation exercises can be individual, collaborative, or competitive, they all serve to get the student actively thinking and performing. Generation activities accounted for, on average, 25.4% of class time, with a range from 5–58% of class time.

Generation Example Class

In Class 31 at Eureka High in St. Louis, the teacher Justin played with emotions, movement, power dynamics, and everyday actions in building a class around Generation activities for his students. The class began with a single student's performance of an ongoing assignment about the students' personal lives, hopes, and dreams. This student performed for almost 27 minutes. Notably, this was a script the student had created herself out of lyrics from shows and songs, so she had generated it herself and then written it down. Then, there were about 7 minutes of Reflection on that performance, and a quick 4-minute Preparation warm-up that students completed in a routine way (this was in March, so the students were well familiar with the pattern of the warm-up).

Then, the class transitioned into almost a full hour of Generation activities and feedback on these activities. Specifically, the students came up with ideas about and then fully improvised scenes in pairs, one pair at a time. At one point as they were setting up the improvisation, a student blurted out:

"I'm going to mess it up!"
Justin responded, "You can't mess it up!"
"I'll find a way," the student promised.
"You can't," Justin answered.

This is the heart of the Generation segment of class. The students learn to try anything, whatever they want, and they cannot mess up (in the way an actor might mess up their lines or their movements in performance). Because the Generation segments of class involve activities that are created in the moment without a predetermined order or script, the students have to both produce and judge simultaneously whether their ideas are valid to be included in the activity. While doing this, they need a mindset of openness and possibility, to try out whatever they are feeling and see if it works. This balance of judgment and creation is at the core of Generation activities.

The longest exercise in this class was the creation of a scene, with the goal of having it lead to an emotional climax. The students sat and brainstormed for a few minutes together while one performer was out of the room so they could enter the scene naïve to their partner's goals. The group of students decided on a scenario in which the first actor had just moved into a new apartment and found a note etched into the apartment's floor that a buried treasure was somewhere nearby. This actor needed to uncover and understand the note and its contents before their roommate came home. When the audience hushed and the second actor came in, the improvised scene began. Note that there was preparation (about 8 minutes) for the improvisation, but it was not a separate Preparation section of class. Justin did note in his interview this was a bit long, but was necessary to set up and be able to generate the new material together.

When the second actor came in, they launched into an explanation of a lost frisbee, a legendary group of frisbee players, and the need to go outside with the first actor to immediately recover a prototype frisbee off the roof. However, the first actor kept scraping the floor in an attempt to reach her goal of uncovering the treasure. This went back and forth for 12 minutes, with all words and actions generated by the students in real time. The first student pushed a couch, the second started yelling about frisbee history. Overall, it was a funny moment. But importantly, this was a difficult exercise in an advanced acting class. The actors had to simultaneously keep track of their goals, their characters, the plot, their generated words, and being in relation with the other actor onstage. In this way, the students were quite successful. They were able to come up with jokes in character spontaneously, and show how their character in the scene was feeling and processing what was happening to them.

They used the technique under study in class, Meisner repetition (an acting technique to get actors used to relying on instincts, in which they repeat the same phrase to each other until it feels natural to move on), to keep the scene from getting stuck in any one place, and the words flowed easily. When the scene was done (at an impasse between finding the treasure and recovering the important frisbee), the class spent 8 minutes talking about what worked and what did not in the improvised scene. Justin noted that because of the scene's movement and flow, they did not need to rely on Meisner-style repetition to bring the pair back into generating text and material, but that it was a technique to turn to when an actor cannot think of something else new to say. He also noted, though, that when generating material, there is a fine line between creating urgency through details and becoming so stuck in the details (e.g., a whole story about a frisbee from the year 1534 entrusted to the character), that it is hard to generate additional facts or pulls the actor out of the scene creation.

Next, a second pair of students did the same exercise with a different prompt: one student needed to gather books to get to class while the other needed help with an important job interview. Overall, this Generation segment of class, including set up, discussion, and incorporating multiple activities within, took up 46 minutes of an 85-minute class, 54%. None of it was prescripted or based on written characters.

In other classes, the Generation segment of class included moving around the room as if an animal; moving in pairs as if your partner was a mirror (a classic improv game); generating new tongue twisters to say during vocal warm-ups; trying to convince a student to get out of a chair using a variety of character tropes, or pairing up to interact with a partner, where you know who you are and your partner has to guess without you directly telling them. In each of these activities, whether solo, paired, or in a group, students had to work with what information to give, what to withhold, create new behaviors and words, and communicate through their actions.

Across our classes, Generation is not just for fun or bonding, although the games and scenes are often fun. Generation activities are a way to get students to come up with many different ways of thinking about a single prompt. Across the schools, teachers discussed this creation as a way to build a physical and mental repertoire for later performance choices, and to become comfortable and familiar with trying out a range of options in response to one initial idea. When faced with a character, a script, a director, and a looming performance, the activities of the Generation segment of class will help students come up with flexible options (see Chapter 8 for a discussion of the related Acting Habit of Mind *be flexible*) and make choices about how to perform (see Chapter 9 for a discussion of the related Acting Habit of Mind, *commit to choices*) freely and easily.

INTERPRETATION: WORKING WITH AND UNDERSTANDING SCRIPTS AND DIRECTION

The third activity category of acting classes focuses on Interpretation of scripts, characters, and direction. This involves reading and understanding a script, engaging with characters and working with directors and cast mates to perform prewritten material. This is in contrast to the Generation section, in which students are creating the material they are performing in real time, while they perform it. Interpretation is perhaps the part of an acting class most available and understood by the general public or education administrators. This is also the section of class most like the life of a working actor, rehearsing and performing scripted work. In this segment of class, students have to interpret the work of a playwright or author and determine how to perform the work onstage.

Important to note is that some scripts are more "open" with lines and directions that are not well-defined and therefore multiple types of interpretation are possible, while other scripts are clearly defined with specific actions written for the character, and even subtext or additional notes on the inner life of the character and how they should be performed. This varies by author, time period of writing, and original source of the material. In all cases, there are various ways any line of text can be interpreted for performance, including not only the understanding of what the character is saying and why they are saying, but the subtext and emotion behind it, how each line fits in with the other characters in the script, and how each line leads from and to other actions happening over the play. Importantly, the Interpretation segments of class sometimes continue to include some improvisation. All acting involves the creation of material, but the key difference between Generation and Interpretation activities is what they are based on and where the prompts originate. When students were working with fully formed characters from scripts, using the lines from the scripts, we considered this to be part of the Interpretation section.

Working with scripts and direction can include sitting down and reading through material, talking through subtext, rehearsal of material that has already been blocked (i.e., put on its feet) or rehearsed, or technical engagement with scripts, including definitions, line memorization, or blocking and movement. Interpretation involves both the physical engagement with the script and the psychological engagement with script, finding out the impulses, objectives, subtext, and reasons behind scripts' writing. Interpretation can also involve the rehearsal, critique, and re-rehearsal of moments of script or even entire acts of a play. Interpretation activities accounted for, on average, 44% of class time, with a range from 4–88% of class time.

Of the four segments of an acting class, Interpretation may be considered most centrally "acting"—students must be able to take what is given to them in a text and figure out how to embody and perform it in such a way that an audience can understand the original intention of the playwright and the interpretation of the director. Students in the acting classroom are learning not just to interpret the words of a script and meanings behind them, but also to interpret the ways in which a director instructs them to act and perform, and to think about how the audience might interpret what the actors are doing.

To take a classical example, a Shakespearean play can be interpreted traditionally, in an all-male cast, set in the 1500s, it can be interpreted with an eye toward making the text and subtext relevant in the current moment, or it can be set in any number of time periods (who hasn't seen a *Romeo and Juliet* set in 1776, 1950, or 1996?). Actors will often have a lot of leeway and freedom in thinking through the backstory and emotional pulse of their individual character, but the interplay of collaboration between actor, director, and playwright is centrally important. Teachers frequently provide wide-ranging context to students about the world of a play and the social and political status of characters or the setting in which the play was written, to give them material to interpret for themselves. This segment of class is where students are learning to not just rely on themselves or a minimal prompt, but to take the sketches of what someone else has done, build off of it, and create something new. Students must now construct from the impulses of the playwright and the director. Students must constantly *think collaboratively* (Chapter 7) here, considering the playwright, working with other students, thinking about the teacher as director, and coming to consensus among different interpretations of the same materials. Interpretation and script work is both technical and artistic. Each individual student will put their own spin on material, but students are also instructed how to call back and think through the ways in which characters are stable throughout the script and how their history and position informs their current words and actions. There is a format to it, but also a freedom.

Interpretation takes skills of improvisation and generation, but also skills of character understanding, reading the intentions of others, and collaboration in order to work through what is meant on the page and how it can be translated for the stage. Interpretation is often the most psychologically minded of the sections of class, as students are now asked to think about a specific person, a character, and how that character is expressed through word and movement onstage. Sometimes, Preparation exercises are called back during Interpretation sections of class when a student needs to use a physical skill or vocal ability to interpret a moment in a script.

This part of class was sometimes seated like an English Language Arts course and based on discussion, and other times it was a traditional rehearsal, with actors on a stage, pausing to discuss and get feedback. Sometimes it was based in pairs or small groups, where students would rehearse a script on their own, giving each other feedback and figuring out how they wanted to stage and perform a scene. The ways in which feedback and *reflection* (see Chapter 10) was used during Interpretation segments also varied. Feedback could come after a full performance of a 5-minute scene or focus intensely on the performance of a single line over and over until it felt and looked right. Some classes filmed students for feedback, others used the rest of the class as an audience, and others simply had students rehearse themselves until they felt ready.

In a way, the Interpretation part of class is a bit like a lab component of a chemistry or biology class. Students in the Interpretation section of class engaged in the actual, professionally relevant art of acting, performing a character as they might do on a TV set or a stage for a play (see Chapter 11 for a more in-depth exploration of the varieties of scene study we saw in our classrooms). The Interpretation section of class shows elements similar to how professionals work sometimes with active feedback integrated into performance, and sometimes with feedback withheld until there is a formal period of Reflection at the end of the class (our fourth kind of activity).

Interpretation Example Class

In Class 11, at Boston Arts Academy, the freshman spent 47 minutes (out of 90, 52%) in various forms of Interpretation activities. To note, the first part of this class was an intensive warm-up and then a formal Reflection segment on the *body awareness and control* that was integrated into the warm-up, discussed in Chapter 3 as an example. From this, the class moved into three different types of Interpretation activities. First, Juanita (the teacher) introduced the idea of "tools for rehearsal." She discussed the different techniques and ideas the students would be using to interpret and think about their characters and their scenes. The students took notes in their notebooks, prompted to think about demystifying the process of thinking about creating a scene as an actor, going beyond what a director or a teacher might be instructing them to do, and taking agency for their own performance and learning.

"There is an ownership and an independent artistry that should be developed inside of you," Juanita said. She pointed out that students could not necessarily rely on a director to tell them everything to do, and by having their own process and ideas, they would be served well in their creation of performance in more professional and academic settings. She noted when it is time to rehearse, the students will need to have tools in the toolbox to work on their own, not just when they are sitting with a director or performing for a teacher.

She spoke then for a bit on REGOT, the acronym of Relationships, Environment, Goals, Obstacles, Tactics. These are all ways for a student to think about their characters, how they exist in a script, and how to interpret what is on the page. This day was focused on Relationships, meaning how each character should be thought about in relation to the other characters in the script. "Based on my script," Juanita had the students write down "what is an event that could have happened in the past between my character and the other character that would show. . . .

1. What the relationship is,
2. What the characters mean to each other, and
3. What the characters accept about each other but struggle with."

This is exemplary of an Interpretation activity for a script—the students have to think about what they are given in the lines of the script, and then create for themselves justifiable additional understanding of the character and their relationship with the action and other people onstage.

Juanita brought the complexity of scripted relationships back to the students' real lives, discussing how they might have a friend who they like, but they wish they would be different in some way. She then asked the students why these three questions would help them interpret scripts and understand their character for performance. She prompted the students to think about how they interact with their own friends in different ways, based on the relationship, the history, and the context of the friendship. She noted, "This is part of making these characters multidimensional. It has to be based in the script because everything we do is based in the script. But 90% of what we create is in our imaginations." The script is only a starting point, the rest comes from how the students create, envision, understand, and apply what is in the script to their own performance style and personality. It is script, interpreted through student, that becomes performance.

After this discussion, Juanita sent the students with their scripts to practice together. They first met in scene partnerships and answered the questions. She then asked them to create a scenario for the characters where the relationship and the answers to the posed questions would come through and from the scenario. Juanita and her assistant ran through a brief improvised scene to show the students how they might, in character, start talking through an imagined scenario based on a script. She noted students must remember to create strictly from what is in the script. Based on their knowledge of the personality of the characters from the script, they were to build on top of that "from everything that's in it. You look at the stage directions, you look at what they say to each other. You look at what they say about each other. You look at what other characters say about them." Juanita laid out how the students would use the evidence in the script to create something tightly connected and make it personal and understandable. If the character is described in the script as depressed, the student should not write in their character analysis that they are a "happy person."

The students were given 30 minutes. They were told once they answered the posed questions they should start "playing with it. . . . Play through to see what else you discover." She encouraged them to spend only 5 minutes or so in conversation, and to focus for the rest of the work period "on your feet to see what you discover." In individual discussion with students while they were working in pairs, she said once students were familiar with the script, the assignment to come up with scenarios was "your playing ground, your agency, your power."

Juanita noted it was not about reenacting the script, but interpreting it to delve into the relationships of the characters. The student should use the script to develop an interpretation improv off of the characters, to better understand what the characters know and feel about each other. She also emphasized that the attention should always be on the other person, not on the self, so that the students were not focused on what they were saying next. "If you're paying attention to the other person, then you are open to being spontaneous with them," she noted.

After the work period, the class ended with a third Interpretation exercise, with the students workshopping the environments they had created around their scripts. Here, instead of working in pairs with Juanita walking around to check in, she pulled a few pairs to the center of the room and had the rest of the students watch as she worked with each pair on what they had created about their relationships. She noted students in these working pairs should not just be relying on the Interpretation through the lens that she has asked for (Relationships), but should be bringing in and combining all REGOT lessons she had taught thus far. In this way, she wanted the students to be working consciously on pulling together their multiple lessons and techniques for the best outcomes.

The students performed their improvised, created scenes and discussions based on their scene's characters and script. After they performed, Juanita paused them, and had them start over, reorienting the students back to what the characters were feeling and thinking in response to each moment:

- "Where were you coming from?"
- "How do you feel about the fact that the scene starts with your waiting? What is the truth of that?"
- "Let's find their humanity."
- "The meat of it . . . is the character afraid of something? Does she believe in herself? Don't let it just be on the surface . . . get to know your characters more."

In other classes, the Interpretation section of class included the following:

- sitting in a circle and reading through a script for the first time with assigned roles,
- class discussion of individual characters' objectives and needs,
- dividing into small groups and some students rehearsing a scene while others watched,
- pairs of students working through the physicalization of a scene while the teacher walked around asking questions and making comments,
- students reading lines to their phones to record for memorization, and
- students performing a scene multiple times with a camera focused on a different student each time, for later playback and discussion.

There were also multiple classes where students were working on monologues, as individual characters, and teachers asked students to try performing on their own, in various ways, such as whispering, or connecting to archetypes previously discussed in class. In all of these ways, the students were asked to think about what their characters were saying in the scripts and why they were saying each line. Word choice, its physical interpretation, and how an audience would understand the performance, were always being played with, whether seated, figuring out movement, or full-out in performance.

Interpretation is often what non-theatre people may think of when they think of an acting class. But it is more nuanced, varied, and contextually driven than a simple scene rehearsal. Across our classes, teachers used the Interpretation section, whether a rehearsal of a single line or a full script, and whether seated or performing, to pull together skills taught in the Generation and Preparation segments of class, and to teach students the varieties of tools and techniques that could be brought to bear on written material. They also built in both formal and informal Reflection to help the students understand how they could improve.

REFLECTION: THINKING ABOUT AND DISCUSSING THE WORK

Scattered throughout the class as well as during a delineated period at the end of many classes, the final type of segment of class, Reflection, went beyond simple feedback from teachers to students. Reflection required students to think about what they are doing, why they are doing it, and how they might be doing it in a variety of ways. One note, to be covered more extensively in Chapter 10, is that *reflect and think metacognitively* is also an Acting Habit of Mind, recruited and integrated into the classroom and underlying many separate activities and exercises throughout class. The difference between *reflect and think metacognitively* as an Acting Habit of Mind and Reflection as a type of class activity is the formality and separation with which teachers use a partitioned and constrained time in the classroom to ask students to formally think about and discuss what they just saw or experienced. Segments of class were coded as Reflection when the teachers had students stop what they were doing and sit down and discuss, not just quick comments while still continuing an exercise (we saw many of those moments, which were instead coded as building and integrating the Acting Habit of Mind of *reflect* into the class segment of the activity). While many different activities incorporate *reflect and think metacognitively* as a way of thinking about the activity, most classes also had a section of time in which students did nothing but reflect on the other parts and pieces of their work, sometimes bringing in multiple other Acting Habits of Mind into their Reflection period.

Reflection was not only about the direct activity of the classroom that had just occurred. Many classes began or ended with a formal period of Reflection on the days' exercises and activities as a whole, on larger issues in the student's lives, or theories and ideas from movies or writings. Reflection also occurred after each of the other three segments, when students engaged in discussion and thinking about both others and themselves—why did they make the choices they made in each of the exercises? How did it go, and why do they think it was successful or not? Reflection activities accounted for, on average, 32% of class time, with a range from 4–97% of class time. This could be verbal or written. Students would often build on each other's comments and thoughts during this time, thinking about how their response to something they had just seen performed was the same or different than how others responded to what had just been performed.

Reflection is necessary for students to judge their own learning and success. Without Reflection on an improvisation, it can be hard to transfer all skills built to scripted segments. Without Reflection on a script, it can be hard to take direction and build a performance. Without Reflection on others' performance, it can be hard to build knowledge of what works and does not work onstage for an audience. Without a Reflection on warm-up exercises, it can be hard to understand how to use the body and voice to create anything for anyone at all!

Reflection is critical and allows students to integrate and apply all of the active learning they have been doing. Generally, the more students can engage in thinking about their behaviors, thoughts, and performances, the more likely they are to take the knowledge they have gained in one area of the class and apply it to other areas of the class. Formalized Reflection periods and activities let students know that this is a distinct way of learning they should be using to their benefit throughout the class periods. Reflection is separated and different from the action and work of acting class because it is a metacognitive skill, and a meta-emotional feedback loop. Students learn if the emotion they were performing was not working for the audience, or did not feel authentic or successful in performance, then they need to think about it in a different way for another go at a performance. Reflection requires stepping back from the here and now and putting the other activities and sections of class into context.

Reflection Example Class

In Class 10, for sophomores at Boston Arts Academy, a few different periods of Reflection on different types of activities in the class led the day. While Reflection was not a majority of the class time (which it was in some other classes, see Chapter 10 for exemplars), this class was a model for how Maura, the teacher, used set-aside periods of Reflection to segment the class and provide students with transitions.

The class began with a verbal and physical word game, where the students had to listen closely and add on to each other's words while also drumming their legs. But it did not go well. The students were distracted, talking to each other, making extraneous noises, and not paying close attention. Maura stopped the class. "Did you like that game?" "No!" the class answered. So, they took a moment of Reflection on why the class did not like the game. "It was hard!" they said. "Like Shakespeare?" Maura asked. The class groaned and laughed. She continued, "You have to think, you have to act, you have to move, you have to listen to other people and respond. Oh, it's so hard! It's like acting."

In this moment of formal and separated Reflection, Maura showed she was paying attention to the students and their responses, and also that these exercises were not pointless, but rather based in the goals students were trying to reach. The moment only took 30 seconds, but completely shifted the class into attention for the next warm-up exercise, where they had to closely watch and respond to each other.

After the exercise, the class sat down to discuss an extension on their juried (i.e., teacher judged) performances. In this period of Reflection on their work and performing it, Maura noted "there's no sense in doing something that sucks . . . it's about doing something difficult, well." She then passed out worksheets for the students to write down and reflect on where their performances were at that point and where they need to go. They discussed a plan of action on how to get their performances workshopped and improved.

Maura asked them to "Think back to our workshop [a guest Shakespearean actor from last week] . . . I want you to reflect on that workshop, and I want to ask you a couple of questions. Did you think she was good at Shakespeare? So, let's describe why." The students reflected she was strong with the words, knew the rest of the script, knew actions, was passionate, etc. "But why?" Maura asked. For this Reflection, she was explicitly asking the students to set aside time to think about past experiences in acting class, and how the experiences they had could be connected back to the actions they needed moving forward for their juried performances.

She asked the students to think about "What are the takeaways? What are the things that you felt from [the workshop leader] that you could incorporate? Things that you felt were accessible that you could do. What motivated you? What did she make you think about in terms of preparing your own characters?" Maura noted that in high school and college, students were exposed to many different kinds of theatre, but perhaps after college they specialize in one type of theatre, like Shakespeare.

She then transitioned into a directed exercise for the students to Reflect on what they needed to do to prepare themselves for the juried performance in four weeks. She had them write their goal for the next week on the white board (i.e., "I want _____") to build a class-wide collage of goals to see what each other were thinking. Maura then brought the class back together again for even more discussion on their warm-up from earlier in the day. She focused on how if they bring some skin into the game and make their exercises a competition and perhaps even a fight, it raises the stakes on their acting and makes the whole performance more interesting. She connected all of these components multiple times over the course of the class to give the students guidance on where they could reflect. She even connected it back to the students' abilities to "find a place in your body where it's urgent. If you can't find the urgency, no one will watch it onstage."

The students then moved into an hour of class in which they engaged in some Generation activities, a brief physical warm-up and some scene study. However, Maura came back around again and ended the class with a 9-minute "I reinforce" Reflection activity. The students discussed their scene partners and other classmates, and noted elements they had done well over the class and the past week. The class ended on a calmer and happy note from having Reflected on a variety of moments that had gone well over the day.

Overall, this day showed the various ways in which Reflection is used and integrated throughout the class. While Reflection was 27% of class time, it was a constant touch point from other segments of class. Students took moments of Reflection from previous classes, outside workshops, their own goals, and on the activities they had just done during the class, in order to integrate and understand them as part of their journey through learning how to act.

Other example segments of Reflection include:

- brief circles at the beginning or ending of class where students reflect on their past week,
- a discussion with a visiting alumnus about how she brings the skills of acting into her college experience,
- a check in about where in the body the students feel the vocal warm-up,
- a discussion about whether the students thought the improvisation they had just engaged in was successful in working together,
- an end-of-class discussion of the difficulties of finding active verbs to portray during scenes,
- the difficulties students had in staying in the moment during an exercise that felt a bit silly, and
- a discussion on how students could use the exercise of the day to figure out how their character should move through space during a scene.

Reflection can also be a faster back and forth, as seen in multiple classes. For example, sometimes a group of students would move between performance and a sit-down Reflection, followed by another group performing and a second Reflection period. What this shows students is that every action they choose for performance should and will be carefully discussed and thought through, and that all choices can be made mindfully and with purpose (see Chapter 9).

Formal Reflection is the core to growth, learning, and development in an acting class. It can be applied to all kinds of activities and actions across class time and goals. Students use Reflection periods to think about how the world outside the acting classroom was connected to the world inside the theatre, how they could improve their own Generative and Interpretive performances, how to change the way they engaged with scripts, and how to bring skills across segments of class. A formal, separated time for Reflection is critical for student actors to improve and gain physical and mental self-awareness, and therefore better acting skills.

PREPARATION, GENERATION, INTERPRETATION, AND REFLECTION ACROSS AN ACTING CLASS

While the general order of these activities within the classroom is from Preparation into Generation, and then Interpretation and Reflection (see Figure 2.1, below), the amount of time spent and order of each type of activity varies by class. Some classes may also start with a period of Reflection, then into a Generative improvisation game, and then into a specific memory-based warm-up for the Interpretation section of class for script work.

We observed distinctions by level and experience of the class and students, as well as when during the academic year the class was filmed. In less experienced classes, more time was spent on the Preparation and Generation pieces of class. In more senior classes and fourth-year classes, there was often a brief Preparation period and then students moved right into Interpretive

Figure 2.1. All 40 Classes by Segment Type, Time, and Order

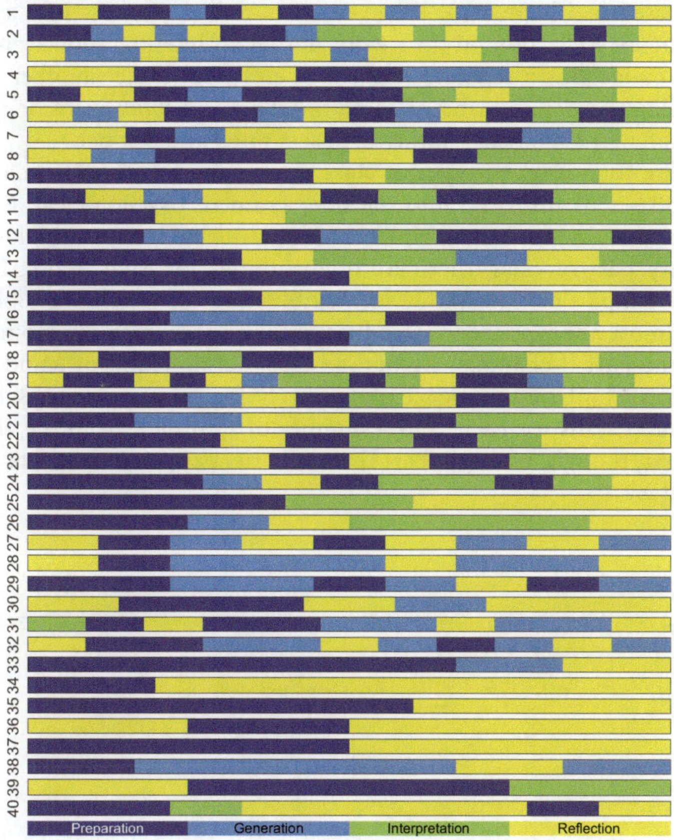

performance and Reflection on that performance. Because the teachers were not consciously or purposefully organizing classes by segment type, but instead by pedagogical goal, the segmentation of class and order was practically never the same. In fact, only two classes that we observed had the exact same patterning of activity types, and these were at the same school, both with Justin as teacher, on a Tuesday and Wednesday of the same class type (Classes 28 and 30). Otherwise, even with other classes at the same school and the same teacher (including a full 2 weeks of observation of the same class with the same teacher), we did not see exact trajectories of activity type. Instead, teachers were being sensitive to the needs of the students' goals and the needs of the time in the academic year.

Each of these segments of class and types of activities can be conducted with an eye to one or multiple Habits of Mind used in acting classes, as will be seen across Part II. Importantly, the content of class is not linear—a Reflection moment can occur during an Interpretation exercise, and Generative activities can build directly from Preparation activities. To note, Reflection moments that take less than a minute or so may be undercounted in our data, as discussed in Chapter 10. When teachers pulled students into a one- or two-sentence Reflection on their work during an Interpretation segment, we did not count it as a separate segment of class, but rather another example of building the Acting Habit of Mind of *reflect and think metacognitively*—active and in the moment—rather than separated and distinct.

These four segment types of class give us the framework to an acting class and set us up to go into the finer grained, psychological aspects of class—the Acting Habits of Mind . . . how students learn to think onstage. For every part of class, there are opportunities for each Acting Habit of Mind. Each part of class allows for flexible usage of whichever tools teachers find most appropriate to introduce to their students in the moment.

In the Part II chapters, we outline each Acting Habit of Mind in turn, with a focus both on the science of the psychological competencies, abilities, and related skills for each, and a number of examples from the classes in turn. First, though, we begin Part II with a brief explanation of what Habits of Mind *are*.

Part II

THE EIGHT HABITS OF MIND TAUGHT IN ACTING CLASSES

Habits of Mind Introduction

Before we can begin exploring the Acting Habits of Mind that emerged through observation of acting classes, we should first clarify what Habits of Mind are. As defined and theorized in education and developmental psychology, Habits of Mind are mental approaches to the world. They are ways of thinking—sets of skills, behaviors, past experiences, and tendencies brought to bear when a student (or really, anyone) needs to solve a problem or complete a task. They are techniques of orienting attention and methods for structuring, thinking through, and solving problems. They are buildable, learnable, and stable over time. They are internalized frameworks to inform the ways a person thinks about, tackles, or understands multiple topics, domains, and new ideas.

Habits of Mind are also dispositional, meaning they are stable for each individual person—similar to how individuals have personality traits that inform their thinking and behavior, people also have habits of mind they use at their own level every day. And, similarly to how individuals can build and shift their traits over time, they can do so with their Habits of Mind. Acting Habits of Mind, therefore, are big and broad ways of thinking, taught and used in the theatre, but potentially usable outside of the theatre classroom.

Positive and adaptive Habits of Mind are fundamentally important to develop for success, both in education specifically and life more generally. But notably, these are not thinking strategies that are easily captured by the kinds of standardized tests taken in high school (see Butler 2020; Sheridan et al., 2022; Winner, 2022; Winner & Hetland, 2000). One way to think about Habits of Mind is that they are "practices" that allow students to use capacities they already have for particular tasks; a method for applying and framing approaches to problems and questions students encounter in their classrooms. They are not easily quantified and testable in the way math knowledge or even empathy have been in the past.

Habits of Mind as a concept was first developed as a way to delineate and organize "patterns of thinking behaviors," "ways of thinking," "systems thinking about outcomes," and "thinking skills" that go beyond simple intelligence into thinking behaviors in education more generally (Costa & Kallick, 2000). The idea of Habits of Mind as trainable, buildable frameworks for thinking has been applied broadly in education for many decades, as domain general ways of approaching learning that can help all students (Perkins, 1995). They have also been applied specifically in various domains including scientific thinking (Butler, 2020), mathematical thinking (Cuoco et al., 1996; Goldenberg et al., 1996), and legal training (Jaquish & Ware, 1993).

While Habits of Mind are flexible to educational and life settings, generalizable across scenario and multiple contexts, they are not exactly "far transfer" skills—they are not psychological abilities per se, nor are they facts or pieces of information to be learned. A Habit of Mind is not a single, set skill a student is taught through acting that can then directly transfer to another academic requirement. Habits of Mind consist of many separable skills. An Acting Habit of Mind is a way of approaching the world that works in acting classrooms to complete acting tasks and solve acting problems. It recruits various psychological traits and abilities. But critically, Acting Habits of Mind could also work to complete tasks and solve problems in other domains. Students may have to be taught how to transfer these ways of thinking. But it is here the possibilities of expanded learning lie.

For example, *being aware of your body* helps actors perform an emotional scene in an acting exercise so the audience can understand what the character is feeling. For the student actor, this Acting Habit of Mind of *body awareness and control* for performance consists of skills including kinesthetic awareness, mindfulness, interoception, and proprioception. Then, as the student approaches the world, with a habit of awareness of their body, this approach could also help with emotion regulation in everyday life (see Chapter 3). What I propose is that once a student has a personal sense of how to use each Acting Habit of Mind, to call upon it and integrate it in an acting class, then the Acting Habits of Mind could be accessible for them and useful for them across their lives.

Call for Future Research

Within classes, some Acting Habits of Mind are more central than others in particular activities, and I hypothesize some students will naturally gravitate toward using some over others across activities. Like any dispositional level trait (e.g., introversion or agreeableness), eventually there will be individual differences in how much and how often students' use each Acting Habit of Mind both in and out of acting classes. This will be a rich area for future research.

In acting classes, the Acting Habits of Mind are complementary to each other: they fit together like puzzle pieces in various ways across various settings. They can also be causal to one another, and cyclical in an activity (see Chapter 11 on Scene Study). Students can move from one Acting

Habit of Mind to another in succession as an exercise or task changes and requirements shift. Acting classes are brimming with activities using and integrating mental habits in the broadest sense. However, our analysis of the 56.5 hours of 40 acting classes uncovered eight foundational, cross-cutting Acting Habits of Mind, separable from one another, described in Part II.

THE STRUCTURE OF PART II CHAPTERS

In Chapters 3–10, I lay out the eight Acting Habits of Mind that emerged from analyzing our 40 acting classes across five schools. Each chapter follows the same structure and includes sections where I define and discuss each Acting Habit of Mind in a variety of ways. First, I give an illustrative moment from a class, and then a concise definition of the Acting Habit of Mind, and a discussion of where it can come out focally in a single activity. While no Acting Habit of Mind is ever used in an activity on its own without any other Acting Habits of Mind, there are a variety of activities from the classes where one in particular is at the forefront.

After defining the Acting Habit of Mind within the classroom as its own mental practice, I go into the science. I connect the Acting Habit of Mind to scientific findings across developmental, cognitive, and neuroscientific research to show its possible application across contexts and critical psychological outcomes. I zoom in to where there is evidence specifically in adolescent populations since the students in our study were all teens. While there is not a one-to-one correspondence between each Acting Habits of Mind and defined psychological skills, there are related constructs to be found across psychosocial and neurological functioning and development. By discussing the science behind each Acting Habit of Mind, the reader can see how the highlighted illustrative acting exercises tie back to skills that could be applied outside the theatre classroom.

After working through relevant psychological constructs, I then describe a series of exemplar activities where the Acting Habit of Mind is used and integrated across each of the four different types of activities (from Chapter 2) in acting classes.

Then, I turn to two focal activities, where a teacher spent a considerable amount of class time on a particular exercise or activity that centered, used, and likely fostered the Acting Habit of Mind. I describe how the activity was set up, how it was engaged in by the students, what the teacher said about the activity in the interviews, and how the teacher's in-class discourse integrated and centered the Acting Habit of Mind. Finally, I end each chapter with a brief summary of the Acting Habit of Mind: its definition, connections back to findings from psychological science, exemplary activities, and how to bring it into future practice and research.

STRUCTURE OF PART II CHAPTERS

- **Illustrative moment** (vignette) of the Acting Habit of Mind.
- **Definition** of the Acting Habit of Mind in terms of the acting classroom.
- **Connections between scientific findings** across developmental, cognitive, and neuroscientific research and the Acting Habit of Mind.
- **Four short exemplar activities** where the Acting Habit of Mind is used and integrated in each activity type: Preparation, Generation, Interpretation, Reflection.
- **Two longer focal activities**, each where a teacher focused on a particular exercise that centered, used, and fostered the Acting Habit of Mind.
- **Brief summary points** for the Acting Habit of Mind's definition, connections to psychological science, exemplary activities, and future practice and research.

I have not ordered the Acting Habits of Mind in any particular way related to how they are presented in acting classes or at different acting levels. Acting Habits of Mind are not scaffolded off each other like reading or mathematical skills. They are instead iterative, integrated, collaborative, and blended. As the reader will see, the Acting Habits of Mind can be centered during entire exercises in an acting class, or they can be pulled in by one line of teaching during a day, and I highlight both usages throughout. They can be activated by both verbal and nonverbal moments in class. While from the outside, activities of acting class may look like games or play, those games and play always have a broader meaning and purpose. Multiple Acting Habits of Mind can combine to support one acting task (see Chapters 11 and 12) and also can combine to support one psychological skill (see Chapter 13).

Readers can therefore approach these eight Acting Habits of Mind chapters in a few different ways. If you are interested in exercises to foster a particular psychological, cognitive, social, emotional outcome, look at the last two exercises described in each chapter, and make sure to download the Exercises Toolbox available online at TheatreEdMatters.com website. If you want to know the variety of ways the Acting Habits of Mind can be used, check out the descriptions in each chapter's section for each acting habit of mind "in Acting Classroom." If you are interested in what kinds of scientific and psychological research is available on a particular Acting Habit of Mind, you will want to focus on "The Science of . . ." for each Acting Habit of Mind. If you just want the gist, check out the summary at the end of each chapter, and the executive summary of the Acting Habits of Mind (and the book as a whole), available online at TheatreEdMatters.com.

To note for all readers, in the executive summary we lay out the eight Acting Habits of Mind and why they are important for development and education. In the Toolbox, we describe the focal activities that may be best suited to engage that Acting Habit of Mind for adolescents. And on the website, we have further reading lists to delve more into the research, and video examples from our classes that are linked to the ways in which we provide examples throughout the book. We hope readers of this book will find these resources helpful and use them widely!

SPECIFICITIES FOR HABITS OF MIND IN ACTING CLASSES

As mentioned above, these Acting Habits of Mind are not necessarily individual psychological skills or abilities that can be directly taught and fostered in development. Acting Habits of Mind are strategies for problem solving or approaching activities. These kinds of strategies are not straightforward or simple, though. This is one of the reasons why theatre and acting classes are such good conduits for these Acting Habits of Mind—the complexity. These are not singular skills that can be isolated—they have to be taught in their fullness of context, and brought to bear on complex ideas, the type of which are always happening in acting classes at all levels.

Frankly, one of the biggest issues we ran across with discovering these Acting Habits of Mind as separable components within an acting class is how quickly, thoroughly, and readily the teachers moved across them. While there are exemplary activities that do put forward one Acting Habit of Mind primarily, just as (if not more) often there were activities that used multiple Acting Habits of Mind simultaneously or in rapid succession. A warm-up could run through *body awareness and control, think collaboratively*, and *be flexible* in a 15-second improv.

In summary, eight Acting Habits of Mind emerged from our thorough qualitative and quantitative analysis of acting classes, teacher interviews, and theoretical writings. They are explained thoroughly, with examples, in the next eight chapters.

Chapter 3

Body Awareness and Control

Learning to Understand and Control Your Physicality

In Class 24 at The Madeira School, our private all-girls high school, a group of students stand in a circle, each with their hands over their chest. They hum up and down the vocal register, varying their pitch and moving their arms in a circle. They repeat this several times, closing their eyes. The teacher, Kelsey, leads them through a series of different sounds and movements they already know. They say "zoooooooo" (while making a circle with their knees), "woooaaa" (circling their hips), "shaaa" (pushing hands out from their stomachs), "gah" (shooting their arms out from their stomach), "maaaaa" (bringing hands to chest and out), "faaaa" (two hands out from mouth), "haaa" (waving hand from mouth), "ba, de, peehhhhhh" (touching parts of their face), "deeee" (hand to forehead), and "reeee" (hand from top of head).

The sounds get louder and higher in pitch as the movements of the arms travel up the body. The students and Kelsey repeat this entire 20 seconds of sound, movement, and arm/body climbing in reverse. This "vowel ladder" is described by Kelsey as a way to warm-up before going onstage. She notes to the students that she does this backstage before performing, and if she cannot feel distinctions among both the body placement of the sounds and the movements themselves before stepping onstage, she runs through it a few times until she can.

So, what is happening in this activity and in this teaching moment? The students are being asked to *reflect* on their behaviors, and perhaps also *release inhibitions*, but most importantly, this moment contains, integrates, and embeds ***body awareness and control***. Students are being asked to control their bodies' movements and sounds, to create distinctions in their bodies as they isolate the pitch and location of sounds, to pair sounds with arm movements, and to be aware of what is happening in the resonance of the sound, shape, and movement as they perform it. This exercise is not meant to be showcased for others—it is about the student themselves learning pitch, movement, and control.

Body awareness and control is the Acting Habit of Mind students use as they learn to understand and control their bodies, voices, facial expressions, and how physicality is performed and portrayed onstage. *Body awareness* is one of the several technical skills of acting. After all, the body is the instrument of the actor in the same way the violin, flute, piano, or tuba is the instrument of the musician, and the paintbrush or clay the instrument of the visual artist. Making your voice louder without actually sounding like you are screaming, being able to whisper theatrically, the need to physically freeze onstage for theatrical effect, the way an actor must "cheat" or turn out to the audience for performance while still making it look like they are naturally facing the other people onstage, are all physical actions that need a high level of awareness and control. Beyond these technical skills, the ability to physically communicate fury, sadness, romantic intentions, and glee are physical as well as mental behaviors. While bodily actions themselves are not psychological necessarily, the control and awareness of all of these actions is psychological. The ability to understand what your body is doing, how it could be read by an audience, and how to communicate effectively through body and voice are cognitively built mental habits.

Body awareness and control is not a passive Habit of Mind that appears implicitly (that is, without discussion) in an acting class. Rather, we found it was an active skill educators are teaching. Our teachers are mindful and explicit that students' awareness of their own bodies and control over their own bodies is both critical and central to learning how to act onstage. As Justin, our teacher at Eureka High, a large suburban general public school in St. Louis, would have his students say every day: "Today I will be mindful of my body, my voice, my imagination, as I focus and collaborate."

This quote highlights for the students that while engaging in imaginative activities, while focusing on the performing work at hand, and while collaborating with their fellow classmates, they must use the Acting Habit of Mind of being aware of their bodies and voices, of how they are physicalizing each moment. This quote shows both the complexity of acting classes (more on this in Chapter 12), and that the body, awareness, and control comes first.

THE SCIENCE OF BODY AWARENESS AND CONTROL

As with practically every activity in an acting class, the use of *body awareness and control* as an Acting Habit of Mind is related to and integrates several psychological skills and abilities across cognitive, social, and emotional domains.

What do we know about the science of *body awareness and control* from a psychological and developmental perspective? To begin, while psychology is centrally the study of the mind and the brain, there has been an increased interest in the body and its role in psychological functioning in the last decade or so. This comes in a few forms. First, we know learning how to read the signals of the body (particularly hunger, temperature, and heart rate)—a skill called interoception (Craig, 2002)—is critical across multiple areas of psychological health and well-being (Khalsa et al., 2018), including in coping with eating disorders (Martin et al., 2019), emotion regulation (Kever et al., 2015), and learning and decision-making (Werner et al., 2013).

Interoceptive ability begins early in development, with infants learning how to read their own bodily signals for hunger and when to use the bathroom. Infants also gain interoceptive abilities from their caregivers; as parents respond to the baby's bodily signals, the baby learns to associate those signals with care and help (Montirosso & McGlone, 2020). In general, the growing psychological control of physical engagement with the world continues to be particularly strong in the first year of life, as children learn to crawl and walk while their body grows and changes almost daily (Adolph et al., 2008). This is paralleled in a very real way for our students, who were all adolescents between the ages of 13 and 18 years old. For many of them, their bodies are changing from day-to-day, too!

As children get older, they learn how to be increasingly aware of their own bodily sensations and limits when engaged in a wide range of activities, from figuring out how to regulate their emotions to keeping balance on the playground and in sports. (Think about the difference between a 5-year-old running wildly and crashing into their dad compared to an 8-year-old who can stop and turn on a dime.) As children approach adolescence, being able to read the signals in their body and control their physical self continues to help with emotion regulation (Cole et al., 2004) and is also indicated in risky decision-making (Dunn et al., 2010). Specifically, being able to read their emotions for information as they make decisions guides teens toward better, and away from bad, risks. As mentioned, one of the challenges of adolescence is that the body the student had last week may not be the same in weight, balance, or temperament as the body they have this week. Acting classes, with their focus on the body, are a great place to learn how to engage with changing bodies, the signals they are sending, and what to do about them as a whole.

As with most scientifically driven questions that involve actors, we have only one or two empirical studies on bodies and acting, but some tantalizing evidence from these studies. In 2022, Dr. Peter Sokol-Hessner, a psychologist at the University of Denver, and his colleagues directly asked whether professional actors had better interoception abilities compared to non-actors, as measured by their knowledge of their own heart rate. However, they also asked the important question of whether actors were more metacognitively aware of their own understanding of their own heart rate than non-actors.

That is, did they know what they knew (and did not know) about their own bodies?

Surprisingly, the actors were not necessarily better at reading their own heart rate. They scored similarly to the non-actors. But the actors were better on their metacognitive awareness. They knew what they could figure out about their bodies, and they knew what they could not. This ability was also tied to some of the actors' grades in their acting classes (as all of the actors were enrolled in graduate MFA programs at NYU). Actors found the entire task easier and more accessible than non-actors. This study gives preliminary evidence that actors may be more aware of their own bodies, although they are not necessarily better at counting and knowing their own heart rate. However, given that acting classes, as we will see below, are more focused on external movements and performance, this study may have been testing the wrong thing! Actor's body awareness may not extend internally to heart rate, but instead perhaps involves a "knowing what you know" and "knowing what you don't" about the actors' own bodies (Sokol-Hessner et al., 2022).

Beyond interoception, psychologists often talk about embodied cognition. Embodied cognition is the theory that the physical sensations of the body tell a person more information about their environment and the best way to interact with their physical world than just "thinking" alone. Embodied cognition further proposes that the body can help make decisions and guide cognitive functioning. In fact, an entire area of cognitive studies called "4e" cognition has come to the forefront, proposing that all cognition is embodied (that is, the body has a role in cognition), enacted (that is, cognition is physicalized), embedded (that is, cognition is not independent from the environment where it happens), and extended (that is, cognition is part of the brain, the body, and the environment). Theorists of embodied cognition propose there is no cognition that occurs only in the brain. Rather, they propose cognition is distributed into the sensations of the body paired with the understanding in the brain (Foglia & Wilson, 2013; Wilson 2002). Embodied cognition theory would hypothesize that training and understanding of links between the mind and the physical body will help the person understand their world better.

While no researchers have tested embodied cognition approaches in acting directly, this theory provides a nice explanation for why actors may have really great memories for long stretches of text (traditionally researched and thought of as a purely cognitive feat). Dr. Helga Noice and her husband Tony Noice, a psychologist and theatrical director couple, found over several decades of experimental research in cognitive psychology that actors who enacted and physicalized roles had long-lived memories for monologues and lines from shows. They expanded this work to show that anyone—actor or not—can use the tools of physicalizing and embodying text, giving it movement and space to help remember (Noice & Noice, 2001, 2006; Noice et al.,

2004), and that acting-based memory techniques can even help our aging memories retain more material (Noice & Noice, 2013; Noice et al., 2004).

In addition to embodied cognition work, theories of emotion regulation have increasingly become more embodied as scientists of emotion (often called affective scientists) have rallied around a new theory of how emotion is created for the mind by the brain, and how we can best therefore control our emotions. The theory of constructed emotion (TCE, for short) is in the direct lineage of the classic theory of James-Lange emotion, and proposes that any emotion someone feels is actually their cognitive understanding of what their body is feeling in response to a stimulus. TCE proposes that our emotions are a combination of many different factors. These include how our body feels generally (Did we get enough sleep? Water? When is the last time we ate?), our understanding of the situation we are in and what it means to us (our cognitive understanding, or appraisal of the context), and bodily changes in response to a stimuli (Are we feeling more awake? More asleep? More positive? More negative?). The bodily sensations our brains are being sent, and how we interpret them, is what this theory proposes comes together to make up our emotional responses (Barrett, 2017).

Then, our ability to read and understand those bodily responses, in combination with our understanding of the context and the language we use to put it all together, equal how we are feeling in the moment. Key, as well, to this theory of emotion and its regulation is that the better we get at putting words to our bodily sensations, the better we are at understanding what we are feeling and why and therefore controlling how we are feeling (known as "emotional granularity") (Barrett et al., 2001). This understanding of our current feelings, and then an understanding of what to do about the feelings—bodily and mentally—is the foundation of social engagement and emotional appropriateness.

Acting classes, as we will see in the next few chapters, fill in many of these emotion-related components: language, contextual understanding, and bodily awareness. Acting classes give additional words for how characters are feeling, teach actors about their bodies and what their bodies are responding to in any particular moment, teach actors how to analyze contexts and situations for what they make characters feel, and teach actors how to embody that feeling for an audience to understand. There is evidence that role play and acting classes are related to better emotion-regulation skills (e.g., Goldstein & Lerner, 2018; Goldstein, Tamir & Winner, 2013). Psychological research has found that in general, higher levels of interoception, embodied cognition, and emotional granularity are all predictive of better social and emotional skills. These come from a sense of knowing and being able to control the body in particular ways—having the tools and tricks to engage with the particulars of your body in that particular moment. This, therefore, may be the link between acting class and better emotional regulation.

Finally, body awareness and understanding are central to kinesthetic awareness and proprioception. Kinesthetic awareness, also called kinesthetic intelligence, is what athletes have as they move around a court or to a ball, how dancers perform, and how gymnasts make sure they can flip in the air two times before landing safely with feet on the ground (Stillman, 2022). We know that kinesthetic and proprioceptive awareness is present in adult actors because the action of presenting onstage requires physical awareness. In some of the limited psychological science on this question, research by Drs. Matthew Berry and Scott Brown at McMaster University show that professional actors change their voices' pitch, loudness, timber, and timing based on characters they are asked to play during a monologue. They also find that professional actors systematically change their vocal characteristics, with high levels of control, based on the personality traits of the characters they are asked to play (Berry & Brown, 2019). However, interestingly, this study also showed that actors, when they were asked to perform a text as themselves, just so the camera could hear them, still change their body and voice from their everyday self. They engage vocal and body control just to be presentational.

These findings, too, show a real sense of mindfulness in the actors. They must have present moment awareness of the state of the body and the way it is projecting outwardly. So often in life, we speak and move without thinking. Acting forces actors to move with thoughtfulness and intention. As research shows how engaging with the body from a mindfully aware place can help with pain management, depression, and other indicators of well-being (e.g., Galla et al., 2015). The connection between acting training and present moment awareness of the body needs much more scientific research, including how it is built in classes and acting experiences.

Now, then, let us turn our attention to what we found in our classes: how this kind of bodily awareness, mindfulness, and control is used, integrated, taught, and possibly fostered in acting classrooms themselves.

BODY AWARENESS AND CONTROL IN THE ACTING CLASSROOM

Each of the segments of class, across activities, includes multiple chances for students to practice the Acting Habit of Mind of *body awareness and control*. In fact, the students used their bodies in some way in every single class, even if only for a few minutes before settling in with a script to read. We did not have any classes where there was no movement at all, and we had some classes where there was practically no stillness!

To look more closely at each segment of class, it may seem self-apparent that during physical warm-ups and Preparation activities students are learning *body awareness and control*, and they are. The ability to meditate, engage in a dance-style warm-up, or do calisthenics, are all ways students can learn about the limits and abilities of their bodies. In addition, however, teachers quite often point out specifically how the students should be using the warm-up exercises to become aware of their bodily states and bring them under conscious control. For example, in Class 5 at Imagination Stage, a group of students were standing in a circle breathing in unison as part of the warm-up. As they did this, the teacher explained "understanding your breath mechanics is really important to create voice." Here, students were explicitly instructed that being aware of how their breath worked, how they could alter their breath, and how to think about breath control would help them have a full voice to speak loudly enough for audiences to hear them when they said their lines.

In Generation activities, *body awareness and control* is used when learning how to express emotions in a variety of ways. In Class 28 at Eureka High, the students had to each say the word "Jabberwocky" in turn while keeping in mind how they verbalized the word, their physical posture, and their gestures. To add to this, they were tasked with expressing an assigned emotion through their physicality within the nonsense word. Each student would come to the center of the circle, say "Jabberwocky" with their assigned emotional expression (e.g., "furious;" "ecstatic") and then name another student and another emotion to take the next turn. As a side note, surprisingly, this exercise of individual emotional expressions through body control was one of the only examples we saw of trying on and playing with emotional expression through generative improvisations. While emotion was often explicitly discussed during the interpretation of lines, the students were not often tasked with simply playing with emotional expression.

In Interpretation activities, *body awareness and control* is central to performing a character. Regardless of which kind of acting theory a teacher ascribes to (and none of our teachers particularly ascribed to one theory; rather they used elements from each major acting theory as teaching tools to get across a particular type of acting lesson, or they conducted different units from different theorists to organize the class), students use their bodies. Therefore, students must be intimately aware of what their bodies are doing, and be able to shape and mold their body and their voice to suit their portrayal of a character for the audience. While award-winning actors are often lauded for extreme changes in their bodies to portray characters, that is not what happened in our classes. Instead, teachers focused on the moment-to-moment movements. In Class 20 at The Madeira School, during the Interpretation section, students were tasked with creating physical expression to go in a script they were studying. Students had to pull verbs or new words from a Shakespearean script they were working on for a larger scene assignment, and then create prototypical physical expressions of those words. They were guided to "script" a single movement to a single verb with a large and physicalized interpretation. Kelsey then paired the words with music, and the students had to physicalize how they would alter the portrayal of each term in the mood of the music. This activity centered the idea that actions and words of characters have a physical element to them, and that figuring out the appropriate physicalization is one way in to understanding and performing a character.

Finally, a Reflection on one's body states can occur at any time, as students are asked to think about whether their portrayal and engagement with their bodies was appropriate for their characters and achieved their performance goals. One Reflection moment on *body control* occurred at Boston Arts Academy, in the freshman Class 11. To note, the students started class with a warm-up including 33 minutes of physical engagement with stretching, jumping jacks, and push-ups, led by the class itself. During this time, Juanita gave feedback and correction to make sure the students' bodies were physically aligned and safe. She then led the class in a guided meditation focused on their physical state and engaging with their bodies in a state of calm awareness. After the end of this physical warm-up and meditation, the students sat in a circle with a notepad, next to their partner for their current scene preparation.

The students were asked "what did you discover and/or experience?" from their physical warm-up. They noted being physically aware of their bodies; being able to feel their back on the floor, rising comfort with being physically close and silent with the other people in their class, and being aware enough to visualize, in the third person, themselves lying on the floor during warm-up. Juanita noted she had discontinued much of the warm-up for a while over the course of the year, and then brought it back, so the students could reflect on where the work of the past year had brought their *body control*.

Juanita then discussed the idea of physical movement and mindfulness as a gift the students could give themselves for better physical and mental health. She encouraged them to trust themselves; just because they are feeling something and experiencing something that could take them elsewhere (in their minds), they should not necessarily follow the feeling. Instead, she reflected that students should and can take moments of physical transformation but stay mentally present, allowing those moments to be a gift to themselves.

In our later interview, Juanita specifically noted she wants the students to feel empowered in their art. She wants to demystify how the mind and the body can be applied to acting, and how the students can use what is already in their bodies and their minds to be the best actors they can be. She wants students to have ownership and independent artistry, so while they will still need directors and producers, they can keep what they already know for themselves. In the class, to end the bodily reflection, she asked the students to write down the physical warm-up and meditation to have it in their "toolbox" to get their bodies and minds ready for when they need to be able to warm-up for themselves. This Reflection on *body awareness and control* lasted 12 minutes.

Across these four sections of class, then, the students are using their bodies to prepare to be physical in their acting, to reflect on how their bodies can serve them in their acting, to explore the variety of physical possibilities in self-expression, and to explore the variety of physical possibilities in character expression. We see these all of these possibilities in our two focal exercises for *body awareness and control.*

Focal Exercise 1: Watching Superman's Physicality

Paying attention to how changes in the body are acting changes, reflective of character performance goals.

One particularly potent lesson for learning *body awareness and control* from a theoretical perspective was given early in the year at Imagination Stage, our private, conservatory stage, in Class 1. Students in the class sat and watched 10 minutes across three different clips from the 1978 film *Superman*, staring Christopher Reeve, in the movie that made him a star. For these clips, Nikki (the teacher) described his performance as "creating its own special effect," and the lesson as her "favorite lesson." Students watched, rapt, as Reeve switched his physicality from the tall, confident Superman to the slouched, nerdy, and meek Clark Kent in order to fool Lois Lane and keep his identity secret. Nikki noted this has not always been how Superman is portrayed, and that students should pay close attention to the way Reeve fully portrays the two characters through physical and vocal choices.

They were asked to think objectively about how he made himself look taller versus shorter, how he walked, and how he changed his voice. They responded with what they saw—the actual physical and perceptual changes they noticed while watching the clip. As it was early in the year, and therefore early in the students' training, they were asked not to make assumptions about why Reeve changed his physicality and voice, but rather to focus on the grounded and visible bodily shifts.

In our post class interview, Nikki noted she gave the students this exercise to give them a goal to strive toward—a way of thinking of acting as a physical exercise they could control. The physical expression and performance of inner thoughts, for Nikki, is what the students should be thinking about at all times when building a character, which requires an awareness of what and where the body is in space, and how its movements are reflective of what is happening inside the character's mind. After watching for 10 minutes, the discussion lasted more than 20 minutes, with Nikki always bringing the conversation back around to what the students actually saw in the film clip and what kinds of physical and vocal movements Reeve made.

She then began to show how each physical choice and movement was in line with his objective as the character (i.e., to hide his identity). If students moved into discussion of the narrative or the character's inner life, she would bring it around again to vocal cues (e.g., a stutter) or physical cues (e.g., his posture). Students pointed out his slouched and shrunken posture, and how he looked down or away when addressing Lois when he played Clark; his mannerisms were more suave, with shoulders back and long strides, when playing Superman. They also noted the differences in his voice. When playing Superman, for example, he used no extraneous sounds, and engaged in more direct discussions, compared to when he was playing Clark.

The students noted even how the movement change was led by the top of his head and the curve of his shoulders, moving down his body to be a complete physical change. Nikki reflected back to the students that this was called "point of lead" work, and was a physical acting strategy they would be studying later in the year, along with animal work (see Chapter 5) and Laban work (both physically driven acting techniques).

Creating a character, Nikki put forward, is not just reading a script, but really thinking through the physicality and body of the character. Through the bodily cues, she emphasized, the students could see what was happening in the character's mind. She pointed out that audiences can really see what the character was thinking through the various facial and bodily changes, at one point even narrating through what Superman/Clark Kent thought in each movement of the body.

Thinking and reflecting on physicality and the way in which Reeve controlled his body was central to all parts of the discussion. In particular, how the physicality was isolated from objective, narrative, costumes, or script, and centered it on the performance of the character himself. This theory-driven activity was also a chance for the students to get used to Nikki's style of questions, reflections, asking students for their opinions, and then reflecting back to them again. It is important to note here that the students themselves were not physically enacting any of these changes or movements, but rather being asked to think deeply about what bodies can do, and how bodies can reflect inner states.

Focal Exercise 2: Wearing a "You Suit"

Learning to tune in and find a third-person perspective on the body.

A second particularly potent lesson in *body awareness and control*, from a practical perspective, was "Space Walking." This activity comes from Viewpoints, an acting and dance theory developed in the 1970s and 1980s. When we observed it in the classroom at Eureka High School Class 33, students already knew this activity and had previously worked on a variety of aspects within their walking, which on the outside looked like simply walking around the stage randomly. However, walking within Viewpoints requires and incorporates a number of different elements, including space (i.e., how they are moving around the space), time (i.e., pacing and speed), level (i.e., are they high or low), and several other variables. Here, the students were playing with multiple overlapping Viewpoints in an improvisation game.

Justin, the teacher, asked the students to begin walking, and once they were in the movement, asked them to freeze. He then told them that they needed to start walking again, but to only think about themselves as having a sense of touch. (An exercise in *imagine and envision* for sure, but grounded in *body awareness and control*, thinking, and processing). He went further, telling the students to focus exclusively on the material, physical experience. He asked them to think about sight as photons touching the eyes, sound as waves touching the ears, and taste and smell as molecules touching the inside of the nose or tongue. In this way, Justin pulled everything back to its actual, perceptual, physical aspect.

The students then began to move around the space focusing in on only their senses. Their movements became slower and more cautious. The students moved purposefully and with a sense of thinking different from how they had been physical before. Then, Justin brought the idea out even more into a cognitive understanding, awareness, and reflection on their own physicality. He instructed: "Almost like an astronaut exploring the space, but it's you exploring the world." This brought up the central point of the activity: he wanted the class to move around the theater space thinking about their own bodies as a "you suit." He wanted them to think of self as a puppeteer and the body we all unconsciously move about in all day as a puppet (much like Descartes would want in his theories of acting from the 1600s!).

In this way, Justin asked the students to make the automatic purposeful. When any of us move around the world normally, we are not thinking from the insides of our body about the way in which we move or physicalize our environment. This acting classroom activity made that nonconscious normality conscious for the students, increasing in a very real and practical way the ways they become aware of their bodies.

The students' walking now became more awkward. After a minute, Justin asked them to freeze again, and to choose where "they" were. Where were the students thinking "themselves," their consciousness, lived? He asked the students to play with this idea. What if they moved their sense of themselves, their "impulses" and their "command center" first into the solar plexus, with the head simply a lens through which information came in? The students considered and moved in this way for a bit.

He then took it another step, and asked the students to pretend they were aliens in their own bodies and environment, exploring their physical senses as new. He asked them to take away the labels that allow looking through or past their senses, and instead think about the history, background, and depth of ordinary objects. By paying attention to the physical sensations without labeling, he wanted them to be curious and explore, in a fresh way, their perceptual world. He gave an example of thinking about the stage floor beneath them not as just "floor," but as something that used to be a living forest. He asked them to consider the history of the wood, the paint, the use of the floor as a stage for productions and assemblies. He asked them to expand their perception and thinking beyond unconscious and automatic processing, into awareness of the present moment and control over how they engaged with it.

This scaffolded activity had the students move into their bodies and away from the automaticity of moving through the world. Instead, they had to be purposeful and thoughtful about their physicality. This exercise is a great example of how to mindfully separate from the body and notice with all senses—of mindful and physical preparation. Justin linked this to reading a script without shorthand, and performing a character purposefully and consciously, *thinking metacognitively*. This also requires a real sense of control. The exercise allowed the students a way to explore and experiment with something new, just using their senses, and not their "understanding" at all. The exercise was all about staying in the present moment and understanding meaning through physical exploration and awareness. The students discussed in reflection of the exercise, that they can manipulate their own physical selves for performance and character—and thus, for the task of acting a character.

BODY AWARENESS AND CONTROL, IN SUMMARY

- The body is the instrument of the actor. In music, visual arts, and writing, students use tools and instruments. In dance, the body is used representationally. But acting uses the body, voice, and face directly to express the character, emotion, objective, and situation.
- *Body awareness and control* is related to the psychological skills of interoception, self-awareness, emotion regulation, and emotional awareness. These are all embodied, multimodal, and kinesthetic ways of knowing.
- Teachers emphasized this Acting Habit of Mind across activities. This included jogging, sit-ups, vocalizing, and mindfulness. Students must learn to understand what they are physically doing, how their bodies feel, and how to manipulate, calm, and change their bodies, faces, and voices to perform for an audience.
- Reflection and correction focused on whether students' bodies are doing what they wanted, how gestures and movements reflect

inner states, and how changing a facial expression can change a character's desires.

- Acting as a character requires both embodiment of the character's voice and body, and control of the self. Mind and body must work as one to move and express.

Chapter 4

Release Inhibitions and Be Playful

Learning to Perform Fully and With Self-Trust

> Two students stand in front of the class, engaged in an exercise playing characters in dialogue. But instead of saying the words of the script, they have to make up words in the moment that convey the underlying meaning of what the characters are trying to say. In this script, one of the white characters is behaving and saying racist things to the Latina character. Unable to get through the line, the white student actor stops the scene, uncomfortable even pretending to say these racist statements in an acting exercise. The teacher, Juanita, sympathetically responds and steps into the stage area with the student. She turns to the student and says, "Your character is living inside a lot of societal prejudices . . . in order to bring these people to life, we have to break through being uncomfortable, in order to say things we may not normally say" (Boston Arts Academy, Class 13).

So, what is happening in this teaching moment? The student is being asked to *consider others* (i.e., her character's mental state) and *commit to choices* (i.e., how she talks while playing the character), but most importantly, this moment embeds the need to *release inhibitions*. The student is being asked to maintain a sense of self-trust and self-efficacy that she will not be seen as racist for performing these actions and words onstage, and that the role of an actor is to let go of the judgment that she personally holds toward the character (rightfully so) and serve the script and performance. As Juanita says, "[B]ecause it's the whole context of the whole entire piece that's going to change the audience's view."

To note, this is a serious exemplar of a students' self-judgment and not wanting to be seen as a racist or prejudiced person getting in the way of their being able to portray a racist character. But, *release inhibitions* can be about many of the blocks that may get in the way of acting as a variety of characters: looking silly or foolish, appearing to know less than the student knows, holding an identity the student does not hold, or acting romantic or hateful toward someone the student has a very different relationship with. Students must learn to have a sense of playfulness about themselves, and to trust their inner sense of self to hold steady while portraying a variety of ridiculous, negative, or sublime behaviors and people in performance.

Release inhibitions and be playful is where a student learns to overcome self-judgment and gain a sense of play. Generally, *release inhibitions* also means releasing embarrassment or self-consciousness; *be playful* means fully and wholeheartedly buying into the play. An actor cannot play unenthusiastically; they must play with their whole sense of self. "I felt like I entered a childish mind," said one student after being asked to approach a prop umbrella like an alien who had never seen such an object before. This requires a sense of buy-in—teachers ask that students do not make jokes or snide comments about exercises or each other because it breaks the magic of the acting classroom. As one teacher said, making jokes is an attempt to "control the situation" in the face of "uncomfortable emotions," whether those are embarrassment, silliness, or some other sense of self-judgment that is particularly relevant for teenagers.

Acting teachers do not just ask students to overcome self-judgment, but to push even further into becoming playfully and joyfully silly. Teachers communicate to the students they must "rise away from" themselves to fully play a character and explore all the possibilities of a character's mental states and behaviors. In balance, this requires a trust of the self—that the student can be silly and ridiculous, and they are not threatening their own sense of themselves as growing, maturing, and engaging. That they can trust themselves enough to let themselves go.

Release inhibitions and be playful can also be about building energy and not thinking—just acting and reacting in a moment without uncomfortable self-awareness and without thinking about how it might work, trusting that after the fact there will be reflection and feedback. In the moment of right now, acting teachers will push students to make a decision in a split second (particularly in the Generative exercises of class) and go with it. In a larger sense, actors have to trust their impulses of emotions and movements across exercise type. They have to overcome any embarrassment and be able to look spontaneous in whatever they are doing, even if they have rehearsed it hundreds of time before and performed those exact moments for years onstage. This balance of spontaneity and awareness, without judgment or blocks, is the hard part, and often a stated goal of many actors (e.g., Caine, 2000).

THE SCIENCE OF RELEASE INHIBITIONS AND BE PLAYFUL

As with the other Acting Habits of Mind, *release inhibitions and be playful* is related to and incorporates a number of cognitive, emotional, and social skills. These include playfulness, self-esteem, self-judgment, self-concept, and the growing awareness of social status and conformity that occurs in adolescence.

What do we know about the science of *be playful* from a psychological and developmental perspective? Playfulness is central to learning in early childhood and an everyday part of life for children under the age of 5 (with one estimate of 48% of their open preschool free time being spent in play, Thompson & Goldstein, 2022). Many scientific papers, some of which I have published with students, have focused on pretend play for very young children and the way it can develop social skills, emotional understanding, and emotional control (see Goldstein & Lerner, 2018, or Thompson & Goldstein, 2019). While the directness of the links between play, in particular pretend play, and outcomes is sometimes questioned (Lillard et al., 2013), there is strong evidence from education that a playful mindset is the best way for young children to learn (Hirsh-Pasek et al., 2004).

Highly fantastical play in particular may be a good way for young children to practice their executive functioning skills, i.e., their ability to keep multiple ideas in mind simultaneously and switch among tasks and goals (Thibodeau-Nielsen, et al., 2020). However, playfulness as a default, and certainly pretend play, begins to become less central as children develop into middle childhood, ages 6–8, and is often thought to be completely done by the time children are age 10. The cognitive and social knowledge that undergirds pretense is thought to transform into other activities, such as an appreciation of reading fiction, engaging in playground games, or playing board games and sports with rules (Harris, 2000).

By the time we get to research on adolescents and adults, playfulness is basically gone completely from the scientific literature in developmental psychology. There is just not a lot of psychological science on what adolescent or adult play is, how it works, or what it may do for teenagers. (Do see the few theoretical or small empirical works here: Göncü & Perone, 2005; Kapitany et al., 2022; Smith & Lillard, 2012; Vadeboncoeur & Göncü, 2018). However, there are a good number of related psychological concepts that could be applied and work as related to *release inhibitions and be playful*.

The first is letting go of a sense of self-judgment and inhibition of newness or silly behaviors that might otherwise constrain the actor. The acting classroom is purposefully a place where students' behavior is accepted across a wide range of volumes, actions, and unselfconsciousness that cannot and do not occur in other contexts. Being open to and trying out new behaviors is critical to figuring out the best way to play a character, but an inhibited actor cannot perform fully.

Linking to the psychological science, trusting yourself to make mistakes and try new things is critical for the development of identity and self-concept. Expanding the notion of what you can and want to do, allowing for behaviors that might seem outside the norm, and thinking of the self as able to exist in a variety of ways and behaviors is all necessary to getting to know yourself and shape your own identity. Particularly in adolescence, where social embarrassment is painful, and even stronger than in younger or older age groups (Somerville et al., 2013), identity development needs a space where exploration is high and self-consciousness low.

Self-concept is also a particularly salient psychological achievement of adolescence (Erikson, 1994; Marcia, 1966). Learning how to separate from one's parents and their expectations and trust yourself is key to having genuine expression of the self, and not just a constructed or inauthentic persona. The major task of adolescent identity development (and frankly, the continued evolution of identity that all people go through as they continue in their lives) is to engage in real exploration of the world; look at the options for identities in religion, career, social activities, attitudes, and the like; and make decisions about how you want to express yourself (sometimes called "dual-cycle processes"; Branje et al., 2021; Crocetti, 2017; Marcia, 1966; Phinney, 1990).

Identity exploration is defined by looking at the commitments you have made in your life, reevaluating them, looking for alternative possibilities, and then committing to those possibilities. This of course does not take place in a vacuum—social relationships, family and cultural pressures, opportunities and risks all play a role (Crone & Fuligni, 2020). This exploration and commitment duality also requires the development of an identity narrative, a way for adolescents to integrate their experiences, relevant moments in their histories, and continuity across behavior and time (Pasupathi et al., 2007). All of this requires a sense of play with self, and a release of rigid expectation and discomfort. Without possibilities and support for exploration, active reflection, and narrative creation, an already difficult task—figuring out who you are—becomes even more difficult and perhaps painful (Branje et al., 2021).

This is where I believe acting classes can play a role, and particularly thinking about and learning to *release inhibitions and be playful* can be important as a process for identity development. *Release inhibitions* asks the students to overcome blocks that may be preventing them from engaging fully in activities and to bring a sense of lightness and ease to exploring something new. Combined with *reflect and think metacognitively* as a norm, and the engagements with narratives that are central to all works of theatre, even improvisation games, the underpinnings for developing a coherent sense of self are present.

Similarly, having an attitude of play and uninhibited engagement can encourage positive risk taking. Adolescence is a prime time for sensitivity to embarrassment, social status, popularity, and social evaluation. It is a "sensitive period" for learning about social information from peers and about social structures (Blakemore, 2008; Burnett, et al., 2009). If a teen actor is focused in on these elements of their experience, they will be too self-conscious to perform. However, if they are surrounded by other students also taking emotional risks and positively engaging with the emotional freedom of an acting class, it could build creative self-efficacy and self-concept. Purposefully choosing to *release inhibitions and be playful* becomes critical in acting training for this age group, as it creates a new culture for the students and becomes a different space than what they may be experiencing in the rest of their lives. This helps students develop an identity as open to new experiences, even if they might otherwise feel embarrassed, and play, to learn from and take advantage of such situations.

An acting classroom provides a way for students to be in social situations in which they are encouraged to look a bit ridiculous—but this does not come naturally. The younger students in our sample (the freshmen) had to be coached through their warm-ups and exercises in a way the more advanced students did not, possibly because the culture for those older students was much more based in playfulness and releasing any self-judgment.

In actors, there has not been much research at all on how engaging in acting classes or the acting profession is linked to a sense of playfulness, releasing inhibitions, identity development, self-concept, or embarrassment and social status. However, the few studies that have been written hint at some tantalizing possibilities. In two studies on the neurological signatures of the self while acting (Brown et al., 2019; Greaves et al., 2022), researchers have found evidence that there is actually a suppression of the areas of the brain that are typically active when thinking about the self. This points to the hypothesis that when actually acting, performers are thinking in the first person as a character, and that requires a reduction of thinking as the self, being embarrassed about the self, or paying attention to social implications of the self in that moment.

With 15 college theatre majors, Steven Brown, a professor at McMaster University, and his colleagues had actors lie in a brain scanner and answer questions, either in role as Romeo or Juliet (a part they were all well familiar with), or as themselves. When they were acting, the participants had less activation in the "self"-focused areas of the brain compared to when they answered questions as themselves, or even when they answered questions about someone else that they knew personally. However, the "other person" focused areas of the brain were just as active when the participants were in role and answering questions as when they were answering questions about a friend. This means that while acting, actors were not thinking as themselves, but were thinking as the character, in both a first- and third-person perspective. Importantly, though, these actors were in an fMRI scanner, requiring them to hold as still as possible, a scenario not well tied to how actors typically perform.

In contrast, with professional actors, a group of researchers from University College London, led by Antonia Hamilton and Dwaynica Greaves used fNIRS systems with six actors performing a scene from *Midsummer's Night Dream* (Greaves et al., 2022). fNIRS is a way to measure neurological activity while allowing the participant to be up and walking around. Here, the researchers looked at how the actors' brains responded to having their names called (versus their acting partner's names). Similar to Steven Brown's findings, Hamilton & Greaves's team found that while acting, the actors did not respond as quickly to their own names as when they were not acting. Their brain responded more slowly! As an interesting aside (and more on this in Chapters 6 and 7), neurologically and physiologically, the pairs of actors who participated simultaneously became more in sync with each other over the course of acting together. Their brain waves began to line up, as did their heart rates. While this work shows the self may be suppressed while performing, it does not mean the self is not part of learning to act. In fact, the opposite is true. Learning to act requires thinking about the self in relation to character and performance and figuring out how to engage with the actions of a play fully. Then, actors must put that aside (release) to play the character.

There is also some published research to show college-aged and professional actors tend to show higher levels of generalized tendencies for fantasy awareness, and even dissociation while acting. But not in a negative sense. Rather, this suppression of sense of self allows actors to bring forward a sense of self for a character (Panero & Winner, 2021). Actors have been found to have higher levels of both fantasy proneness and dissociation in their daily lives (Panero et al., 2016; Panero et al., 2020; Thomson et al., 2009; Thomson & Jaque, 2011). However, other work has found that keeping a sense of current awareness and a perspective on the current moment is critical for productive performing in character (Konijn, 2005).

These two concepts—of the suppression of the sense of self while acting and the development of identity through *release inhibitions and be playful*—may seem in opposition to each other. However, they work well together if thought of in terms of learning how to act. While learning how to act, students have to explore, think about, reflect on, and engage with how they understand characters, perform for audiences, and relate the work to their own life and experiences in order to build the realism for the characters for themselves. However, once they are actually performing, they have to leave all of that behind (a lesson I have been taught by several acting coaches) and engage fully in the moment of the play, the moment of performance. Therefore, it may be that identity processes are built through the purposeful engagement with a variety of activities and personalities in acting class, and then set aside while performing the other, a sense of self and self-concept fully realized in the background. This is the dual process of identity development as formulated by research psychologists. First explore, then commit and see how it works, being open to more exploration as necessary (Crocetti, 2017).

To this end, in the one experimental study I know of with children, together with an undergraduate student, Brooke DeBettingnies, I showed that children aged 10–11 in improvisational theatre classes improved in their self-concept after a one-semester improv course. Here, we randomly assigned children to either take a semester of improv or a semester of study hall. In the middle of the year, we switched the kids—the ones who had been taking improv moved to study hall and the ones in study hall got to take improv. The findings were good, but a bit nuanced. There was improvement in self-concept, but only for the students whose self-concept began at lower levels. Those who had higher levels of self-concept retained their positive self-view over the course of improv and study hall, but did not improve. However, those with lower levels of self-concept improved through their engagement with improv, and retained that improvement even when they moved to study hall (DeBettingnies & Goldstein, 2020). Given that other studies with young children had not found improvements in self-concept as a result of acting classes (Freeman et al., 2003; Kardash & Wright, 1987; Wright, 2006), it may be that focusing on those who begin at lower-than-average levels is where theatre can have the most effect (Emler, 2001).

CALL FOR FUTURE RESEARCH

Acting classes engage with ideas of the self, identity, and self-concept. This is likely related to the ways in which students are asked to try out behaviors and emotions that are new and perhaps a bit socially awkward, but also the sense of playfulness and self-trust that is necessary in theatre activities. Future research, however, will have to distinguish when and how acting classes (versus acting performances) engage a sense of self, and how the process of exploration and commitment to a personal identity is linked to exploring acting exercises and characters.

Now we turn to how *release inhibitions and be playful* was integrated and embedded in acting classes themselves—how teachers engaged in fostering the use of this Acting Habit of Mind across activity type and centered it in some activities.

RELEASE INHIBITIONS AND BE PLAYFUL IN THE ACTING CLASSROOM

Any time students engage fully in an activity without a sense of self-awareness preventing them from fully engaging, they are able to *release inhibitions*, and anytime they engage with joy, an emotion teachers brought into most classes, they are able to *be playful*.

In Preparation activities, *release inhibitions and be playful* is integrated in any kind of warm-up where the students have to shake out their bodies, say silly tongue twisters, and stretch their faces into grotesque shapes. These are actions and activities unlikely to appear in any other classroom or moment in the students' lives, in the school day or other kinds of activities. But these are central in the beginning of each of the acting days. Students are learning how they can engage in the joy, play, and freedom of theatre in these warm-ups and bring the mindset of *release inhibitions* into the character work for later in the class. We saw this often.

At Boston Arts Academy in Class 15, the students started class with tunnel freeze tag, where they had to chase each other around the room, making tunnels with friends to crawl through when they were tagged. In Class 12 at Boston Arts Academy, Maura had the students stand in a circle at the beginning of class to pass around silly body and face expressions, yelling and shouting. She said, "I want you to act silly. I want you to go big and go hard." In Class 1 at Imagination Stage, Nikki had the students toss a ball around the circle in a set order, saying each other's names. Then she added additional balls and tosses, and then reversed the order, until the game devolved into chaos and laughter. She introduced this activity by saying, "Exercises might make you feel silly or weird. . . . In those moments it's important that you acknowledge that you feel silly but then try to move past that and take the exercise seriously." She then had the students go through a series of relatively silly dance poses with loud pop music behind the cues, including the instruction to "smell your shoes!" In Class 4 at Imagination Stage, Nikki had the students roll their hips, and told them, "Don't let my staring at you make you uncomfortable in any way."

In Classes 2, 3, 5, and 7 at Imagination Stage, Jewel's standard warm-up included unusual sounds, facial gestures, tongue movements, and random words with encouragement to be "louder louder louder!" In Justin's classes at Eureka High School, students had to sing songs together, paired with movements, and pass silly movements around the circle, with each student taking a leader role at some point. Students in these classes started more embarrassed but ended joyfully. They even used childhood rhymes such as "Down down baby . . ." At Madeira, Kelsey's warm-up included silly sounds and body movements, including a "lion face" where the students all looked at each other, laughing and making giant faces. At each school, teachers found this Acting Habit of Mind at some point during the class, most days.

In Generation activities, the improvisational games teachers set up often required overcoming inhibitions to silliness and *be playful*. One such game, the Android Game, might look familiar to recess games for a group of elementary school children. Here, at Eureka High in Class 27, one student was secretly told they are the "android" and can "infect" the rest of the class through winks. At the same time, the rest of the class had to determine who is the android through accusing each other, throwing each other in the "recycling center" (when correct in their accusation) or "jail" (when incorrect). After a while, Justin, the teacher, stopped the class and let the remaining androids peek at each other, to then work together to target the remaining humans. It was a silly, playful game, and students created strategy and technique, but also lots of laughter, and the students fully engaged. Justin noted in his interview that he wanted them to play without thinking about it too deeply. None of the students acted too "cool" for the game, or as if it was beneath them. One can imagine, though, that if a student tried to suggest playing this game at lunch in the high school cafeteria, it likely would not go over well. This activity also built ensemble and got the class communicating with each other (i.e., *think collaboratively)* by allowing them to let down their guards and simply play.

In Interpretation activities, *release inhibitions and be playful* is central to performing a character. In a scene study at The Madeira School, Class 26, in which Kelsey is working with the students to build a scene, delving into their characters' motivations, intentions, and desires, she asked them to think about the reasons why lines are being said in each moment of the script. In one moment in *Tartuffe*, Kelsey was working with a student whose character is shifting from one tactic to another rapidly across the scene. The student made physical motions of soothing another character, but could not articulate what she meant for the character to do in that moment. Kelsey urged the student slightly to trust herself and her intuitions. She wanted the student to overcome some shyness and say what she thinks. "Your hand gesture is indicating it, in what kind of a way? . . . You have an instinct! Go ahead!" she pushed.

On the next line, the other student in the scene began to move away from her scene partner in response, but stopped herself. Kelsey says, "Do it! You had such great energy." In this way, she is gently encouraging with students to overcome the blocks they may have around saying what they think, physicalizing actions, and playing with ideas they are creating in response to a script. Students are tasked to trust their instincts, to *release inhibitions* around whether they are "right," and to play with ideas they are having.

Theatre only works if it is done at size and scale—unlike television or movie acting, which is very subtle, when students are being trained to be actors in a theatre (and in this class, a classical theatre piece that is satirical in nature), they have to physicalize inner states with large overemphasis. This is different from how students are asked to portray almost any other state of knowledge or behavior in the rest of their academic lives, and for adolescents, this requires them to overcome the social and personal embarrassment or unusualness of those actions. Developing the ability to *release inhibitions* to the goal of performing full-out is therefore a particularly relevant skill set for this age group.

Finally, students are often asked to Reflect on whether and how they were able to *release inhibitions and be playful* during their exercises and activities in class. In Class 2 at Imagination Stage, taught by Jewel, the class was engaged in an improvisational exercise in which they have to describe the physicality of a character they have chosen (e.g., a grandmother) and then their partner had to become that person, and improvise conversations in character.

After the group tried it in pairs, Jewel brought one student up in front of the class to do a bit of back-and-forth working on the embodiment of the character. The student was timid, projecting self-awareness of the silliness of holding up an imagined shirt and describing it, and unable to overcome her own embarrassment. Jewel said, "Inhabit her so I don't feel like you're thinking about it, you're just being her," asking the student to *release inhibitions* she might have around performing this Generation activity. After this exercise, Jewel brought the class into a circle to Reflect on what they had just engaged with in the exercise. She said a number of quotes in conversation with the class to ask them to overcome their self-judgment and be in the moment of play onstage, including: "It's okay, you're going to be uncomfortable, right?" and "You have to be willing to inhabit somebody else and not show me."

The students had a discussion about how this made them think about details in the person's body. They also noted that it was a bit easier to *be playful* when they were engaged with each other in conversation, compared to when they only had themselves to focus on. Jewel noted that this was because "You were trying so hard to listen that you weren't acting. Does that make sense?" When the students were really engaged in the action of acting, they were not also commenting on it. One student noted she was more at ease in the second performance, and Jewel responded that was indicative of releasing the "self-conscious" nature of acting.

She discussed *release inhibitions* in terms of the audience needing the actors to just be in the reality of the moment, and not "indicating," that is, projecting or overtly showing the audience what is happening in the character's (and the actor's) mind. By indicating, Jewel says, the students are not trusting the audience. When the students are able to release blocks they have about performing the actions of the characters, they will not have to indicate to the audience what the character is feeling, thinking, or doing. The audience will be able to read it in their actions.

Jewel had them write in their journals:

> "You don't have to be right. You just have to create."
> "It's not about perfection, it's about playing to create character."

People in daily life do not comment on their own actions. In fact, commenting on your own actions is a style of comedy—think *The Office* or *Parks and Recreation*, where characters look into the "documentary" camera to note when something is funny or ridiculous. Finally, she ended with,

"This was an experiment and for some of you it worked and for some of you it didn't and that's fine," importantly noting that activities in class do not have to be deadly serious for them to be useful, and that not every student has to pull something from every class. Holding acting exercises with a sense of ease and play is central to building an Acting Habit of Mind that students can engage fully, without tension, even if they are not sure what they are doing. This Reflection on *release inhibitions* lasted only 7 minutes of a 2-hour class, but set the stage for scripted scene study that took the rest of class.

Across these four sections of class, then, the students are learning to become unselfconscious, to release self-judgment, and to allow for the playfulness, silliness, and lack of inhibitions that can help them to both warm-up and perform fully. They are learning to open themselves to engage without winking to the audience that they are above the character or the play they are performing. They are overcoming any senses of self-doubt, shyness, or embarrassment about their own ideas. They are gaining instincts to perform at the size of a theatre, thinking about how they can exist onstage with a level of realism and relaxation and ease that makes a performance engaging to watch. We see all of these possibilities in our two focal exercises for *release inhibitions and be playful.*

Focal Exercise 1: The Whoosh Game

Use the fun and silliness of a game to bring up energy and let go.

"We need something to energize us a little bit!"

After a relatively low energy warm-up, Nikki had the students at Imagination Stage, Class 8, pass around an energetic "whoosh" from person to person in the circle. She wanted the students to use a big strong energy with their arms and then add additional movements: a "bang" can stop the "whoosh;" a "bridge" that causes the "whoosh" to skip the person next to you; "suspension bridge," causing the "whoosh" to skip two people; "tunnel," which allows the person holding the "whoosh" to move it across the room to anyone else in the circle. Additional rules came into play—you cannot "bang" a "tunnel" or a "bridge." Each word had a paired gesture and rule change. If this all sounds a bit confusing and a touch overwhelming, it is for the students as well!

It took several minutes of slow turns through the game to get the students to fully understand what was and should be happening with the game's interactions and movements. Finally, Nikki added "clown car." When called, "clown car" required all the students to dance their way to a new spot in the room while also singing a silly circus-themed song. Nikki then added the final rules: students must be quick and fast and should not think, as any hesitation or an error will cause an assignment of lap running around the classroom.

As can be read simply through this description, this is a silly game, complicated in both its usage of executive function (pairing nonsense words with rules and movements) and in its social cues (wanting to move as quickly as possible and wanting not to mess up for the class). The students would not only break the rules of the game for not moving quickly and on instinct, they would be punished.

In her interview, Nikki stated that she used this activity to raise energy and get the students hyped up to engage in the somewhat tedious work of blocking out a scene (putting the actors where they need to stand, which can take a long time and gets boring when it is not your turn to be placed). Yet the "whoosh" game also serves the psychological purpose of integrating and using the students' abilities to overcome any sense of self-judgment or "looking cool" in service of working together and getting the game right. Students were asked to have energy in their movements. If they were self-conscious or put too much focus into any one piece, saying the words, making the movements, or singing the song, they would not be able to keep up. Nikki even noted to students' "fake it till you make it," to get a student more involved in the singing of the clown car exercise. Play is not a bonus here. It's required.

Focal Exercise 2: The 1,000-Year Exercise

Know how to hold your own space, and do not apologize for being there.

In Eureka High, where students take acting classes as electives for fun, trusting yourself in performance and not engaging in self-judgment while performing for others was centered in a silent Generation exercise entitled "The 1,000-year exercise" (Class 27).

Here, students were instructed by Justin to lie down as if they have been sleeping for 1,000 years. When he clapped and began playing some prerecorded ethereal classical music, the students were to wake up slowly, stand up, and walk forward to the edge of the stage. While doing this, they were instructed to look as far as they possibly could and imagine viewing far beyond the horizon and thinking of someone, something, or a goal that they wish for. The students were assured that they would not have to share their deepest desire of wanting that morning. Instead, the desire was picked to motivate the exercise. For students to *release inhibitions* in engaging with their inner sense in this way, they must have a sense of trust for the teacher—that he would not require them to share their desires, and that an honest engagement with wanting would not come under comment.

To ease them in, Justin first performed for the students. They were silent as they watched him perform this exercise for them, and it was obvious from watching that he felt no sense of self-judgment or inhibition while walking and looking. The students actually said "Wow!" and "That was good!" when Justin finished his first showing. He asked them to Reflect on what they felt he was giving and portraying for them.

The students noted facial expression, body position, and stage presence. "Is it an X factor?" Justin asked rhetorically. "Only some people have it, naturally?" No, he promises them. Stage presence is merely an actor who knows how to hold their space and not apologize for being there. If actors can stay grounded with focus, balance, and calm, they have the basis from which to play any and all other types of characters. For the students, this exercise is about learning how to be in space without apologizing for taking up space. This means no extraneous movements, no shirking or shrinking away from the spotlight and from the eyes of the other people in the room. Instead, the students were asked to think about what it might mean to take up space and then practice that calm presence during the exercise.

"There's no way you cannot be interesting if you are truly yourself," Justin says. In the interview, he noted students are often concerned about being enough onstage. This exercise uses *release inhibitions* as an explicit strategy to take away some of those fears. "Watching someone not worry about entertaining, or being funny, or being cool. It's like a magnet for the audience." Lack of self-judgment brings the audience to the actor, and lets the student actor perform honestly and authentically.

Next, each student was asked to complete the exercise, in groups of three or four, but working independently of each other. Students watched and quietly observed each other performing the exercise. What is critical about this exercise is that it is not complicated—the body movements are just walking and standing. The facial expression is meant to be natural and come from the inside. There is no script or complex movement to remember or to get information across to the audience. The actor is tasked with having a "want" that they move toward, and to do so without self-awareness and without self-judgment, but nothing else. It is a perfect example of how to teach intuitive performance and trust in the self without having any additional information to think about or respond to.

In the reflection on this exercise, Justin asked the students, "Why is this interesting to watch? Why is this difficult to do? What were you (the student) feeling as you did it?"

Students then discussed the different ways each person fulfilled the exercise, why choice of focus changed physicality and how interesting that was, and how individual the start of each movement choice looked to the audience. There was a real emphasis on the individuality of the exercise. The students talked about how it was a moving exercise, to be focused on one desire through the movement and perhaps feel the emotion resulting as well. As students learned, each individual actor can perform the same prompts in vastly different ways, that audience members can see those differences, and that all possible choices are valid in their performances. Through this they learn that being true to your own process can aid in performance to achieve the goal at hand.

RELEASE INHIBITIONS AND BE PLAYFUL, IN SUMMARY

- Acting can be a vulnerable art: actors must use their own bodies to portray actions that in "real life" would be considered immature, silly, embarrassing, or even racist and antisocial.
- Across very different kinds of actions, actors must release any inhibitions that would stop them from fully engaging with the material and the performance. While sometimes this is serious (as in the case of playing a racist character), it is often silly and playful.
- Students must develop a sense of personal vision and expression. They have to trust their ideas and impulses as worthy of performance, without self-judgment or self-restriction.
- Acting teachers talk about full performing by learning self-confidence through developing a role.
- Many Preparation and Generation exercises in acting classes are silly and embarrassing. Students are asked to perform without feelings of embarrassment, and given continual encouragement from their teacher and peers.
- Often, actors have to make a choice, quickly, without thinking, and subsequent actors have to go with it or the scene fails. Through performance decisions, students gain a sense of self confidence and self-concept of what works and what does not for them, onstage.
- A self-aware actor is not pleasurable to watch, and students must learn to be fully invested in the character without commenting on them.
- Beyond the acting classroom, being able to *release inhibitions,* trust yourself, and retain a sense of *be playful* is critical to the development of a strong sense of identity.

Chapter 5

Imagine and Envision

Learning to Create and Think Beyond Perception

> To prepare for the end of the semester at The Madeira School, Kelsey is working on scenes with pairs of students, the class serving as audience (Class 26). The language is heightened and poetic, not the way teenagers in the 21st century talk to or about each other. She has two students perform a few lines from *Tartuffe* by Moliere and then gives corrections to the student playing Mariane, professing her romantic interest in the off-stage Valère.
>
> Kelsey stops her, saying, "Oh I think you can confess more."
>
> To illustrate the idea of "more," she follows up with: "Have you ever had a crush on a celebrity or something? Yes, I see it in your face! (The class laughs.) Remember how we talked a little bit about personal separation and stuff? Celebrities are great because it's not an actual personal attachment that could become emotionally harmful to me as the actor. It is a great 'what if?' So, in this magic, 'what if' you are confessing your love for this celebrity to the person who could actually introduce you to them?" As the class starts to giggle, Kelsey looks on with a big smile. "Aha! It's so good! This is a safe way to do the emotional replacement." The students then return to the scene, heightened sense and portrayal for the confession of love for Valère in place.

So, what is happening in this this teaching moment? The students are being asked to *consider others* in thinking about the mental states of the characters and what they want, and perhaps also *commit to choices* in picking firm actions that their characters can portray. But most importantly, this moment contains the Acting Habit of Mind *imagine and envision.*

The student is being asked to *imagine* their celebrity crush—a real person they have emotional experience with in their everyday personal lives, and *envision* what it would be like to use this person in place of the fictional character in the script. The student has to talk about this celebrity even though they are not there, and while the student cannot replace the words of the script to be about the celebrity crush and their feelings about the crush, they have to *imagine*, recall their feelings and imbue the performance with those feelings.

Imagine and envision is the Acting Habit of Mind where students learn the ability to create outside of the perceptual here and now, their current sensory experiences, and apply it to the actions and needs of the onstage, present moment. This is where students hone and shape their creative thought and inner "mind's eye" to work for them in acting situations in which the visual scene, sound, smell, taste, feel, previous moments, depth of knowledge, and background are simply not available. Students work on their acting in a classroom setting, and perform it on a stage or set where there will always be pieces of the real world missing. Thus, the ability to *envision* themselves fully immersed in the scene and world of the character is necessary to create realism for an audience.

Imagine and envision is not a passive Acting Habit of Mind, but an active part of the creation of exercises, scenes, and moments in class. If acting is the work of creating naturalistic story for an audience out of nothing, then the ability to *imagine and envision* is key to developing the skills of performing. It is necessary for all acting work—from a sketch of an idea that leads to a fully improvised scene to a developed script imbued with a real sense of place and time. Students must *envision* both external perceptual experiences (e.g., sounds, smells, temperature) and internal feelings and goals (e.g., sadness, fury, manipulation). The "magic as if," noted by Kelsey earlier and used across several other of our classes, is the act of *imagining* what the world of the student would be like if they took something they know and turned it into something they could perform. This can mean pretending a class activity is a real audition, pretending the classroom is an alien land, pretending your fellow classmate is your daughter, and on from there.

THE SCIENCE OF IMAGINE AND ENVISION

As with each of the Acting Habits of Mind, *imagine and envision* has a rich scientific literature, and the ways in which it is used in acting classes are related to a number of psychological skills and abilities. These include findings on how mental imagery and imagining work generally, and also the more specific abilities of mind wandering, pretense, counterfactual thinking, mindfulness, meditation, and dissociation. Many of these are also related to creative thought and output.

Imagination, like pretend play, is central to children's development, and skills related to imagination continue to develop over time. However, imagination is not just the ability to create exciting fantasy worlds filled with dragons and unicorns (although it is also that). In psychological science, research on imagination shows its connections to a variety of cognitive functions, including being able to consider alternatives to the current moment (counterfactuals), remember the past, and visualize objects or settings (Byrne, 2016; Harris, 2000; Pearson et al., 2015). This means most uses of imagination are actually highly realistic in nature (e.g., imagining what you might have for dinner tonight if you cooked at home versus got takeout). Similarly, there is a recent movement in the study of children's pretend play to show that given free choice, most preschool-aged children will head toward play and imaginative activities that are tied to the real world and could actually happen, rather than those of high fantasy and far off non-realities (Harris, 2021; 2022; Taggart et al., 2018; 2020; Weisberg & Sobel, 2022; Weisberg et al., 2013). This is because the neurological basis of all imagination is the real world, memories and experiences you have already had.

In adolescence, as mentioned in Chapter 4, pretend play does fade away. However, the uses of imagination continue to refine and develop. Counterfactual thinking is the ability to imagine and envision alternative reality states. Although often framed as meaning just thinking about how historical events could have played out differently, causing different current states (Bryne, 2016), counterfactual thinking also can be used as a form of social comparison, meaning how differently would one's life be if they were more like a model of another person they know (Olson et al., 2000). This type of social comparison can be harmful, particularly when teens spend a lot of time comparing themselves upward to an imagined "better," especially when that "better" is a false or highly curated individual on social media. Upward social comparison via social media is associated with higher levels of depression (Broomhall et al., 2017; Vogel et al., 2015) and poorer body image (Carlson Jones, 2004). However, social comparison with those who are less fortunate can increase gratitude (Nicuță & Constantin, 2021) and possibly can be trained (Lomas et al., 2014). (Though it may also be linked to schadenfreude, or pleasure at others' misfortune.)

Imagine and envision also can be engaged during meditation in a controlled and directed manner. There is a substantial and growing set of scientific findings supporting the positive use of meditation for outcomes as disparate as stress and well-being (Ganesan et al., 2022), mental health (Fincham et al., 2023), emotion regulation and interpersonal relationships (Sedlmeier et al., 2012), compassion (Kreplin et al., 2018), and learning (Henriksen et al., 2020). Other research has found that for creative action, meditation may increase creative thinking by increasing cognitive control (Müller et al., 2016), mood and personality (Ding et al., 2015), or by focusing attention with full awareness (Baas et al., 2020). However, the strength of these findings, the contexts under which the studies take place, and who funded, ran, and wrote up the study all vary widely; "silver bullet" beliefs about meditation (that it can solve all problems) should be approached with caution, as mindfulness itself is very hard to study (Davidson & Kaszniak, 2015).

Less controlled forms of *imagine and envision* include mind wandering and dissociation. Both have been tied to creative action and outputs across behavioral, artistic, and neurological studies (Preiss et al., 2020). Mind wandering is considered any thought that is not tied to the perceptual here and now of a situation. Neurologically, in the brain, it looks fairly similar to the ideation stage of creative thought, when an individual is thinking about the possibilities of new ideas (Fox & Beaty, 2019). College students' tendencies toward mind wandering has been shown to predict their creativity, but only when the mind wandering is controlled in some aspect (Agnoli et al., 2018). However, other work has shown that mind wandering does not necessarily predict divergent thinking (Murray et al., 2021).

Call for Future Research

Meditation was used in several of the classes studied, as warm-up and focus exercises both for individual students and for pairs. But future research will have to delve into how meditation in acting class is used for imagination, and its effects on creative outcomes both in and out of the class. Other future work could explore how the guided mind wandering of *imagine and envision* in acting classes may be related to creative ideation and performance in and out of classroom.

Similar to mind wandering, dissociation is considered a lesser controlled imaginative experience. Defined as a "break" in the integration of cognition, body awareness, memory, and perception, and often related to negative forms of psychopathology (DSM-5TR; APA, 2022), dissociation for actors has been thought of as blurring the boundary of imagination and reality. However, there is very little research on the topic (Panero, 2019). In 2016, we looked at one form of dissociation, hypnotizability, and whether college-aged acting students felt more hypnotizable than music students or non-arts students. To test this, we gave students self-report measures of imaginative suggestibility (that is, how vividly they reported imagining various scenarios), fantasy proneness, and whether they became absorbed into fiction and narrative. Actors scored higher on all of these measures than did our two groups of non-actors, suggesting that learning how to act may allow students to become more in touch with alternative and imaginative forms of consciousness (or that those with higher levels of imaginative consciousness choose to major in acting). In addition, the results suggest actors have a greater ability to create imagined sensory experiences. These findings are in line with what we see being trained in our acting classes (Panero et al., 2016).

In follow up work, Panero and Winner (2021) found that when actors act, they score higher on measures of dissociation than when non-actors act. However, as a whole, actors do not show higher levels of dissociation. Instead, actors tend to show higher levels of flow (that is, the positive experience of losing track of time while absorbed in a task) and higher empathy (that is, being pulled into and experiencing the emotions of others). On a standardized measure of dissociation, student actors in college level conservatory show higher levels than the general population, but their scores do not increase as a result of 6 months of intensive training (Panero et al., 2020). Taken together, the links between dissociation, fantasy involvement, and positive mind wandering and flow are ripe for future investigation, but happily the more negative forms of dissociation (such as amnesia) do not seem to be associated with acting training and experience.

These different varieties of imagination, however, likely rely on the same cognitive mechanisms. Specifically, the cognitive ability to quarantine the real world from the imagined one (Leslie, 1987), the ability to think about the imagined world visually, given what is perceptually known about the real one (Pearson, et al., 2015), and the control to think about what you may want to imagine at a particular moment (Liao & Szabó Gendler, 2010). Imagination can be neurologically encoded as verbal information and/or visual information (Pearson & Kosslyn, 2015). This underlying similarity points to the ability of acting classes to therefore shape and mold how actors learn to use *imagine and envision* skills for the variety of creative and goal-oriented outcomes necessary to perform characters and perform everyday imaginative tasks.

Now, then, let us turn our attention to what we found in our classes where and how the skills and approach of *imagine and envision* are used, integrated, taught, and possibly fostered in acting classrooms themselves.

IMAGINE AND ENVISION IN THE ACTING CLASSROOM

In Preparation activities, *imagine and envision* is integrated in any kind of warm-up where the students have to meditate or pre-plan what they will be doing in class that day. For example, in Class 38 at McKinleyville in Humboldt County, the students engaged in a meditation in which they thought through the lengthy improvised group scene they were about to perform for their teacher, and imagined how their character in the scene would behave, making choices along the way in the meditation. In Class 9 at Boston Arts Academy, the students were guided through a solo meditation, thinking about themselves as an empty vessel, with no negative energy anywhere in their systems, focusing on letting go of what had happened to them so far that day. Then, they were paired up for a "toe to toe" and looked at each other, imagining what they needed to be successful that day. The Focal Exercise 1 below, on using and portraying animal imagery, also begins with a meditation.

In Generation activities, students use *imagine and envision* when creating improvised scenes from minimal prompts. In several schools, after purely physical warm-ups, students were asked to move around the room imagining themselves in different kinds of psychological relationships with each other, and envisioning how that would change their movement and perspectives. At Eureka in Class 29, students were engaged in an exercise in which they had to simply walk around the room, and when teacher Justin said "freeze," they had to stop all together, simultaneously (at this point, an exercise in *think collaboratively*). However, Justin raised the stakes, telling the students to secretly pick one person in the class and imagine them as a predator, moving around the room avoiding them, while not letting them know. After a few minutes, he raised the stakes again, asking students to imagine a second classmate as a protector, trying to stay close while continuing to avoid the imagined predator. Finally, Justin had them flip who they were imagining as predator and protector, and change their behavior accordingly. Altogether, this set up and improvised set of movements and mental states took 8 minutes of class, with students shifting rapidly through envisioning what the environment would feel like under conditions of predator, protector, and prey.

In Interpretation activities, *imagine and envision* allows the students to see their characters in their mind's eye, and work to portray what they envision for the character. For example, at The Madeira School in Class 21, a quick 3-minute exercise had the students walking around the room until they imagined seeing the character they were working on for a monologue assignment across the room as a statue. Once they envisioned the statue, they were asked to walk up to it and see how detailed they could imagine the positioning of the figure, how it looked. They were asked to envision the expression on the statue's face, whether the character-statue wore a private or public emotional expression, any props, the shape of bodies for the monologue moment, etc. Once the students walked around the imagined statue for a minute, they then took two steps "in" and became the statue they had just imagined. Teacher Kelsey told them to recreate "down to the finest detail of the facial expression, the lines in their face, the energy behind it" the statue they had just imagined. Then, she had them increase their engagement and specificity of the statue. This exercise very directly tasked students with imagining a physical form and expression in their heads, as specifically as possible, and then making it a physical reality. They gave the statues a title, perhaps as a line or word from the monologue, before moving on with the class. Kelsey noted during the interview for the day that this *imagine and envision* exercise, brought into the students' bodies, was particularly good for getting into character.

Students are often asked to Reflect on their performance and *imagine and envision* what the performance might look like if they were to change some aspect of it. For example, in one class for seniors at Boston Arts Academy, Class 14, the students spent almost 90 minutes performing scenes from a movie, with a full camera and monitor set up. Maura, the teacher, filmed them performing 2–3 minutes of the scene, with the camera focused on just one student at a time. The class (which, by this point of the year, was only six students) then watched each individual perform, gave feedback, and discussed, reflecting on what they had just seen. In these moments, because of the closeness of the camera and the singular focus on one student, they could clearly Reflect on their performance in the moment of watching it, and then take that visual as a basis for how a different choice might look on camera. Maura repeatedly gave each target student the question "What would it look like to do something different?" As the students each watched themselves, they had to *imagine and envision* what their performance might look like under another choice. After the discussion, each student went back and performed a second time, implementing that imagined choice.

Across these four sections of class, then, students are engaging *imagine and envision* through meditation as a way to center and focus themselves for class, by embodying imagined shifting relationships amongst the group and enacting that difference, envisioning imaginary objects and targets in their classrooms to act with, and imagining how different choices in their performances would look. We see all of these possibilities in our two focal exercises for *imagine and envision.*

Focal Exercise 1: Animal Imagery Exercise

Using animal metaphor to envision the physicality of a human character.

One longer exercise that used several different variations to integrate and strengthen students' *imagine and envision* abilities was an "Animal Imagery Exercise" at Imagination Stage in Class 4. To begin, teacher Nikki had the students lie down and close their eyes, taking a moment to get centered on the homework assignment they were given the previous week. That assignment was to research and really look at videos of an animal of their choosing. Their first task in class was to think of the animal they had picked and "play some video playback in your brain" about how the animal moves and what it looks like. Nikki even turned off the lights to give the students a dark and quiet space in which to do this first imagery exercise component.

The students then slowly got up and began to move around the space in the form of their animal. They were warned this was a serious exercise, and that they should not be laughing (an element of *release inhibitions*—see Chapter 4). They had to be fully "in" the envisioning of themselves as the animal. They were instructed to try and replicate the movements of the animals as best they could. The students were not tasked with trying to be exact in their movements or transfer an exact replication of the animal's movement to an audience, but rather to use these movements for themselves. This was a personal exercise—the students were not supposed to interact or talk, but rather to explore the room individually as their physicalized, envisioned animal. Keeping the lights off kept the students from being too visually engaged with each other.

Then, they were asked to move on to how the animal might move during the act of play. The students used their homework of watching videos to envision how they could transform that for themselves. They then ate as the animal—hunting or getting food from others. Next, they had to explore a moment of fear, either from being hunted or from sound. How does it make them act? Do they hide? What is their defense? The students were then asked to be aggressive and defend themselves. Finally, they were asked to sleep and rest. Whenever a student was not fully performing the movements of the animal, Nikki gently asked what kind of animal the student was envisioning and how it was connected to the behavioral goal.

The acting goal for this exercise, noted by Nikki in the interview, was to consider a different style of movement, and then to transfer their image of what the animal looks like to how a human body might communicate similar, animalistic behaviors and actions. Once the students finished performing as the animals, Nikki had each "go to sleep," then wake as their animal and transition from animal as animal into animal as human being with as many of the characteristics of the animal as possible. This part of the exercise took approximately 5 minutes. The students were then imagining themselves as a human character, with the same characteristics as an animal.

Once the group had practiced and explored, students were asked to do their movements individually in front of the class. Students moved around the space as the animal and then transformed into their human character. The students in the audience were asked to guess which animal, which characteristics, and give feedback about what they saw and what they liked. The transformation from animal to human and back again was meant to be subtle, almost magical—not a direct shift.

The students discussed their own animal choices (a koala; three kangaroos; a panda; a penguin; a cat; a lion; a pigeon; a sloth; a walrus; an otter) and how each of them transferred the animal characteristics to human characteristics. They discussed how animal characteristics could look like human emotions given the simplicity of some animals (e.g., how kangaroos are particularly aggressive and perhaps nervous; pandas are weighty and kind of lazy; sloths are slow; penguins are awkward; otters are playful; pigeons perhaps a bit paranoid; and cats, curious but cautious). When the students' statements of what they were trying to get across did not match what Nikki saw from the enactment, she noted it, to make them aware of how they should be thinking about the connection.

Finally, the students moved to a circle for a formal Reflection period. They were asked to think about the takeaways from the exercise and performance. Humans imprint qualities on animals, through literature and cultural knowledge, and these then get expressed in acting, too. Nikki gave an example of an actor she was directing in a play who used a specific image of a cat with its claws out when approaching a scene partner to be both wily and play a trick on the other actor. She discussed how actors could take small moments and turn them into something larger for production. The students reflected on how they could use this idea of animal imagery and movement in real acting rehearsals after getting a script.

Taken together, the meditation, group improv, individual performances, and feedback was meant as a way to *imagine and envision* a variety of characteristics that could be pulled from other sources. Nikki kept focusing the class back to physical qualities—what were they seeing in their mind's eye and each other's physicality, and how did what they saw relate back to their imagination around the animal and their characteristics. Nikki pointed out the usefulness of imagery translation and transformation as a way to take what might be useful and leave behind what is not quite human enough. She focused on how the exercise was meant to help the students understand how physical qualities are translatable into psychological qualities, by thinking about what the movement reminds the students of, what does it makes them think of, and how they can *imagine and envision* the transformation of an animal with all their characteristics into a human with human psychology? Nikki also reflected that the exercise would help students *imagine and envision* what a full character would be from a few distinct characteristics.

While this exercise required a *release of inhibitions* (Chapter 4; as Nikki said, "If you can stop commenting on yourself, it's really good"), and *physical and body awareness* (Chapter 3; to move as the animal), the primary goal here was *imagine and envision* the world as the animal, and then take that awareness and imagined creation into the rest of their actions. From the meditative imagery's first moment through performances and discussion, this section of class took almost 75 minutes. Of note, it also crossed multiple types of activities—there was a meditative warm-up, a generative improvisational section, an interpretive performance section, and a reflection, all around the idea of imagining and transforming that imagining. They had to create and think beyond their own bodies and experiences of reality the entire time.

Focal Exercise 2: Raising the Stakes Through the "Magic As If"

Using imagined experiences to heighten performance and envision the situation on top of reality.

Another focused lesson in *imagine and envision* came from Maura for the sophomores at Boston Arts Academy in Class 10. Here, the students were working on their "juries" or final exam scenes. Maura introduced the exercise by saying that if the students simply stood onstage and performed their scenes with only the movement and instructions from their directors or teachers, it would be a very boring scene to watch. She wanted the students to think about how they could personalize and add their own burgeoning acting skills and techniques to performance. To make it more interesting, she put forward, the students needed to focus on raising the stakes. She referred back to a few other exercises from class (e.g., going faster in the warm-up, or trying to find hidden money in the classroom) as examples of how to get a sense of internal motivation and urgency in their bodies (of course, harkening back to *body awareness* as a foundation for acting classes). Maura noted "you have to find a way to make these scenes really personal and urgent."

She then introduced another technique the students could use. The "magic as if" (also noted in the opening vignette), a technique from Konstantin Stanislavski (1989) where the actor puts their own reality into a situation, drops into that reality, and, as a result, creates high stakes for a moment. This requires imagining what those alternative realities or circumstances might be, and envisioning what the reaction to those heightened situations should look like. Then, if this alternative reality works, it can be a strong, emotional, real moment for the audience to watch.

Maura brought two students to the center of the classroom to play through a few lines from their current scene from *A Midsummer's Night Dream*. They were timid and not very emotionally engaged with the lines. So, she showed herself as an example, begging Helena to stay, *as if* the actor was her daughter, and instructing the student to act *as if* she (Maura) had disgusting breath and hands. This caused laughter from the class, but made the point. The magic "as if" allowed the student to respond not necessarily to the words the character was saying, or even to the way in which Maura herself was acting, but instead to imagine that the lines were said with a particular underlying meaning and then react according to that envisioning. This allows the action onstage to heighten beyond baseline and raise the stakes for actor and audience. Then, the two students performed again, obviously having to *release inhibitions* to put themselves into their heightened performances, but going for the raised stakes and getting a laugh and cheer from the crowd.

Later in the exercise, there was even a moment where Maura gave a quick note about onstage combat, where one student grabbed another, that it was the job of the "victim" student to make it look like he was really hurting her, even though he was holding her very gently. This mismatch between what the students needed to show to the audience and the reality of what it would feel like to portray that scene requires an external *imagining* of the self in the moment as well as *body control*. Being able to *envision* what the scene looked like for the audience, and how that was different, necessarily, from how it would feel to perform it from the point of view of the actor, is necessary to keep everyone safe, while giving an authentic vision of what a fight would look like.

As Maura said for any kind of performance: "You have to make it as if you've been in this position before and feel some sort of personal way. . . . You have to start collecting those feelings you have inside, 'and this was like the time my mother told me this,' and use them in the moments of the scripts where you can find a connection." Maura notes that this is not "faking" the moments, but making them personal and real at the time of performance, by layering and connecting the personal with the script and character though *imagining* what is needed and the metaphor to the self. Altogether, this introduction to the "magic as if," discussion of its application, short example and set up for next activity, and applying the discussion took 8 minutes of a focused lesson to then apply across scenes and activities, but it was a concentrated focus on the use of *imagine and envision* to enhance a scene.

IMAGINE AND ENVISION, IN SUMMARY

- Actors must be able to imagine what their character wants and needs, what they will look like when portraying a character, and create multiple possibilities for relationships, emotions, and objectives, all from scripts or seeds of ideas.
- When performing, actors must be able to *imagine and envision* everything from the temperature, scenery, sounds, and fourth wall, to backstories of characters' relationships and what their character was doing in the immediate moment before they stepped in front of the audience.
- Learning to *imagine and envision* involves thinking about both the physical and psychological possibilities for a character portrayal. Student actors must be able to go beyond the words of the script and the characters, connect given circumstances back to their own lives, and use that active *imagining* in the moment of creation.
- This ability to *imagine and envision* is related to how we all create counterfactuals, think through decisions, and take action to achieve goals in our everyday lives.
- In our classes, students learn and practice this Acting Habit of Mind through engaging in mindful meditations to prepare an agile and open mind for new scenarios, develop complex physical imagined characterizations, and *imagine and envision* feelings and reactions they might have never themselves experienced.

Chapter 6

Consider Others

Learning to Think About Others' Behaviors, Minds, Emotions, and Perspectives

> In Class 5 at Imagination Stage, where students are working on monologues by presenting them in pairs to each other, Jewel walks from pair to pair, making small comments. With one pair, she points to a line in the script and asks the student actor, "Why does [character] say this? Why does she feel the need to say this at that point in that moment? In life, this is not just an acting scene, why do people tell you what they're telling you?" Jewel then goes on to provide a few possibilities to add to the student's thoughts: "What if she's frightened? What if her parents are really super strict? What if she's the kicker on the football team and won't be able to wear the dress of homecoming queen?"
>
> Jewel keeps walking around. To another student, she asks, "Why did [character] sarcastically comply?" To another, "Why does [character] decide to do it? If she thinks it's stupid . . . the whole thought of doing this is dumb, what makes her actually do it?" To other students, in turn, "Why does your character do that? Because you do have a sense of duty to your friend." "Why did [character] skip class?" "Why is [character] attracted to her?" "Why doesn't [character] care about her future?" In each of these repeated questions to the student actors, she waits for the student to think through the answer to the "why" questions behind the lines and behaviors, and then moves them to the next moment of the script.

So, what is happening in this teaching strategy, repeated student by student across the activity of monologue rehearsal and preparation? In these questions, which we saw in many variations across most of our classrooms, Jewel is pushing the students to explicitly *consider others*. In this case, the "others" are their characters. The students are being asked to think about the reasons why their characters are saying what they are saying, why they are making the choices written out in the script, and why the characters are the way they are for the actors to portray. Jewel is asking them to think about and name the thoughts, feelings, beliefs, desires, motivations, and behaviors of their characters. She is asking them to use their abilities to *consider others* in service of portraying a realistic character from the scripts' words.

However, as seen below, *consider others* is not just used in service to understand and interpret why the characters are behaving in ways according to the script. It is also used when students are giving feedback to each other, when they are moving around the room in warm-ups, and when they are reflecting on putting together a performance.

Consider Others is where students learn to think about how other people think and react to the world around them. Because theatre is necessarily about the vastness and variety of human experience, students need to be able to think about people they have never encountered in real life, people whose lived experiences are far outside their own lived experiences, and how they would think about, react to, and engage with the world.

It is not just about the inner life of the person, though. It is also about considering behaviors, voices, and physical choices when watching each other for feedback—how does the outside reflect the inside? In scripted work the students only get words and perhaps some hints on inner life from how the playwright notes the way the character says their words. So, a secondary task the students must learn is how to pay close and careful attention to the physical cues they are getting from actors and colleagues, and how to read and respond to those cues in character. They must become amateur psychologists (and I often say that psychology and theatre are basically two different ways of answering the same question: why do people do what they do?) and recognize and understand patterns of behavior and the motivations and emotions that undergird such behavior.

As Juanita at Boston Arts Academy noted, her overarching pedagogical goal for several of her freshman-level classes was constructing relationships between the characters in the scenes, and doing so by having the students get together and ask questions to find out what the relationship is. She wanted students to ask probing questions, to understand each other's characters, and therefore know how to build the relationships with each other. She noted for Class 13 (the juniors at BAA) her goal was to get students to "be able to take each other in" and "structure a strong point of view" for each other. But she also wanted students to consider the minds of the audience when putting together their performances. She wanted students to show them character, but also remember performance is meant to entrance and entertain. As she said in Class 15, actors should keep in mind that most audiences want to be active, mentally engaged members of performances: "You want to give your audience an 'x,' it's like an algebraic equation. . . . If you give the audience everything, why would they sit there?"

Throughout our acting classes, students are being taught, explicitly and implicitly, to think about other people in a purposeful and reflective way. Not just reacting to them as we react to each other in social situations in everyday life, but to engage with the inner worlds of other people, and how that inner world is reflected in behaviors. Making this an explicit goal was built from warm-up through performance and feedback.

THE SCIENCE OF CONSIDER OTHERS

Like our other Acting Habits of Mind, *consider others* is linked to a number of foundationally important cognitive and social skills. However, *consider others* is also unique from a developmental science perspective as being particularly important and relevant in the adolescence age group, a particularly high time of social sensitivity and enhanced mentalizing abilities (i.e., thinking about other's minds; Blakemore & Mills, 2014). I believe *consider others* is a central part of every acting class, across age group and level, so its emphasis in classes for adolescents, which we investigated here, is likely not a coincidence.

How do psychologists and developmental scientists think about and study *consider others* and its requisite skills? The process of (1) recognizing that other people in your life have an inner world; (2) figuring out their thoughts, beliefs, desires, and emotions; (3) trying to recognize (visually) or parse out (through analysis) the content of those beliefs, desires and emotion; and then (4) figuring out your own response to the inner states of others, has many names under which it is studied (e.g., cognitive empathy, emotional empathy, theory of mind, mentalizing, compassion), and also unifying concepts (i.e., interpersonal intelligence; emotional intelligence) that have made their way into the popular imagination. Here, I will take the constructs separately while also connecting them back to what we know as a whole.

Acting requires making meaning out of behaviors. The very nature of theatre is that there is subtext and meaning behind words in the script. This primary skill—figuring out that there is meaning and subtext under the words said by a person, and the content of the mental and emotional states that underlie the words—is called "theory of mind." Theory of mind has been studied intensively and extensively since the early 1980s, in primary form in infancy (with a lot of controversy, Barone et al., 2019; Onishi & Baillargeon, 2005; Poulin-Dubois et al., 2023), in early childhood, and through its more complex forms in adolescence and adulthood (Dumontheil et al., 2010; Hughes & Devine, 2015; Kuhn, 2000).

Related to theory of mind is the understanding of other people's emotional states, and the emotional response we feel in return, called in the scientific literature "cognitive empathy" (understanding the emotions of another) and "emotional empathy," "affective empathy," or, more often, just "empathy" (feeling the emotions of another). While the history of all this terminology is too much to get into here, it is likely that all of these processes rely on the same behavioral, learning, and neurological systems (Preckel et al., 2018; Schurz et al., 2021). Another term that is often used in the science of adolescent development in particular is "mentalizing," meaning thinking about the mental states of another person, and considering their emotions, motivations, and beliefs when thinking about them. It is this term, mentalizing, that is probably most similar to what I mean by *consider others* as an Acting Habit of Mind.

Critically for our study, the adolescent brain is particularly primed to enhanced processing of both one's own social emotions and the social and emotional actions of other people (Blakemore, 2008; Dahl et al., 2018). While this mentalizing is still anatomically developing in the prefrontal cortex through the early twenties, and a full understanding of behaviors as representations of inner states continues through the life span (Kuhn, 2000), the extreme focus and growth of these skills in adolescence makes it a ripe time to learn how to think about and develop a Habit of Mind of *consider others*. As Sarah-Jayne Blakemore, a preeminent scholar of adolescence neurological development states, in adolescence, the social brain is "always on" (Blakemore & Mills, 2014).

There are a few additional key areas where the skills related to *consider others,* that is theory of mind, empathy, and mentalizing, show up in the psychological literature. This is where the majority of my lab's and personal experimental and empirical research in the effects of acting classes has focused. A recent meta-analysis (statistical analysis of multiple studies) looking across types of theatre and types of empathy measurement found a positive but moderate overall effect of acting training for empathy skills (Lewandowska & Węziak-Białowolska, 2020). However, direct testing of students themselves (rather than parent or teacher report), and importantly, with an active control group (receiving a different activity or intervention), is rare.

In 2012, Ellen Winner and I found that a year of acting training, compared to a year of active control visual arts or music training, increased empathy in both 8–10-year-old children and freshman in high school (aged 14–15 years old). However, only the older age group also showed an increase in understanding of other people's mental and emotional states (i.e., their theory of mind), while the younger age group stayed stable over a year of acting classes. We hypothesized that this was because these acting classes were more focused on *body awareness and control*—the physical expression of character and emotion—rather than explicit discussion of the characters' inner lives. In contrast, the high school students engaged in far more discussion of why characters said and did what they did compared to the elementary school students (Goldstein & Winner 2012).

Other work has found exciting evidence of increases in recognizing mental states in autistic adolescents as a result of acting in a performance (Corbett et al., 2019; 2023) or participating in an improv theatre camp (Guli et al., 2013). While previous correlational work had shown varied findings (sometimes positive associations between theatre and empathy, sometimes not, e.g., Goldstein et al., 2009), these more quasi-experimental and experimental research studies provide evidence for the idea that social skills are trained, recruited, or fostered in acting classes for adolescents.

In younger age groups, children who role play stories (as compared to just reading them) show higher empathy as a result (Gil et al., 2014), and elementary school–aged children whose parents report lots of role play also show higher theory of mind and empathy (Goldstein & Winner 2011). Children who participate in multi art interventions including dance, music, theatre, and visual arts also show higher social–emotional skills after participating in these interventions (Andersen et al., 2019).

As mentioned above, mentalizing, empathy, and theory of mind, combined with awareness of what you are feeling and how to regulate it, is often conceptualized as emotional intelligence, or EI, originally proposed as its own skill in 1990 (Salovey & Meyer, 1990). I discuss EI and its use of multiple Acting Habits of Mind thoroughly in Chapter 13.

In schools, the combination of understanding your own emotions and understanding others is often labeled as social and emotional learning, and taught in social and emotional development courses, which have propagated from elementary school through high school across the United States. These courses typically have units on empathy and thinking about other's emotions. They even sometimes contain improv exercises and light role play. But these interventions often fail, particularly for teenagers (Yeager et al., 2018). One hypothesized reason is interventions do not take into account adolescents' needs for self-determination, talk down to them, or are prescribed instead of allowing students to engage for themselves. Generally, explicit teaching of social and emotional skills is less successful than both implicit teaching and experiential learning (Zinsser et al., 2015). Therefore, the implicit learning of others, minds, and emotions that may take place through the active study of characters in acting may be more successful than explicitly learning about them.

Importantly, but less direct, learning how to consider others' perspectives, emotions, beliefs, desires, and knowledge is the basis of compassion and prosociality (Gilbert, 2019; Preckel et al., 2018). Approaching others with interest and curiosity for their inner worlds is necessary to be altruistic. Most psychological theories of prosocial behaviors begin with theory of mind and perspective taking of the other (Imuta et al., 2016). Then comes the emotional engagement of knowing how that feels and that something should be done to help. This then leads the person to want to engage in compassionate and prosocial behavior. While it is not a direct correspondence, and research has shown that other elements (such as whether the person is part of your in group, or whether you can help) can make a difference, almost all compassionate behavior and prosocial actions contain elements of considering others' current situations and perspectives. Thus, building an Acting Habit of Mind to *consider others* could have considerable downstream effects.

Now then, let us turn our attention to what we found in our classes—where and how students were asked to integrate and use their abilities to *consider others* acting classrooms.

CONSIDER OTHERS IN THE ACTING CLASSROOM

In Preparation activities, *consider others* is integrated in any kind of warm-up where students have to pay close attention and react off each other. But it is also used when students have theoretical discussions about the nature of acting to prepare them for the exercises of the day. For example, in a theory discussion in Class 18, a group of seniors at Boston Arts Academy were introduced to the topic of the day by Maura as "the skill of listening." She referred to three quotes written on the board:

> "Acting is about listening and reacting."
> "The big secret in acting is listening to people."
> "Acting is mostly about listening. Just focus on what the other person is saying and acting takes care of itself."

She discussed how this kind of careful listening and reacting to others is actually quite hard to do because you have to put all your attention on someone else. This full attention to others is rare in our everyday lives. And while this skill that is hard enough in everyday life, it is particularly difficult in acting because the students have a script! Therefore, they already know what they are going to say. Acting in this class was discussed as a way to really focus in on someone else and make your close attention and understanding of that person be the guide to the performance rather than a preconceived notion of what you are going to do or know ahead of time.

Maura noted for the students: "The instinct is oh I'm going to think about me while this person is talking. . . . You find yourself pretending to listen and being active listening fake. So, the hardest part of film acting is to push through that level of not listening or listening fake, and actual listen like you don't know what's coming next. . . . You let your heart watch somebody's face . . . you can't pretend because as soon as you pretend, we can see it."

She did note that all the rest of the students' acting training up to that point does not go away, but that the central act of listening and paying attention to the other person is the focus of the actual act of acting in that moment on camera. She then sets the students up to perform scripted scenes for a camera and then watch for feedback, while thinking about how they are paying attention to another person for real, not pretend, and reacting authentically to that other person, even when they know all the words in advance. They have to pay careful attention—more than one would normally in life. A difficult task to be sure, but central to the habit of closely and carefully *considering others*—both the other actor in the room with them, and the other character that their character is performing with. They have to consider carefully the messages the other character is giving them, and try to react appropriately both given their listening and their consideration of the words.

In Generation activities, students must make sure they are pay attention to and *consider others* in their improvised activities, sometimes integrated into the activity itself, for example, when having to build off of another student's jokes. But often teachers set up explicit improvised activities in which they pay close attention and *consider others*.

At Eureka High School's advanced acting Class 28, students sat across from each other in chairs. In pairs, they engaged in an improvised activity in which they had to observe each other closely, just sitting and looking at one another. First, they had to list out all the objective truths they could about the other person's appearance, clothes, and demeanor. The students repeated these truths back and forth to each other. Then, they asked each other "provocative" questions, nothing over certain preset boundaries of consent, but still focused on what might make the other person feel uncomfortable or delve into their inner being. This exercise forced the students both to pay close attention to each other's external presentation of self through clothes and facial expressions, and their internal sense of what would make their partner uncomfortable or thoughtful. Justin discussed this as playing with their partner and being present with them in the moment in which they were communicating.

In Interpretation activities, *consider others* is central to performing a character. A student must deeply consider and understand their character in order to portray what they are saying; playwrights purposefully make the lines of a script have deep subtext and multiple possible meanings. For example, in Class 26 at The Madeira School, Kelsey pointed out how the actors needed to think about the emotions of the characters being shown through behaviors. "You perceive that I am angry because I am challenging you. Emotions are perceptions, which is why it is very difficult to act it out, which is why we act it out through tactics." Here, Kelsey is pointing out how the students need to be thinking about the tactics and behaviors they are displaying as a way to think about how their inner states can be made external for the audience, and for their fellow actors to have a reaction to. The actor knows the emotions of their characters, but they need to translate that to behaviors. It is theory of mind integrated into the exercise of intention reading for a character.

Students are often asked to Reflect on the ways in which they interpreted and understood the inner lives of their characters. For example, at The Madeira School, the students spent Class 22 formally presenting their monologues for grading from Kelsey and commentary from their classmates.

After being asked to take a moment and envision their imaginary monologue partner's facial expression (an exercise in *imagine and envision*), the students presented their complete monologues, all Shakespearean. "As we do observations for these, for our fellow classmates . . . we're going to give just a little bit of a piece of a critical response. So instead of saying, 'I liked, I disliked' whatever, say, 'things I noticed, that struck me, that I wondered about.'" In this way, Kelsey is focusing the class to make their Reflection moments for their classmates considering what will be most helpful, and to have carefully noticed and paid attention to what was happening in the monologue moment that they could reflect on.

Each student in the class took a turn making a specific comment to the actor who had just presented, noting what they noticed, were struck by, and wondered about. Students discussed the sounds the actor made, how she shook her voice, the way in which the presentation reflected inner emotionality, and how the actions of the actor added to what was strictly in the script. "Get away from opinion, and into observation," Kelsey said, prompting the students to tie outward physicality to inner mental states.

Across these four sections of class, then, the students *consider others'* emotions, behaviors, words, and thoughts. They are thinking about listening to each other in character, perceiving the emotions of their characters from the words, reflecting on how their fellow actors portray inner states in monologues, and thinking about their classmates' hidden inner lives. We see all of these varieties of *consider others* and thinking about others' mental and emotional states in our two focal exercises for *consider others*.

Focal Exercise 1: Improvising Characters From Drawings

Building a full picture of a character starting from a few details.

In Class 2 at Imagination Stage with teacher Jewel, the students began a long improvisation exercise in which they built a character with a partner and then created a scene where that character was interacting with others, followed by a Reflection period. They started by standing back-to-back in pairs, with one student describing a picture of a character they had brought in from home. As they did this, the other student was tasked with transforming their bodies into the character. This required both of the actors to *consider others* through perspective taking: the describer had to think about how to best let their partner know what they wanted them to do, and the performer had to interpret and transform into what the describer was saying. At this point, the character transformation was mostly physical, the two students trying to match description to action. Jewel encouraged the students to think about where the character physically "leads from" and where their voice "is," meaning how their physicality was expressed and experienced by others. This requires a sense of physical perspective taking from the performer, and thorough feedback from the describer to cocreate the character as a fully realized human being. Throughout the exercise, the first student had to stay in character, physically and mentally, even when having a conversation with their partner about their own drawing. The describer really had to be explicit about how they thought about and conceptualized the character in the drawing, their body, voice, personality, and inner life. The actor then had to think about how to take those characteristics and embody and portray them.

After each of the students were in character, Jewel gave an example with a student she had previously paired with. The student did a great job portraying an old man, squinting at what she has to read, and awkwardly walking across the classroom, obviously stiff. Jewel described how this exercise requires being physically neutral to be able to "receive" any character given for portrayal in the exercise. She also described how to purposefully create and think about characteristics in the character that are different from the actor—to have a sense of self-knowledge and a sense of distinction from the knowledge of character, too.

After this description, the students began to walk around the room as their characters. Jewel warned them to *imagine* as they walked, and that they will be tasked with some challenging movements based on their understanding of their character. For instance, she told the students not to just walk in circles, but to think about what their character would do as a real person—stop in front of someone, look at something, sit, etc. They then paired up, still in character, and talked about what they had to do so far that day.

Throughout the exercise, Jewel prompted them to think beyond labels or simple definitions (e.g., as a "teacher") to the other ways in which a person is more than that. "Start to find the person. And remember we all have different faces that we show to different people." The students were prompted to think about the complexities of other people. They were asked to think about the characters they play not just as archetypes or single personality traits, but with the same fullness of character they may use to think about themselves or a close friend. She then had them walk around the room with different circumstances—how would their character behave if they were late? If they forgot something? If they were trying to convince a partner of a business venture?

They then wrote in their journal noting what did they get or not get out of the exercise and how can they apply it to their scene work. The students wrote quietly in Reflection, thinking about how creating that character from scratch and having to think about the fullness another person is much more fully realized than reading on a page. In this way, Jewel had the students reflect on how *consider others* in the form of the minds of the improvised character would transfer as a skill to the scripted character. She wanted them to think about how they got deeper into the improvisation, maybe they stopped working so hard as an actor, and let the character come through a bit more clearly.

Students reflected on how they started with a stereotype but then moved into more specificity on how they interacted with other people. One student reflected how he started putting a story line on to his character and that helped him. Jewel responded: "Isn't it cool how that story line helps you start to relax into the character? That's why we use our imagination to fill in what doesn't happen with the given circumstances" (what the background and history of a character tells you about their current moment). Another student reflected on using characteristics from a real person they knew to fill out the improvisation.

Then, a student talked about struggling with her improvised character, and Jewel pulled her up to the center of the classroom stage to talk through what she knew about the character and thought about the character while she was becoming the character. Altogether, in this part of class that spanned both a Generation and a Reflection activity, students were primarily being tasked with thinking through the minds, movements, and goals of characters, and then use *consider others* for how they understood those characters for themselves.

In the post-class interview, Jewel said one of her overarching pedagogical goals for the day was to get the students to learn how to break a character down and to embody their physicality—so, learning how to take a whole, live, human character to consider the component parts of their mental and physical world for portrayal. Literally, a technique for thinking about the inner and outer lives of others!

Focal Exercise 2: Holistically Reflecting on a Mask Unit

Formally thinking through what the audience understood and took from a devised masked performance.

At Arcata, one of our rural public high schools in Humboldt County, students had a more theoretical and traditionally pedagogical way of being asked to *consider others* during Class 34—a long Reflection period. The week before they had worked on a mask exercise in which they had created their own masks and then worked on a pantomime while masked, which included dramatic structure, music, and performance of the resultant 3-minute solo for the class. This was a unit on physical theatre and mask work overall, and the Reflection was the end of a major project and unit. They had worked on physicalizing a character without a face (since they were masked) and thinking deeply about creating a narrative structure and plot without the benefits and ease of words or facial expressions. On the day of the observation, teacher Melanie asked the students to complete a worksheet with a series of questions about the experience from their own perspective. Then they had to pair up and discuss.

In this discussion, students shared their answers to the worksheet and then discussed what they might want to share with the whole class. This involves *consider others* in thinking about how their responses combined with their partner's responses might engage the rest of the class with the work. Melanie spent some time engaged in individual consulting with the members of the class in partnership. The first set of questions was about the emotions students were portraying, and perhaps experiencing, in their mask scenes. One student said, "I liked to make a face under the mask because it made it more authentic for me, which I believe made it more believable for the audience." *Consider others* was also centered as the students were asked to reflect on how they thought about their classmates' solos, and their reflections on what made the classmates' solos effective or not. They were asked to think about their classmates' intentions for performance, how those intentions came through in the choices the performer made, and how they were able to communicate plot and character through their performance. The students had to reflect on their own understanding and where personal meaning came from, and whether that was reflective of what they thought the creator was trying to give to them.

They also had to think about whether they felt any emotions while watching their classmates, and if so, whether those emotions matched the emotions they were watching; they discussed whether there was a right or wrong way to be thinking about these performances; they discussed how it was different to think about what someone was showing you, versus feel what they were feeling, versus to have an emotion such as "reactionary . . . like, this was tense." This was an intensive, reflective discussion of what students saw others doing and how it affected them—thinking about how the actions of others played out in the emotional lives of the audience. This requires *consider others* in a variety of ways—character, actors, and classmates.

There was additional discussion of watching an actor express an emotion and specifically think about "why" that actor was expressing what they were expressing and how it might be motivated by various things the students were seeing. They also discussed how the different emotions were connected to the audience. One student said, "I think people tend to relate to sadness more than any other emotion. . . . Because every single person in their lives has had a little bit of sadness. . . . So when [an actor] puts themselves out there with a sad emotion, you can be like, 'I know!'" Melanie also talked about the distinctions about being emotional "with" the person onstage, versus "for" the person onstage—the clear distinction between cognitive and emotional empathy and sympathy. The students then picked a scene that stood out to them and discussed the actions of the performer that made that scene stand out in particular. As one student said, the scenes that stood out did so because of the job of the actor "to portray and project their feelings as actors to the crowd."

CONSIDER OTHERS, IN SUMMARY

- Acting teachers spend a lot of time asking students: "Why did the character do this?" "What is the character's history" "Why do they say these words in this moment?"
- Student actors must consider the minds, the words, the physicality, and the emotions of others, both connection and similarity to self, and in conflict to what they themselves might do.
- Once students are performing, they also must consider and observe what other actors and characters are doing onstage, and react in kind.
- Observe and *consider others* is built into group exercise warm-ups and improv games in which actors react to a partner and build off of their improvisations; this is the basis of scene study when students must determine how to portray a character.
- Students not only have to *consider others'* minds and emotions, but also others' physicality, and think about how their own physical status is presented to others and the self.
- Beyond the acting classroom, *consider others* is critical to empathy, a sense of belongingness, and creation of relationships.

Chapter 7

Think Collaboratively

Learning to Actively and Purposefully Communicate, Engage, and Work With Others

> The group of students in Class 10 at Boston Arts Academy stand in a circle. They are playing "yes," a simple warm-up where one student makes eye contact with another and the second student has to say "yes" before they can move across the circle. The second student then looks around for someone to make eye contact with and say "yes." The students must be looking at each other, listening and watching carefully to make sure they get to take their turn in time, or they will be eliminated. The ultimate goal is to make sure all students are given a "yes," with no repeats. As this is happening, Maura reminds the students to "make sure you hit everyone, guys, share, take care of each other." She repeats this several times over the 12 minutes of the exercise. "Take care of each other. Make sure you include the whole class." When one student loses, she mentions, "Sometimes you're out because your partner doesn't do their job!" As students continued to get eliminated, Maura tells them to pick someone to root for, and then the class gets really rowdy.

In these quotes, Maura is reminding students to not just pay attention to their own, singular role in the game, but to go beyond just thinking about others' mental states and *think collaboratively* about the whole group. She wants them to center the goal of ensuring everyone in the group is included. The game is nonverbal except for the "yes," so while the students are being asked to *release inhibitions* and buy into the game, it also contains the objective of taking individual connections between two students and turning them into an exercise in *think collaboratively* as a whole class.

Think Collaboratively is where students learn to communicate, engage, and work with other students actively and purposefully. It is where students learn to build an ensemble from the disparate group that walked into the classroom. It is where students work to understand their own ideas, movements, behaviors, and emotions needed to integrate with others' behaviors, emotions, and goals in order to portray a scene onstage. Students learn to *think collaboratively* through careful understanding of how their wants and needs as actors mesh with the wants and needs of the other people they are working with onstage. They learn to work as a unit to keep each other's goals and needs in mind as they move through their own needs and goals.

Collaborative goals are being consistently framed by the teachers in exercises, discussions in class, and their interviews. Teachers would discuss exercises as a "great way to bring a group together" (Jewel, Class 3), or discuss with the students the need to engage as an ensemble (e.g., "you have to care more about each other than yourselves in that situation"—Jewel, Class 7) when they were playing a game. For example, Jewel said, "By the end, I felt like you were becoming an amoeba-like character," when the students created a moving form together onstage (Class 7). Nikki (in Class 1) said her overarching pedagogical goal was "building ensemble" to make sure the students knew theatre was not about lead and side roles, but that the students needed to "move and breathe together" and trust each other. Justin, during Class 31, said his goal was to get the class to "develop as an ensemble" and noted that this required the students to connect in an authentic, truthful, and vulnerable way.

THE SCIENCE OF THINK COLLABORATIVELY

Think collaboratively is related to a variety of psychological abilities and constructs considered "21st-century education skills." These skills are framed as the skills students (and everyone) will need in the 21st century, as culturally we cannot know what kind of jobs or skills will be necessary due to how technology will continue to change society (Chalkiadaki, 2018; Charleroy et al., 2011; Geisinger, 2016). While the list of skills varies depending on which researcher, educator, or policymaker is writing it, communication, collaboration, and intergroup understanding are often included (frequently with creativity, character, and critical thinking—sounds like the Acting Habits of Mind to me!).

Teamwork, leadership, being a good partner, and a collaborative group member are all critical to building ensemble and connection both in and out of acting classrooms. Importantly, in adolescence, there is a growing sense of group identity with peers, both in the sense of conformity, and in the sense that socialization with peers becomes primary over engagement with parents (Smetana et al., 2006). This also comes with a growing affective (i.e. emotional) commitment to group engagement and thinking (Stets & Burke, 2000). Motivation for peer acceptance becomes stronger in adolescence than in childhood or adulthood (LaFontana & Cillessen, 2010; Newcomb et al., 1993). This peer motivation can protect adolescents from social isolation, but also can be related to bullying or other negative outcomes. Orienting groups to autonomous social connection with each other (i.e., building ensemble) can help steer them toward prosocial actions rather than negative outcomes, as can providing healthy adult relationships that include guidance, acceptance, and personal connections while still holding high standards (Yeager et al., 2018).

Much in the same way there is an adolescent search for personal identity (as discussed in Chapter 4), there is an adolescence search for a group to be a part of, a "group identity" (Erickson, 1994; Marcia, 1966), which primes teens for higher forms of social learning and the fast adoption of new social norms, cultural norms, and change (Crone & Dahl, 2012). This is often why adults cannot keep up or understand quickly changing adolescent slang—it is part of their group identity formation! Rituals of engaging together in an activity can allow for group identity and formation, which points toward collaborative theatre as a particularly potent way to engage with this psychological construct.

There is also a growing desire for intimacy with a group of peers in adolescence, and a social sensitivity that underlies the desire and ability to make and keep close friends (Blakemore & Mills, 2014; Brown 2004). This change is underpinned by structural and functional changes to the social brain in adolescence, and the ongoing onset of pubertal hormones may have the effect of increasing motivation to maintain group status in the social environment (Terburg & van Honk, 2013). In fact, close peer relationships in adolescence are a stronger predictor of healthy adult relationships than even romantic relationships in adolescence (Allen et al., 2020). Such close intimate relationships remain important across the lifespan, both in the romantic sense and in terms of making and maintaining group bonds and friendships (Hartup & Stevens, 1999; Hruschka, 2010).

The ways in which acting classes build group rapport and help form ensembles have been used in a wide variety of settings outside of high schools, including in companies for team building and for groups to come together in search of social justice. This is often focused just on the Generation segment of class, with improv exercises and warm-ups being the entire and central activity. There is a small cottage industry of theatre companies creating experiences for companies to bring employees to collaborate on improv games, to use the sense of *release inhibitions* and *think collaboratively* to build a sense of belonging to a group and build relationships (e.g., Dudeck & McClure, 2018; Koppett, 2013). In educational settings, improvisation classes have been shown to increase feelings of collaboration (Sawyer, 2004, 2014). And, there is a long history of theory and research on Theatre of the Oppressed, created by Augusto Boal, specifically for the purpose of devising works of theatre focused on a system of oppression or other struggle that a group is going through, to give them agency and voice, and to bring them together as a collaborative group to work on solving problems (Boal, 2013).

In the only direct test I know of looking at how acting classes are associated with *think collaboratively,* my doctoral student Megan Stutesman and I conducted a collaborative study with the Commonwealth Theatre Center in Louisville, Kentucky, and their associate artistic director, Julane Havens.

We used their internal student and teaching rubrics to look at the possibilities of collaboration as a growing student skill over time. This theatre had put into place an end-of-semester rating system, where teachers thought about students' creativity, problem solving, initiative, and communication and collaboration, taking into careful consideration their level in the conservatory theatre program and what each kind of skill would look like in the class the student had just completed. We looked both at teacher ratings numerically and their qualitative comments about students in the classroom.

Students gained across skills over the course of each semester they were in the program. However, as the students moved up in level, their growth was slower each semester. This shows a particular possible pathway to how these students learned psychological skills in acting classes, and particularly to *think collaboratively*. They are getting better year by year, but as the acting class gets more difficult, skill growth slows. This is indicative of acting classes teaching Acting Habits of Mind, which must be differentially applied across classes, rather than a rote skill that can be applied blankly. In their comments at the end of each semester, students and teachers noted students' gains in abilities to work in groups, respect their peers, and receive others' ideas (Stutesman et al., 2022).

Now, then, let us turn our attention to what we found in our classes: How thinking and communicating collaboratively, with ensemble, is used, integrated, taught, and possibly fostered in acting classrooms themselves.

THINK COLLABORATIVELY IN THE ACTING CLASSROOM

In Preparation activities, *think collaboratively* is integrated in any kind of warm-up where the students have to cohesively engage in an activity and work together to achieve a collaborative goal. For example, at Eureka High School (St. Louis) in Class 29, students had to walk around the space, and then stop moving all at the same time. This began with teacher Justin giving them "stop" and "start" times: "Our goal is to stop together as one unit and not to hear any extra shuffling, talking. You hear 'freeze,' boom! You all stop on a dime." This progressed into Justin getting the students to change tempos together, saying, "We're looking for transition where you all change at the same time. Not a cascading of movements. You change as one unit." Then, after a few minutes, Justin stopped telling the students that a change is happening and that instead they should direct their own changes silently, paying close attention to nonverbal cues. The goal is "to have the additional change and the whole group change space between be very, very small, happening all at once because you're so aware of each other." The students then walk for a few minutes, paying close attention to each other's movements to match up how they are walking around. He notes that students will need to be aware not only of the people closest to them on the classroom stage (this was a class of 24 students), but also the students who are standing very far away on the other side. He discusses the concept of "soft focus," meaning students need to be paying attention to the whole space at once. He contrasts this to the "laser focus" of other kinds of academic classrooms, such as a singular focus on your own math problem, blocking out the other students in the math classroom. The students start with larger shifts (from very fast to very slow) but eventually begin to be more subtle in the ways they are able to influence each other. Pushing the idea of group cohesion in even a warm-up period tells students how important it is for them to use and to integrate *think collaboratively* about the group throughout the day.

In Generation activities, *think collaboratively* occurs whenever the students are engaged in an improvisational exercise where they have to work with, to think about, and to pay close attention to each other while developing material as a group. In Class 7 at Imagination Stage, students had to pair up and guide each other around a classroom Jewel had set up with chairs and materials strewn all over the place. One student was blindfolded in each pair, and the other had to provide guidance only with their voice, with physical intervention only allowed if the blindfolded student was in danger. Jewel introduced the activity by noting the students had to "care more about each other than yourselves in that situation." Here, the students had to think about the ways in which they were talking to their paired classmate, where they were, and where their blindfolded partner was, as well as how they were engaging with the rest of the class and the classroom itself. This led into a discussion of safety in acting and how acting is a vulnerable place to be. Actors have to be aware and hold in safety, emotionally and physically, the other people onstage. *Think collaboratively* means thinking about how your fellow actors and all the people involved stay safe.

Jewel noted: "You may not be best friends in here, but that doesn't mean you don't have trust in the ensemble. You guys have been together for a year and a half . . . so there's trust there." To create group trust through collaborative exercises and creating space and action together is fully integrating the power of approaching problems with a mindset of *think collaboratively*. Students engaged in this collaborative trust exercise for 22 minutes, and then engaged in almost 30 minutes of discussion on its meaning. But the exemplar of practicing this, embodying it, was necessary.

In a short Interpretation activity that centered *think collaboratively* at The Madeira School in Class 24, students began working on the physical actions of their monologues (blocking), by working with just the ideas of "toward, away, stay" line by line. Basically, the only decision students were tasked with making was whether a moment in the script prompted movement, and if so, in what direction. The students worked with partners for the first few lines in front of the class so the rest of the students could see the exercise. Teacher Kelsey noted, "We started to see them come together, look around . . . some things like that gives us some ideas to play with. In terms of relationship with each other." The two students had to *think collaboratively* about how to move toward and away from each other to portray to the audience the reality of relationship of the characters as well as how they themselves understood the lines and the blocking of the scene. While just a simple exercise, the key is that the students had to *think collaboratively* on their interpretation of the roles for the movement choices. This required taking another's opinion into account, communicating their own opinion, and coming to a consensus.

Students were asked regularly in Reflection periods to *think collaboratively* about their group work and how they can strengthen it. Reflecting on whether the collaboration as a group was as strong as possible can help the students build up to a performance together. Students must work together in groups and ensembles, pairs and trios, to stage a scene. Even when giving a monologue, students still have to *think collaboratively* with their director, and eventual lighting and sound designers.

For example, at Imagination Stage in Class 8, students were rehearsing the performance of *Antigone* that they were preparing. To begin the performance, they had to walk in a circle and say an opening set of lines in unison. They took a few minutes to form their circle and decide which way to face and walk, but then began to match their pace and footfalls without talking. They continued walking together, all feet simultaneous, for a minute. Then, they began to speak all as one, the opening verse to *Antigone*, the scene they were studying that week. Nikki paused the scene for Reflection on why they were not perfectly in sync, and what they could do to become more in sync, including focusing more on walking, not the words, and how spreading apart physically from each other might help. Nikki noted their pitch did not have to be identical when they do start talking, but that they need to pace themselves to be the same. The students then discussed which foot was better to start, and how to stay focused together, and to keep a circle shape while walking.

Across these four sections of class, then, the students are being instructed in how to *think collaboratively,* and implicitly asked to do so when they have to work together to create cohesion onstage, think about each other's safety, move together without previously discussion, and build a scene. We see all these possibilities in our two focal exercises for *think collaboratively.*

Focal Exercise 1: Bean Bag Toss and Running Blind

Working together in games to build trust and to build ensemble.

At Imagination Stage in Class 1, students spent almost 40 minutes of class in a collaborative, communicative game called Running Blind. First, the students formed a large circle and threw a beanbag around while saying each other's names, making sure they knew each other's names. They did this for long enough that every student had a chance to throw and catch the beanbag, beginning a sense that they are one collective ensemble with a set order of tosses. A second beanbag was added, and then a third. The students had to keep multiple tasks in mind as they listened for their own name, tossed a beanbag while saying someone else's name, watched for other students' throwing their beanbags, and made sure they are staying in the order. Once there were four beanbags going, Nikki had them reverse the order of the tosses. Even this simple toss game with names cements the idea that the students have to work as a unit to create a successful experience for all; no one student can direct the actions, and no one can be left out or fail to participate, or the whole experience will fall apart. Instead, the students have to think as a group, together, with each member helping other members. And they have to figure out what that means to *think collaboratively*, the distribution of attention and focus around the room.

"If something goes wrong, just pick it up and keep going," Nikki says. She reminds the group to relax as it gets more frantic as more beanbags are added, and the names come fast and furious. The exercise then goes one step further where the students can no longer say each other's names and have to rely on eye contact and body language to keep the game going. At one point Nikki tells a student, "That's not making him [a classmate] look good," reminding the student that their job is to be a good teammate.

After a break for the set physical warm-up, Nikki pulls one student to the center of the room and has them put on a blindfold, keeping the other students to form a large circle around them. The students spread out around the classroom to ensure equal distribution of sighted students. She introduces that the blindfolded student has chosen "to put his trust and safety into our hands, and we are going to take that trust and responsibility seriously." The blindfolded student's goal is to walk as normally as possible, and the classes' goal is to guard the blindfolded student from walking into furniture, walls, or debris on the floor. The blindfolded student is asked to just experience the room, and all students are reminded to take this seriously and to play along together.

After the first student went though, Nikki said it was all too easy and she was adding a second blindfolded student. With the additional of a second blindfolded person, the students come up with the idea of a new floating student in the middle of the room to make sure no blindfolded students hit each other. The students adjust the perimeter of the circle to fill in for the walking students, and Nikki asks for quiet. After each walking, they have a moment of Reflection, talking about the sensory deprivation of walking blindfolded, the feelings of fear and then ease as they worked their way through the exercise together. The students on the perimeter discussed needing to keep themselves calm to keep the walkers calm, discussing and noticing how the emotions of the students affect each other during the game. Nikki notes "no acting"—the students are not supposed to have characters or intentions or goals in this game, it is purely about working in a group.

She adds smaller goals as different students put on the blindfolds and walk, for example, "making them feel as safe and comfortable as possible." As the students went further into the exercise, Nikki prompted them to discuss why they wanted to remain silly versus focusing and paying attention and helping each other, working together nonverbally to make the exercise a success. Using eye contact and signals to communicate, she says, allows them to "make this about [the walkers], not about yourself. Make them feel safe. . . . Trust . . . I know it's not an easy thing."

When the students then have three blindfolded classmates, including one who is wearing a sling on one arm, Nikki notes, "It's not on her, we have to create an environment where she feels relaxed. If we are calm, they will be calm too."

This requires *think collaboratively* at multiple levels. The students must pay attention to multiples of their classmates, not just the one who is blindfolded. They have to pay attention to the students who may be helping as well as the student who is wandering the room blindfolded, and think about the best pathway and trajectory for the blindfolded student to include everyone in the class. This shows the students how learning theatre and learning how to act is a collaborative activity. Theatre requires ensembles and groups and listening to directors. During a formal Reflection period, Nikki asked, "Why do we do trust exercises in an acting class?" A student replied, "Because as an ensemble, you have to trust each other." If something goes wrong, you have to trust everyone in the group to solve the problem.

What is interesting, Nikki notes, is that it is rare that something goes wrong. It is also less common that you have to do high-risk stunts, and while large physical scenes do happen, they are not the everyday experience in theatre. Instead, every day, everyone must fulfill their roles, and the group of students will be spending a long time together and performing for more than 2 years, so they have to have group trust. However, Nikki also prompted the students to think about how acting classes often ask actors to do things or think about things that might make you feel weird or silly (*release inhibitions*). Actors do not want to feel like the other people in the classroom are going to judge you or make fun of you, and a priority to *think collaboratively* can help.

Focal Exercise 2: Group Mirror Work

Bringing a group together by thinking about shared leadership through movement.

In Class 3 at Imagination Stage, about 9 minutes in, teacher Jewel divided the class into groups of four or five students, and had them build on the classic partner mirror exercise in a larger group focused on collaborative manner. Without speaking or verbal cues, the students all had to follow the movements of a leader. Before this group part of the exercise, the class had started with just partners, and then a 2 minute "share out" Reflection period where they discussed what was easy and hard about the partnered mirroring. Once the class was in small groups, one person became the "front" of the diamond, facing one way in the classroom. Then, the students began, with one student leading. Other students could either step to the front or turn the group to face another way, with another leader in front.

The leader had to be thinking about their own movements, whether they are clear enough for the class, and how to make sure their group is doing something interesting. They also had to make sure they were not centering themselves too much or taking over for too long. The followers had to pay close attention to the leader and mimic their body movements as they watched. But they also had to simultaneously consider when they might want to take on leadership, or how to share leadership possibilities with the other students in the group. Altogether, then, this is an exercise in *think collaboratively* and focusing on how the group is functioning and working together. In fact, after the first iteration of the exercise, while the students are in a moment of Reflection, Jewel says to write down the exercise in their notebooks because it is "a great way to bring a group together" in case the student ever wants to teach.

In addition to integrating ensemble building and group cohesion, this exercise helps with thinking about individual member's contributions to a group. This was reflected in a student saying about the exercise: "Even though everyone was moving in unison, you could still notice specific interpretations." Jewel then reflects that even when you cannot see someone's face, and you are not directly interacting with them, there still needs to be "that sense of connection with them" onstage. Just like with most of the exercises, even when they are not direct performances of characters, our teachers prompted students to think about how the exercise could be used in rehearsal, teaching, or other forms of theatre. In this way, she is bringing the collaborative nature of the exercise back to the collaborative nature of acting performance itself.

Next, the students started the exercise again, this time in two larger groups of eight students each. The rules also changed slightly, where any student at any point can come from the center of the group and take up the leadership position. This new scenario is teaching students to think about how a group is working in the moment, whether it needs a new leader, whether the person who is leading currently needs to be leading, and whether the student feels they are the right person to step in to that role in the right moment. And, they have to figure it all out without talking to each other about it. Jewel prompts the group to first focus by taking a deep breath in unison.

Finally, after all the students had a chance to participate, and most a chance to lead, there was a longer Reflection discussion about how no matter who you were acting with, they will always be a different person as the character. Jewel prompted the students to always think about the collaboration between the character and the actor as the person you are interacting with on the stage. This is *think collaboratively* in a different sense than ensemble building or individual contributions, perhaps, but still thinking about the variety of sources (character, personal) that go into a performance, and how to imaginatively combine them into the best, equally contributing, outcome. Altogether, the small group mirror exercise, large group mirror exercise, and several small periods of formal Reflection took about 18 minutes of class.

THINK COLLABORATIVELY, IN SUMMARY

- Actors must learn how to be part of an ensemble, communicating and working together. There cannot be cliques or small pairs of exclusive friends in a class or a play's ensemble.
- Teachers set up exercises that can be completed only when the group of students work together to create something larger than any one of them could create on their own.
- Students must always remember that any performance is not just theirs alone, but placed within a group of other student actors, choreographers, directors, and others. Part of learning how to act is thinking about the context of other perspectives that create the work of theatre.
- Beyond the acting classroom, being able to *think collaboratively* is critical to communication skills and working in pairs and teams.
- Student actors are taught to not just think about other people, but to think about how to collaborate, communicate, and engage actively and purposefully with others to create a process and product beyond what they could do alone.

Chapter 8

Be Flexible

Learning to Be Open and Try New Ideas Until One Works Best

> One student stands in the middle of a circle, the others around her, stone-faced and still. She jumps around, makes noises, quickly approaches and walks away from each student in the circle saying "Honey! I love you." But it is not working. None of the other students are laughing. She tries yet another student, who also stays stone-faced. Kelsey says, "That tactic didn't work, try something new" (Class 24).

So, what is happening in this activity? The student is being asked to generate ideas, to *consider others'* points of view and humor, to *release inhibitions* about being silly, and to *embody* and say funny actions. The group is being asked to think about objectives (make someone laugh; don't laugh) and tactics (ways to get the person to laugh; ways to keep from laughing). But in this particular moment of Kelsey's suggestion, she is asking the performer to *be flexible*. She is encouraging the student who is experiencing failure (no laughter from the other students) to try something else, something new.

Be Flexible is where students learn to be open to new ideas and try different options for their acting to see which one works best. They learn to be open to failure and overcome set ideas about perfection. An open and flexible mindset, where students try on different actions, think through and practice different ideas to see what works, is key to learning how to act a character.

Acting classes require students to try on different characters and perspectives, but even within those characters and perspectives, actors must try different ways of performing to determine what feels true and real to the character. Students start with an instinct and analysis, but must move flexibly to other instincts, or to different aspects of their analysis to find the right answer to the problem of how to best perform a character. Without the ability to *be flexible,* a student performing might get stuck in a rigid idea of what a character and performance should look like, and not discover the best way to get their ideas across to an audience.

Students are also required to *be flexible* in the ways they collaborate and take ideas from others. While I talked about *think collaboratively* in the last chapter, *be flexible* is key to allowing collaboration to flourish. Flexibility is the key to learning anything new, and it is the key to solving problems in new and creative ways. Flexibility within constraints of character, collaboration, and script is thus key to success in performance.

The Acting Habit of Mind being recruited and trained in an acting class is to overcome the idea that there is only one right answer to any open problem, or that not getting it right is a problem. Instead, students are asked to be nimble, adaptable, and responsive to feedback and ideas as they arise. As Jewel said at Imagination Stage: "Get out of your head that there's one way to say it" (Class 7), and as Juanita said at Boston Arts Academy: "Keep it open" (Class 17).

THE SCIENCE OF BE FLEXIBLE

Flexibility is about openness to new ideas and ways of experiencing the world. Like our other Acting Habits of Mind, the use of *be flexible* throughout acting classes incorporates and is related to a number of important psychological skills, including openness, creativity, grit, malleability, and cognitive control.

To start, to *be flexible* requires a sense of cognitive control, as students must be prepared and accept changing from one way they might have been performing or engaging with an exercise to a new, different way. In adolescence in particular, cognitive control and task switching actually improves (i.e., becomes more flexible) both over childhood and in comparison to adulthood (Crone & Dahl, 2012). In general, cognitive malleability increases, particularly for social cues (Blakemore & Mills, 2014). This means adolescents are more able and more likely to make changes, particularly in response to friends and peers.

While adolescents traditionally have been conceptualized at being open to more risks, and in particular negative risks such as substance use, physical challenges, risky sexualized behavior, and violence, the ability to engage in more flexible thinking and openness to risk can also be used in a positive manner. In acting classes, *be flexible* asks students to engage in individualized positive risk taking in response to the same prompt or originating point. Taking risks in a theatre classroom and doing something unusual or daring (i.e., *release inhibitions and be playful*) may allow adolescents to channel their needs to take risks in adaptive ways (Duell & Steinberg, 2021). Particularly when a social situation is set up to endorse positive risk taking, the burgeoning ability to adjust goals and priorities flexibly can help steer teens toward adaptive and positive health and social justice outcomes.

To be sure, *be flexible* is not just called upon when given explicit feedback to do something different. Many of the generative improv exercises in acting classes require flexibility to others' ideas and physical ways of moving. There is evidence from studies of the adolescent brain that teens are particularly able to have flexibility to adjust their intrinsic motivations and goals as they receive feedback from peers (Crone & Dahl, 2012). *Be flexible* in a group means being open to the social cues you are getting from others, and being able to fit in with the social scene that is being created before you. This is why social movements in culture are often led by teens and emerging adults (Ginwright & James, 2002; Hope et al., 2016). Adolescence is a key time to see how there could be multiple different outcomes in society, paired with a sense of social connectedness and growing awareness of injustice (Heberle et al., 2020). Positively, participating in civic movements and activities such as voting, volunteering, and activism as a young adult is positively associated with mental health behaviors later in development (Ballard et al., 2019).

Another area that *be flexible* in acting classes may connect to developmental science is through the practice of divergent thinking. Divergent thinking is the ability to come up with multiple responses to a single prompt and is the key to the "brainstorming" part of the creative process (see Chapter 13). Creativity across many fields at many levels (whether a famous professional chef, a local entrepreneur, or a weekend artist in the garage) requires being open to trying new ideas and actions, making mistakes, generating many new ideas, and then being able to pick the best one. Often, being able to come up with many different ideas is used as a way to measure creative potential, or the underlying cognitive aspects of creativity (Reiter-Palmon et al., 2019).

In fact, there have been a few studies that have linked experiences in improvisational theatre classes and divergent thinking. The connection seems obvious, given the underlying task of flexibly approaching answers to a question. Mathieu Hainselin and colleagues at Université de Picardie Jules Verne worked with students age 11 for 11 weeks in improv class, and compared their creative thinking before and after the class to the creative thinking of a group of students engaged in a sports program. They found the improv group had better divergent thinking after their course, compared both to before the course, and to the group who only did sports (Hainselin et al., 2018).

In a related study, Peter Felsman and colleagues at the University of Michigan found that even a brief experience of improv exercises (only 20 minutes), compared to 20 minutes of social interactions, increased divergent thinking and uncertainty tolerance, which is the ability to be emotionally comfortable with variability and unpredictability. Importantly, when uncertainty tolerance is high, people are less likely to have anxiety or depression (Felsman et al., 2020). In a group of college students, Carine Lewis and Peter Lovatt at the University of Hertfordshire found that both verbal and musical improvisation can predict creative output, although it is hard to know in this study whether the verbal improv or the musical improv was more important for causing change (Lewis & Lovatt, 2013).

Beyond improvising and creativity, the personality trait of openness, particularly to new experiences, is well-studied as connected to creative potential and creative behavior (Feist, 2019; Oleynick et al., 2017). Individuals who score high on openness when taking personality tests tend to be more creative in their lives and in their careers (Ivcevic & Brackett, 2015; Silvia et al., 2009). I deal more directly with the science of the creative process in Chapter 13, as there are more components to being creative than just being able to come up with many possible outcomes, but being open to new possibilities is key. While creative action and creative thought requires the creation (literally) of something new, openness is how you get there. Without a level of openness to new connections and new ways of thinking, without *be flexible* to guide and think about your character, movement, or engagement with others from a new perspective, it is unlikely that an actor will be successful. Learning how to approach tasks with the Habit of Mind of *be flexible* could be a pathway.

Beyond just cognitive flexibility and divergent thinking, a significant amount of research has shown that taking a flexible mindset to your own abilities, personality, and intelligence can help overcome setbacks and failures, bolster achievement, and even lower stress. Having a "growth mindset" has become a catch-all term in educational psychology, and is often misapplied to mean simply thinking positive, or that students just have to work harder to overcome systematic failures and oppressions (Moreau et al., 2019). However, there is a variety of evidence in favor of interventions that promote having a growth or incremental mindset toward personality and intelligence. This includes a wide variety of findings such as personality change and lowered stress cortisol (Yeager et al., 2016); intelligence change and increases in standardized test scores (Good et al., 2003); and that a single session of learning about how personality is malleable can decrease risk for anxiety and depression in adolescents (Schleider & Weisz, 2016). However, there are also controversies and questions about publication bias and the strength of such interventions for actual outcomes (Burnette et al., 2022; Macnamara & Burgoyne, 2022; Yeager & Dweck, 2020).

Call for Future Research

Given the role flexibility plays in keeping open the idea of growth and change, future research will have to investigate the possibility that learning to *be flexible* to changes and new ways of engaging with prompts in acting class might generalize to ideas around how malleable personality, intelligence, creativity, and achievement are.

Now, let us turn our attention to what we found in our classes: How the approach of *be flexible*, open to multiple choices and options, able to move amongst options without issue, is used, integrated, taught, and possibly fostered in acting classrooms.

BE FLEXIBLE IN THE ACTING CLASSROOM

In Preparation activities, *be flexible* is integrated in activities where the students are prompted to critique and be open to critique. For example, in Class 2 at Imagination Stage, the students were preparing to work in pairs for a Shakespearean monologue, first translating it into English and performing the English translations, then performing the original verse. In her discussions of how to work at the interpretation of the monologue, teacher Jewel said, "Every single person, including me, could use improvement. I want real notes."

She prompted the students to give each other actual critique and discussion of what was going well and what was not, and she wanted them to head into the exercise with the mindset that improvement is the goal, that no one would be perfect. This is a cue to *be flexible,* as Jewel noted that to get better you need to *be flexible* about what you are doing, and not too precious about how you are working. Instead, students need to be able to take critique and use it going forward. Likewise, she is noting no one is above critique; learning how to give critique is also part of the training. The students need to understand and know how to help others approach the work with flexibility to allow them to improve. There is not necessarily a "right" answer in theatre as there is in math or on standardized reading tests. Instead, there is a goal to get better, and to be open to change in order to continually improve. So, as they prepare to watch each other, they are bringing the mindset of flexibility for improvement to the forefront.

In Generation activities, students must be flexible in the ways in which they perform improvisational exercises, creating and ideating new movements and ways of engaging with the tasks and prompts given to them by the teacher. For example, in Class 33 at Eureka High School in St. Louis, the students were participating in an exercise in which they had to think of themselves and move around the classroom "wearing a you suit" to bring awareness to their own physicality and how they interact with the world.

Teacher Justin asked them to find an object in the room to explore "not as your teenage self" but as an alien creature, new to Earth, totally unaware of what the object is or what it can do. The students had to bring a blank mind to the object, release their preconceived notions about what the object is meant to do, and instead explore it for its physical properties. As themselves, they were tasked with interacting with the object with a different mindset than they would have taken in their real lives. This is definitionally thinking outside a set use of an object, divergently and flexibly about all the ways this known object could be unknown. Students had to break out of typical uses and into unusual uses, based on their physical responding to the object. In fact, when done in a psychology laboratory experiment, the students' answers to these questions would be their scores on a creativity task!

After a few minutes, Justin reminded the students: "Try not to jump to a conclusion immediately about what it [the object] is for. . . . Try to be playful with it. [Use] the language of play, the language of touch, the language of experimentation. Not the language of definite labels." This is encouragement to *be flexible* with a sense of *be playful* or experimentation, and not to close off to new ideas, to allow for the lightness of not a lot of consequence for that particular moment. Together, the potential of *be flexible*.

In Interpretation activities, *be flexible* is central to creating and eventually performing a character. For example, in Class 19, the students at The Madeira School were working on Shakespearean monologues, and thinking about the sounds of the words, vowels, and consonants in each line. Teacher Kelsey attempted to get them to think about the sounds of the words themselves before thinking of the meaning, and how sound alone could lead to how the lines would be said. Students were tasked to think about, based on the sounds, the emphasis of the language for their character.

Kelsey introduced the idea of thinking about text as guidance. "What I want to give you the freedom to do is have more emphasis. . . . You have more freedom than you think." Critical here is that even with classical words, and a fairly strict interpretation exercise of sound and emphasis, she was still highlighting for the students their freedom of choice and flexibility to get the effect they wanted from the script. Here, the student performing was not a native English speaker, and upon hearing that she could be flexible with this exercise of analyzing, interpreting, and understanding the difficult language of Shakespeare, she was more relaxed and happier, and dove into the work of script and sound analysis with enthusiasm. Students come away with the idea that flexibility can be built into even the strictest of scripted environments (even though students often do not consider flexibility with Shakespearean language and interpretation at the beginning of their journey into this particular way of speaking).

Students often are asked to Reflect on their performance and think and discuss how they might make it different in future performances to improve the quality, the effect on the audience, and the realism of the character. In one example, at Boston Arts Academy Class 14, the seniors were 2 weeks away from the end of the semester, working on their final, filmed scenes. Maura had the students run through the full scene, and then asked the actors a series of questions about their characters. Note, this was several weeks into their process with these scenes. They had already gone through the rehearsal and generative ideation with these characters. This was full scene performance for the camera.

Yet after each scene performance, teacher Maura would start a period of formal Reflection with the students. She would ask:

- "What did we learn in this scene that was really important?"
- "This scene is awkward . . . why is it awkward?"
- "Your character . . . what is he doing?"
- "When you're not talking, what are you doing?"
- "What are you doing when she's listening?"
- "Why did she come to this party?"

She ended this series of questions by asking the actors to think about how to make the scene flow better, how to raise the action of the scene even though they are sitting still, and how to truly listen and pay attention to each other.

Maura then stopped the class to go through with each actor and ask them, "What are you doing? What else are you doing?" She got the students to list off and Reflect on a number of different behaviors they were doing while performing—they had to keep coming up with ideas, each different from the last—to determine different ways of thinking about the same actions and the same characters. Even though she was not directly telling them to *be flexible* in their thinking, she was requiring it as part of the Reflection on the scene and the exercise. If you list the things you are doing, she would say, then you move into what the essence is of what is under what you are doing, and then the "as if."

In Chapter 9, Commit to Choices, I describe how Maura, and all the teachers, move from the flexible Generation of many different options to making one choice to perform. In this Reflection, she is getting the students to think more deeply about the scene and how continued analysis changes the choices they make. She is getting the students to understand what the characters want and need, what the script is telling them, while also getting them to think about how they, as actors, can *be flexible* within their performances to make them better and truer to the character. This period of Reflection is meant to break the students away from what they had been doing up to that time, and into what else they could be doing to make their performances better. This kind of Reflection, thinking about why students make the choices they made and how making different choices comes with deeper understanding, is integrating the habit of *be flexible*.

Across these four sections of class, then, the students are learning and working on *be flexible* when thinking about how they will give and receive critique on their work, how they improvise responses to their environment, the possibilities for choices they make while bound to the script, and going more deeply into their analyses of characters. We see these possibilities and more in our two focal exercises for *be flexible*.

Focal Exercise 1: Interpreting a Script to Develop Atmosphere

Showing how different options to the same prompt have different effects.

At Boston Arts Academy, in Class 12 with Maura, the students worked on *be flexible* over the course of an hour of loosely scripted improvisational exercises to get them familiar with the idea of atmosphere. The day began with a preset fight that was a surprise to the class. Maura had set up that two students would be in the middle of the warm-up and begin to get into an argument, building into a full-fledged screaming match with threats of violence. The other naïve students all reacted swiftly and with a lot of energy—it changed the way the room felt immediately.

From this fake fight (that the students were all very impressed with!), Maura began a discussion of the concept of atmosphere and a list on the whiteboard of all the different atmospheres that could be used in a simple, open scene. She noted that atmosphere changes when behaviors change in the environment and shift the feeling in a room. To start her examples, she had the students stand in a very tight circle and hop up and down quickly to get a sense of how physicality could change the way a room felt. She then had the students leave, to see how atmosphere could change. She asked a student to describe "not what's happening, [but] how does the room feel?" The students then came together and came up with a long list of environments and atmospheres. This created the groundwork for *be flexible* in possibilities.

Once they had the list, Maura told the students their task would be to think about their space and environment not just as a classroom, but how it felt, and what adjectives they would use to describe it in order to physically react to it. Importantly, this is using the students' abilities to *imagine and envision*, and their *body awareness and control*. However, what came next made it an exercise to show the students possibilities for *be flexible*. The students paired up and were given "open scenes" where there were just a few lines and words to portray. Maura asked them to each pick three types of environments, different for everyone, to use to frame out the scene.

From those preliminary choices, they had to determine the relationships between the characters and how they would interpret the script. After a short rehearsal period, pairs of students performed the scripts for the class. Notably, even though the words were exactly the same across all performances, the scenes were interpreted and performed dramatically differently dependent on the atmosphere, environment, and character choices the students made. The class then Reflected on how the choices caused the variety of outcomes they saw.

Sometimes the scene felt playful, and sometimes it was tense. Students chose characters as broadly different as a mother and son on the playground, friends in the cafeteria, strangers at a bus stop, two friends in college, and even two dogs! The students talked about the energy as a result of their choices, and whether it was smooth or awkward. They guessed at the atmosphere choices, and how approaching the scene from a variety of environments made a world of difference. Importantly, while Maura followed up each students' performances with small corrections and changes, she was mostly pointing out the different ways in which the scene showed its atmosphere.

They also discovered how flexibly one line could be played, depending on which direction they went in. The script included the lines "eat the orange" and "what is that purple"; the pair that played the scene as dogs chose to make "eat the orange" mean "chase and catch the orange car," while the mother/son pair used "orange" to mean the actual food. As Maura said later, "Orange and purple can mean anything. You guys are very creative . . . the beauty of it is that you don't all have to play the same character. You get to do your own thing. No one's character is going to be alike." The hour-long exercise ended with a quick discussion of always noting the atmosphere as important and how differences in atmosphere make differences in characters.

While not explicitly talking about *be flexible*, pointing out the clarity of different atmospheres gave the implicit message of how varied a single scene could be depending on the choices that were made by the students. The rapid succession of performing the scenes really showed a lot of different options quickly, gave weight to the ways students could build atmosphere thoroughly without needing much background, and allowed the students to see how lines could be open-ended and dependent on different choices about environment. Altogether, the exercise encouraged the students to think about how many different ways atmosphere could affect outcomes for performance, and the many different *flexible* ways in which atmosphere could be applied. And as a note, this idea was also inherent when the students were later engaged in more formal scene study in groups. Maura told them: "We're in the experimental phase. No idea is a bad idea and don't make someone feel bad for something risky." "Honor the risk" that each classmate takes, and allow, therefore, for openness to new choices and flexibility in making those choices.

Focal Exercise 2: Hop-Skip-Clap-Jump

Switching tasks quickly and flexibly, while keeping the current moment in mind.

One exercise that centered *be flexible* from a very basic psychological perspective was a warm-up we saw multiple times at Imagination Stage (Classes 2, 3, 4, 7), and that is commonly and broadly used in acting classes across levels and types. Sometimes called the "opposites game," this begins with the students following short commands from the teacher, such as "hop," "clap," "slow motion," as they walk around the room. This requires close listening and attention, but not necessarily the Acting Habit of Mind *be flexible*.

What comes next activates *be flexible* through the basic cognitive ability of executive functioning. While often only practiced for a few minutes (2 to 4 minutes was the range in our classes), students have to be invested fully, and paying close attention. A mistake or mess up is quickly apparent (e.g., when a student spins upright but they should be laying down), but students take these lightly, laughing and quickly moving on.

After going through the set of commands in a straightforward way, matching movement to words, Jewel or Nikki would then call "jump" . . . but the students had to clap, and when they would say "spin" the students would shimmy. This game had been repeated often enough that the students were quite familiar with the repertoire of possible movements, but the calls changed each time the game was played, as did the pairing of which calls went with which opposite movements. Sometimes students were given additional commands while listening to the opposite calls, such as only being allowed to move at right angles around the room.

When asked how the students thought of the game, they said "it is to wake up your mind . . . and wake up your listening skills and your focus." In other versions of this exercise, almost any two movements can be paired and switched, groups can work to mix three movements, leaders can create longer moments to be switched, and students can lead and make up the movements and switches for themselves (Spolin, 1986).

In rehearsal and performance, actors must be able to keep in mind their lines, the emotional state of their character, the placement of the audience, and at the same time be in the performance and slightly removed from the performance to ensure they are in the right place. And, they have to be able to shift the balance of what they are paying attention to *be flexible* in response to the audience and their fellow actors. This engagement in performance is an executive functioning task too, well-served by this warm-up forcing cognitive flexibility.

Altogether, this exercise prompts students to be prepared for change, and to have an agile mind that can switch from goal to goal quickly. In fact, this acting exercise is used almost literally in psychological testing for measuring basic cognitive abilities. In neuropsychological and cognitive development laboratories, there are standard tasks, named the "go/no-go" task or the dimensional card change sort (DCCS) task, in which the person being tested looks at pictures, for example of a sun and a moon. When shown the sun, at first, the person says "day" and when shown the moon, they say "night." However, then the instructions are switched, and when they see a moon, they are supposed to say "day" and when they see the sun, "night." While in the acting class the students are engaging in the physicalized form of this responsiveness and switching, people's abilities to respond quickly and correctly in a psychology lab is the standard way of assessing executive functioning (Zelazo, 2006).

Call for Future Research

As executive functioning develops steadily with age, and is correlated with cognitive control, goal-directed action, concentration, and even SAT scores and physical health (Zelazo & Carlson, 2012), it would be fascinating to see whether and how the acting warm-up task and the standard cognitive task are related, both behaviorally and at a neurological level.

BE FLEXIBLE, IN SUMMARY

- Students are asked to show quick flexibility among their choices and create multiple pathways to engaging with material.
- Students are given instructions to not always go with their first instinct, in warm-up, improv, or performance. Instead, teachers instruct students in taking critique and feedback constantly and consistently from their directors, peers, and teachers. This involves integrating what could be changed and used into a new iteration of the performance.
- Beyond simply engaging with the single monologue or individual performance, part of being in an ensemble and working with a director is *be flexible*, being willing and able to do what the ensemble or director needs.
- *Be flexible* allows students to try out options until they find the one that is most effective for the character and the moment of the show. Student actors are taught to keep themselves open and flexible to new ideas, to grow from idea to idea, and to let go of an idea that is no longer working for them.
- Beyond the acting classroom, *be flexible* is critical to problem solving and working with others.

Chapter 9

Commit to Choices

Learning to Make Firm, Bold, and Definitive Decisions

> In a class discussion at The Madeira School on scansion in Shakespearean writing (the process of analyzing the rhythm of poetry and verse—arguably more of an academic exercise than acting one), Kelsey makes a clear distinction as to why the homework of careful literary analysis can make all the difference in performance. She says, "This is how [Shakespeare] gave us a clue in to character, to what might be happening. Because remember, [Shakespearean actors] didn't have the whole play. I would love to think that he weaved all of this in . . . and we may be reading more into it than actually existed in Shakespeare's brain space, and that's okay too. If it helps us, if it gives us clues, why not use it? If it helps us, great, if it hurts us, we make a different choice. Acting is a series of choices" (Class 19).

So, what is happening in this teaching moment? The students are learning the various ways in which they can interpret characters and *consider others'* mental and emotional states. They also are learning how to *imagine and envision* how words would look performed onstage. But importantly, they are learning Shakespearean clues to make and *commit to choices*. Kelsey's goal is to show them how to work with, and past, the difficult language of Shakespeare's time, and to follow the clues he leaves through the rhythm of the words (not just the meanings of the words themselves) to show the choices they can make about characterization and action.

Commit to choices is the flip side and partner to the Acting Habit of Mind *be flexible*. Acting students need to think through all possible options for their character and performance, but in the end, they have to come to a conclusion about what the character wants, needs, and is doing, and then make a firm and singular decision about what their performance will look like given those wants and needs. This is a necessary precursor to physically understanding how their body and voice create that performance onstage (using *body awareness and control*).

It is almost impossible for an actor to physicalize two different character objectives at the same time. Trying to perform and communicate a few different mental and emotional states simultaneously was pointed to multiple times by teachers across many classes as "muddled" or "difficult to read." More concretely, this means when the audience is meant to understand and pull a central point of view from the work, an actor who is not clear on what their character is doing and what they are trying to get across will not be understood by the audience. Therefore, a choice, clearly made, fully committed to, and clearly performed, is necessary. There is, of course, flexibility both before and after the choice is made, but in the moment of performance for the audience, the student must learn to *commit to choices*.

Here, the Acting Habit of Mind being recruited and trained in an acting class is to make decisions, even if you are not 100% sure of the outcomes or outputs, and to move with action to bring those decisions to fruition.

THE SCIENCE OF COMMIT TO CHOICES

Commit to choices as an Acting Habit of Mind is about making decisions, being concise and simple in those decisions, and keeping a broader goal and objective in mind while moving forward into action. While there is a large modern and historical literature in psychology about decision-making (from Edwards [1954] taking theory from economics and applying the psychological science of the day to Wedel et al. [2023] modeling individuals' eye movements while making choices), here I will focus on the psychology of risk taking and tolerance, the necessity of focus and mindfulness for committing to choices, and the psychology of keeping larger goals and objectives in mind while making smaller choices.

Commit to choices is often studied in the psychology of adolescence through the lens of decision-making. Popularly, teenagers are "known" for taking unnecessary risks and making "bad" decisions (a complaint that is as old as at least Socrates; Dahl et al., 2018). However, the truth is more complicated. Taking a risk is not inherently bad. When adults can structure environments to promote developmentally constructive risks, the decisions of adolescents pointed in a positive direction can be harnessed for creativity, exploration, social bonding, and new and exciting challenges and skills (Duell & Steinberg, 2021). Importantly, framing risk taking as a positive endeavor during development, rather than only focusing on negative outcomes, actually can prevent students from taking irresponsible risks (Telzer et al., 2022).

Risk taking is a hallmark of adolescence, particularly when the risks are taken against parental or school rules: the need for autonomy becomes particularly strong in this age group. In general, risk taking is defined by the potential for a negative outcome, and uncertainty about whether that outcome will occur (Duell & Steinberg, 2019). During adolescence students are particularly accepting of uncertainty in outcomes (Tymula et al., 2012), which may allow for higher risk-taking behavior. Encouraging adolescents to make and *commit to choices* for themselves can promote necessary independence (Duell & Steinberg, 2021). Teaching and encouraging students to not only *commit to choices*, but to follow them through, evaluate, and *be flexible* to new choices, can teach students how to deal with their natural desire to engage in risks and make autonomous decisions for themselves. I hypothesize the safety of the theatrical setting and acting classroom allows students to honor their sensitivities to status and purpose while making acting choices. This could teach strategic, positive risk taking. The theater also can be a space where while there might be uncertainty about outcomes in choices for the stage, but the negative possibilities are minimized.

To be able to *commit to choices* also requires impulse control. An actor cannot just let out whatever impulse comes into their head while in performance—this may be a hallmark of the Generation activities of class, but is maladaptive in the Interpretation activities of class. Once an actor makes a decision, they have to stick with it, at least for that initial iteration of performance. Practicing this ability may have a long tail of positive effects. For example, as mentioned in Chapter 8, Be Flexible, part of the creative process is coming up with many ideas, but another part of the creative process is choosing one idea and applying it to the problem at hand. Often the best solutions to problems are multiple ideas combined into one choice. However, most creativity theorists agree that you cannot try multiple ideas simultaneously in response to most creative problems. Most of the time people do not have enough cognitive or behavioral resources to do so. Instead, what a creative person needs to do is find one solution that feels good enough to try in the moment, and try it out as much as possible to its logical conclusion. Only by committing to a singular idea and trying it out will you actually be able to see if you are brainstorming the right ideas to solve the issue at hand (Sawyer, 2021). This requires control of alternative impulses and a need to be focused on a goal. Cognitively, for thoughts and actions, focus and control abilities increase over the course of adolescence (Luna, 2009), and such control has positive effects. For example, college students who score higher on measures of impulse control have higher grades, higher self-esteem, better relationships with others, and less substance abuse (Tangney et al., 2004).

Making a choice, whether risky or not, also requires motivation and keeping in mind a goal. Being able to hold a single goal in mind can lead to both higher academic risk taking and achievement (Meyer & Turner, 2006). Cognitively, this is related to mindful awareness of goals and the ability to hold these goals continuously in mind. In acting, this is often related to the "meta objective" of a character in a play (e.g., Stanislavski, 1989). Related to making decisions, mindfulness abilities (which are often included in acting class warm-ups) are related to self-knowledge, and therefore to making decisions and choices that are related to personal interests (Schultz & Ryan,

2015), as well as improving the emotion regulation skills necessary to maintain a choice when it may feel difficult to do so (Roemer et al., 2015).

Being allowed to take risks, make decisions, and see them through can also help develop a sense of confidence and autonomy—key in adolescence, and also critically important at other stages in development. At this developmental stage, adolescents must figure out a new way to understand and project who they are (that is, their identity, as discussed in Chapter 4). But the way to do this is through trial and error. Trying on different decisions, in concert with parental expectations, peer feedback, and personal sense of motivations and goals can be one strong pathway (Dahl et al., 2018) to a secure sense of identity. Acting requires the actor to be not only in collaboration with a director and cast, but also autonomous in their interpretation and understanding of a character and the choices they bring to that performance. Engaging with choices through autonomous exploration can reinforce positive self-image (Allen & Loeb, 2015; Duell & Steinberg, 2021), and adolescence seems to be a particularly specific time of neural enhancements in sensitivity to novelty and learning from situations where the feedback is variable and imperfect over time (Dahl, et al., 2018). Altogether, this means training an Acting Habit of Mind of *commit to choices* is accessible and possibly generalizable to our students, in and out of the classroom.

Now, then, let us turn our attention to what we found in our classes: how this idea of finding a singular choice in an array of options, committing to it, and turning it into action is used, integrated, taught, and possibly fostered in acting classrooms themselves.

COMMIT TO CHOICES IN THE ACTING CLASSROOM

In Preparation activities, *commit to choices* is integrated in any kind of activity where the students predetermine what it is they will be working on or how they will approach a text or exercise. For example, in Class 38 at Northcoast Preparatory School, an International Baccalaureate–level theatre class in Humboldt County, the students are preparing to go into an exercise that takes 54 minutes. In this improvisation exercise from March 12, 2020, the students are told they will have to pretend to be a parent who is concerned about their child coming to school with COVID-19.

Before beginning any Generation of material, Jean, the teacher, has the students all lie down and think about what kind of parent they are going to enact and how they are going to act. Once the students have made this decision, they head out of the classroom to get into character. Then, they each come in to an improvisation where they interact with each other, have a group meeting with a "principal," acted out by a guest teacher, and talk about COVID-19 fears and restrictions. The choice they make in the Preparation period has to carry them through the entire improv.

This is an advanced move, where the students have to pick something they know ahead of time will carry them for most of class, and they have to build a full character off of it. During the Preparation period, Jean had also instructed them to pick a quote to create their character and use during the scene. One student chose "you can't find happiness where you lost it" while another mentioned she couldn't pick a quote and had a few that she wanted to engage with, and was instead thinking about pretending to be like her father. She noted after the fact that once she started the improv, she realized that "it did not work that way" and by not making a choice about a quote to pull herself through, it made the exercise very difficult. Overall, this Preparation period, and the students' willingness to make a strong choice and stick to it, showed how committing a singular and specific choice affected the rest of the exercise. As Jean said, "The thing about preparation is that it's really important in acting. The more details you bring in . . . the more it helps you in your character."

In Generation activities, students must *commit to choices* when improvising characters because they do not have a script, words, or known personality to help the audience see and understand the performance they are giving. In the Class 4 exercise described in Chapter 5, for *imagine and envision*, where the students at Imagination Stage had to bring in an animal movement and match it to a human character, there were several moments in which teacher Nikki was also discussing and emphasizing that in the imagining of the animal and recreation of the animals' movements, the students had to make super specific choices about what to transfer to the human character, and what to leave behind. She asked the students to Generate movement for the animal in the act of play, eating, in fear, aggression, sleeping, and to explore. This first part was about trying on all the possibilities. However, then for the performance of the animal as a human, Nikki asked them to "bring as much as possible of the animal while still looking like a normal person." The students had to create a character, based on a broad exploratory exercise, in order to firmly choose how that performance would look as a human. When watching a performing student, Nikki told the others to "take stock of the choices she's making" along the tempo of movement and transformation qualities. She had each student reflect on the qualities they choose to bring with them, and which they left behind.

In Interpretation activities, *commit to choices* is central to creating the moment-to-moment behavior of performing a character. For example, at The Madeira School in Class 23, the students sat with their scene partners and their script to "score" their scripts with verbs. This meant determining the objective for each character in each moment: What did the character want from their partner, and why were they saying each line? While this is also an exercise in *consider others*, key to this moment was that Kelsey continually told the students to think of just one verb, just one objective for each moment (beat of the script), and to clearly choose that word for that moment. In particular, Kelsey emphasized a strong and helpful verb choice for performance, pulling out an actor's thesaurus book of verbs to help the students make singular *choices to commit* to. She cautioned against choosing verbs that are "so general they aren't going to help." Only in the clarity and commitment to a single, firm, clear choice for each moment would the later creation of physicalized performance be clear to the audience. "Work on getting just one of those verbs down on paper . . . you always want to go for the most intense, specific thing you can." This would allow the students to "create that tension that we see as drama. That makes it interesting to watch."

Students are often asked to Reflect on how they *committed to choices* and what that caused them to do onstage. Heading back to Class 38, at Northcoast Prep in Humboldt County, after *commit to choices* in the Preparation period as described above, and then engaging in the exercise for almost an hour, the students sat together for a period of Reflection. One student said it was hard to stay in character the whole time given the decision they had made about what kind of character/parent they were going to portray, and how it played out over the course of the exercise. Another student reflected that thinking through "how I would be as a parent helped me to stay in character." A third student took what they knew about parents, their "social judgment" and "underhanded commentary" about parents and "showed it," while a different student said they wanted to be the "most aggressive and hard to deal with parent" and felt they had done a good job following through with that attitude. Finally, one student reflected that they had made a choice that their parent character was there to learn and not get into discussions with other parents. This made the improv hard to engage with, as the student felt they were "stuck in an environment" and they had just sat silently most of the time in the exercise. Jean noted that it was "good that you held on to your intention." "I held on to it," the student answered, "but it made for a very silent character."

Across these four sections of class, then, the students are learning to make strong and definitive choices before they head into an exercise, while they are generating material and transforming their performance responses to prompts in real time, as they work with difficult scripted materials, and when reflecting on how their choices shaped what happened onstage. We see all of these possibilities in our two focal exercises for *commit to choices.*

Focal Exercise 1: Archetypes and Monologues

Using classical theatrical "types" to try out firm choices as a start to complex characterization.

One particularly potent lesson in learning to make firm choices and commit to them, even if just for a moment of performance, came from The Madeira School Class 19. The exercise began with a quick discussion and word about archetypes (e.g., sovereign, trickster, warrior, caretaker, etc.) in classical theatre. Archetypes, Kelsey explained, are culturally ingrained ideas about a certain type of person, which most often show up in classical drama, such as Shakespeare, Moliere, Greek tragedy, and commedia dell'arte. With Shakespeare, Kelsey noted, actors are dealing with archetypes in many of his characters.

To begin, she had the students listen to different words (e.g., upright; responsible; gravitas; important) and walk around as if they were embodying and experiencing that word. As the students found their versions of the walk, they interacted with a partner using Shakespearean lines "Fail not our feast" and "Courage man, the hurt cannot be much" in the style of the archetypal character. The students did this exercise across four different archetypes.

Then, they had to think about their own assigned monologues, and which of the four archetypes might work for their monologue. Even though a singular archetype cannot be perfectly applied to a complex Shakespearean character, Kelsey asked the students to make a firm choice (and try not to play a bit of multiple archetypes) and to work on their monologues within that archetype, both physically and with their voice in the moment. "I want to pick, for now, you can always try another," she noted. "Either using the walk or the words, pick one of those for your character. We're going to take these archetypes and expand them later, but for now, pick one."

While Kelsey emphasized that the archetypes were individualized to the performer and the students had some flexibility, she also emphasized that the students needed to fully "just give it a try. . . . See how it feels," even if they were not sure. As she said, "This is putting your character in a box, briefly. With Shakespeare, we already talked about him inventing a full human character. Going towards realism. He's veering us away from the boxes of commedia. We're taking one moment to put them in a box and see what it feels like." Once the students were on board having chosen an archetype and moment from their monologues, Kelsey asked the students to "find a body position from your walk that feels indicative of this archetype. A statue that you can create of this archetype." After saying their monologues as that archetype, she switched it up and had them say their monologues as a different archetype, showing the students what it would have felt like with a different choice. Like in the exercises teaching students to *be flexible*, here Kelsey was showing them how committing to a different choice would provide them with new and different information about their character and the performance of that character. "What happens if he's the trickster? See what happens!"

This archetype exercise and script performance was a simple way to apply firm choices to a specific and complex character from a Shakespearean script. Importantly, Kelsey let them try on and try out four archetypes, walking like them and saying a single scripted line, before asking them to *commit* a single choice to try out. While real characters are complex, with multiple motivations, personality traits, contextual effects, emotions, motivations, beliefs, and desires (just like real people), the performance of all that complexity only works if it is simple and clear in the moment (i.e., "Clear and simple as the truth," as the book on writing by Francis-Noël Thomas and Mark Turner states).

Actors have to boil down the complexity of a real person into a relatable, specific character for the audience to understand from their seats. This specific exercise on archetype choices, and short, simple word choices to apply to the character was a first step for Kelsey in building out more complexity into the characters as they progress through the script in later classes.

In the interview, Kelsey noted an overarching pedagogical goal was to have students find clues within their Shakespearean scripts to use for character choices—particularly in finding ideas within the text that could lead them to make a choice about archetypes, and connecting archetype with monologue. This in-depth text work was meant to lead the students to make choices about the text to perform later in the class. Kelsey also noted for two later classes in the week, Classes 20 and 21, she wanted each student to make strong verb (i.e., what action to take), tactic, and overarching objective choices for their monologues so they could proceed with understanding.

In this way, she noted choices both come from understanding and lead to deeper understanding. Each activity in these classes was related back to the idea of making a singular choice, and making these choices could increase students' understanding of the text. Calling attention to verbs, finding different ways to find verbs, and physical and vocal workshops, were all in service of making and committing to firm tactic choices for the monologue assignment. In Class 22, at the end of the week, Kelsey assessed whether the students were able to understand and use the concepts of picking a tactic, an objective, and an obstacle choice for their acting.

Focal Exercise 2: Reading Children's Books

Using simple texts with multiple characters to perform a singular, firm, bold choice.

A second training exercise in making firm and singular choices for performance came from Imagination Stage in Class 8. Here, the students were tasked with bringing in children's books from home and giving a dramatic reading for the class. They had to use voices for characters, change vocal timbre, pitch, and accent, all while still staying seated. This was relatively late in the year, after the students had been working together for more than 6 months, giving them a level of familiarity with both each other and Nikki's expectation for performance.

This was a homework assignment, so the performance had not yet been seen by Nikki or the class. Each student performed their book in turn and then was given feedback from both the other students in the class and Nikki. Children's books are an interesting assignment for teaching students how to make choices, because they involve both narration from a narrator, and often dialogue and character voices. The books are short, and sometimes rhyming as well, so the students did not have a large amount of material to prepare, but often the books had multiple characters within the book. The first student who read her book (*The Gruffalo*) used a British accent to speak one of the character's lines. As she did this, Nikki said, "Good! Really commit to this, because then it's going to be a big change."

Nikki wanted the student to fully engage in the accent, to not laugh or giggle at herself while making the accent (going back to *release inhibitions*) and to push the performative nature of the accent to its fullest so the audience could respond to the change between character voice and self-voice. She did note that the students should not confuse an accent with a character voice, that the voice choice needs to be more than an accent. The students also gave feedback along the same lines: "When you committed to a voice, the voice was very good. . . . So just keep in mind when you commit, good things happen." Nikki loved this feedback so much she asked the student to say it again and filmed it!

The feedback for this student ended with Nikki reflecting positively: "You had choices, they were there. The snakes' 'ssss,' the accent for the owl, the low voice for the fox and the lower for the Gruffalo. You just need to make bold choices, you just gotta commit more, make it bigger." Overall, this was an entire exercise and performance in choosing one way to perform a book (ostensively after perhaps trying and rehearsing a few different options at home), and making that choice firmly and with emphasis in its performance.

The second student then read *Another Mother*. The students gave feedback that while the character voices at the beginning melded together, the student got better over time and made more clear distinctions between the different characters she was performing. They had a small discussion over whether the student's basic narration voice was an intentional accent, or just the way she sounded when reading presentationally. Nikki's feedback was that while the selection of the book was good, the student could have gone even farther with the accents of the various mothers in the book and her performance of their distinctions, and given them "each really really specific mother voices." So, Nikki here was again emphasizing the specificity of the choices that the students were tasked with making for this exercise, and how success in this exercise would be predicated on making firm, bold, singular choices, and enacting those choices to the fullest. The firmer the choice, the better the distinction, and the better the distinction, the better the actor.

COMMIT TO CHOICES, IN SUMMARY

- Important for every moment in acting class is to make singular choices about the objectives, wants, emotions, and physical movements of a character in each moment of performance.
- Student actors are taught to make firm, bold, and definitive choices, and explore each choice fully, while not holding on to it so firmly they become stuck in a bad decision.
- Muddled choices, where a student tries to make two or three decisions simultaneously, or thinks of a character as holding multiple perspectives and emotions at the same time, becomes difficult for an audience to read.
- Throughout both discussions of acting theory and actual practice in the classroom, teachers tell the students to think about meta-objectives and minor objectives for the character they play, to think through their options, imagine which may be best for them, decide, and go for it.
- Even when a student's choice is completely wrong, and could not possibly apply to the character in performance for real, they are still pushed to learn something from the full, if incorrect, application of the character. It is never framed as a mistake; it is framed as a trial and error, with the errors becoming learning moments.
- Beyond the acting classroom, being able to *commit to choices* is critical to achieving goals and completing important tasks. Being able to think through possible counterfactuals and then firmly going toward a goal can help students with perseverance and achievement.

Chapter 10

Reflect and Think Metacognitively

Learning to Thoughtfully Consider Your Own Actions

> The students have just spent a few minutes moving around the classroom in a pantomime as their character. They are asked to pause in a statue, still in form and action. Teacher Kelsey tells them to increase the specificity of their statues, that is, the performative nature of them. "I want you to take it from a 4 to a 7" in intensity while staying still. Then, she tells them to think about what their statue would be titled, what would be a single word or short line to place on their statue in its current form. Then, they break out of the statues, and come back into a circle. Kelsey asks them, "What was that like? . . . What did you feel when you were in the pose of the statue? What did you title yours?" As the students share their observations of what the pose made them feel, how it related to their characters, and why they chose their simple titles, Kelsey discusses this statue exercise as a way to separate yourself from the character, and give yourself the mental space you may need for the heightened emotions of the character onstage. It is a way to step into a sticky moment that may require a level of commitment that is not necessarily common in everyday life (Class 21).

So, what is happening in this activity? The students are being asked to integrate their understanding of their character into a single action, to show *body awareness* of their character, and to *commit to choices* for a single physical action in a stature. But most importantly, this moment of naming the statue and then coming back together in a quick circle to discuss contains and requires students to *reflect and think metacognitively*. The students have to integrate everything they know about the character's life, wants, objectives, needs, and emotions into a single physical position and a single word or phrase. This ability to take a step back from the details of the character and look at it from a broader perspective is integral to the habit of *reflect and think metacognitively*. This is also a way to engage with what may feel like strong, overwhelming, or difficult emotions, as the drama characters often experience is the height of the most intense emotions in human lives. That can be difficult for a teenager (or, in reality, many people) to engage with truly and fully. Using *reflect and think metacognitively* can give some distance.

The students have to be able to engage with the material from a perspective of *reflect and think metacognitively* as well as engaging in the details and specific moments—they have to be able to do both. This habit of constant and continual reflection on the activities of the classroom and how the students felt about and felt they did in these activities is rare in any other kind of environment, but central to building performances and the third-person/first-person nature of acting. Actors must both perform and be aware of the impact of their performances. They cannot be fully lost in a character, acting and physicalizing blindly. In fact, *reflect and think metacognitively* is so central to learning how to act that the teachers in our classrooms use it in two ways—both as an immediate Acting Habit of Mind integrated across the classroom into most activities, and as a separate, formalized component and activity type in class.

Reflect and Think Metacognitively is where students learn to thoughtfully consider their own actions and the actions of others. Students learn they cannot just prepare and then perform. As teacher Justin noted in one interview, "The reflection was reinforcement over and over . . . to get them to understand what they were doing and the front loading of information." Students learn that to improve in acting, they need to be consistently checking in with themselves, and taking feedback from others. They learn how to *reflect and think metacognitively* about their own actions and performances, and to adjust based on what they think occurred in the moment, and they learn how to think about their thinking around performance. In parallel, they learn both how to give reflective feedback to others, through observation and noticing, and how to take those observations and noticing from others and incorporate it into their own work. Part of this is learning how to *think collaboratively,* so the students can take into account what the director/teacher and other members of their ensemble think is working or not working, and part of it is learning how to step away and back from what just actually happened, into its effects.

Importantly there are two ways *reflect and think metacognitively* works for the students. The first is formally in periods where the whole class sits down and talks about what just happened, or in the critique portions of rehearsals where the students give a performance and then hear feedback on that performance. The second is informally where the students are constantly thinking about their own work and performance as they are engaged in their work and performance. *Reflect and think metacognitively* allows for building complexity through engaging in simultaneous performing and critiquing of activities at the same time.

Reflection often begins with an observation—a noticing and seeing. The students are taught how to *reflect and think metacognitively* by first observing what they have just seen or what they have just experienced in themselves. They are taught to start with just the facts—the pure perception of what just happened. Then, they can move to the meaning: What did it mean or signify when they saw the particular expression or the particular movement in themselves? Then, they can make broader connections to the meaning and how it changes over time, or what it means in the broader context of the rest of the activity or the rest of the class.

Often, the teachers would ask for a moment of *reflect and think metacognitively*, and the students would begin with what they thought was happening internally. The teacher would bring them back to "What did you see? What did you observe?" Other times, a teacher would ask the students to note, "What did you see that you liked, or what did you see that you thought worked well?" This served to engage the students' critical eye for performance—what did they enjoy and what caused a reaction, and how was that connected to the actual perceptual experience of the performance onstage. While deeper psychological meaning is always present on stage or screen, anytime we are engaging with humans in a narrative, the projection of that deeper narrative and psychological state has to come through behavior, and particularly through observed behavior by the audience. Therefore, the students learning to act must always be aware of how their behavior is being observed, and all the various ways and tricks that the students can use to change that behavior to make it better and more observable to the audience members.

In Class 30 at Eureka High School, Justin noted his pedagogical goal for the class was to give the students a chance to articulate feedback and figure out how to give reflective critique in a positive and constructive way. In Class 34 at Arcata High School, teacher Melanie also noted an overarching goal of both critiquing others' work, but also being able to engage in self-reflection. She provided a handout to guide students for the goal and set up the class to work in pairs (see the Focal Exercise 2, below). Nanette, in Class 37 at Eureka High in Humboldt County (not to be confused with Eureka High School in St. Louis), also noted modeling and practicing the language of feedback would increase reflection as a skill, as their goal for the class.

Together, *reflect and think metacognitively* is the Acting Habit of Mind being recruited and trained in an acting class to be able to understand, think about, and have distance from, your behavior and performance, and thus know what needs to change and improve.

THE SCIENCE OF REFLECT AND THINK METACOGNITIVELY

Like our other Acting Habits of Mind, *reflect and think metacognitively* is linked to a number of other psychological skills, but also, it is a psychological skill in its own right. In fact, reflection is central to learning and making purposeful steps toward cognitive change and increasing knowledge.

It is how people are able to transfer knowledge they have learned in one domain or context to a different domain or context. To that end, *reflect and think metacognitively* is not necessarily considered to always be explicit and purposeful—you do not have to have conscious reflection to come to an understanding of your own cognition. This can often be based more in knowing emotional reactions or motivations, rather than explicit knowledge states (Koriat & Levy-Sadot, 2000).

Generally, metacognition is defined as the "the knowledge, monitoring, and control of one's cognition" (Marulis et al., 2020, p. 47). It is considered second-order cognition, or thinking about thinking. While very young children do not have much ability to engage in thinking about their own memories, knowledge states, or abilities to learn, it becomes more conscious over development (Kuhn, 2000). Instead, what young children do is purposefully learn about logical thinking and scientific reasoning, particularly through their formal education and through interactions and asking their parents questions (Danovitch et al., 2021; Mills, 2013).

Children's meta-memory, or their ability to remember what they know and what they have learned, develops through middle childhood, and has long been studied as predictive of how well children do academically (Wellman, 1978); it is perhaps even more important than intelligence (Veenman, & Spaans, 2005). Through and past middle childhood, with purposeful use of critique, questioning, and constructive discussion about tasks, knowledge, and reasoning, children can learn to *reflect* on what they are being taught or how they are thinking, and begin to build metacognitive skills (Brown, 1997). Learning that knowledge is constructed, how to figure something out, how to know what you know and what you do not, continues to develop through adolescence and into young adulthood (Kuhn, 2000). Then, in adolescence and into young adulthood, metacognitive confidence, that is, the ability to know how well you have done on a task, continues to become more accurate, and allows for better understanding of effort needed to complete tasks (Weil et al., 2013). In general, this also enables children and adolescents to move from learning and retention strategies for knowledge that are more general and less useful into strategies that are more personalized and helpful to the individual (Siegler, 1998).

Beyond learning, *reflect and think metacognitively* abilities and tendencies are implicated in other areas of development and functioning (Kuhn, 2022). In adolescence, reflection is critical for identity development, as discussed in Chapters 4 and 7. To build and to understand which personal commitments (in religion, academia, personality, etc.) an adolescent wants to keep in their lives, and which ones they are more open to change or want to work to change, requires reflection on current status and commitments, and metacognition about the process for finding a new outcome (Branje et al., 2021). In therapeutic contexts, insight and metacognitive understanding of the self has been investigated as a critical component for recovery from a variety of disorders including psychosis, schizophrenia, and alexithymia (Gumley, 2011).

Reflection is a part of many mindfulness practices for noticing and being aware of the body and the mind are doing, and this links to emotion-regulation skills, as discussed in Chapter 3. The more an individual can know what they are feeling, the better they will be at knowing what to do about it (Barrett et al., 2001). This can also help with behavior change in a psychiatric sense (Schuman-Olivier et al., 2020). And becoming a good consumer of information and news in the age of social media, misinformation, and the Internet requires critical thinking and reflection skills about the source of that information, whether it is coming from a factual source or as an opinion, and how to be able to tell the difference between truth, lies, and spin (Ku et al., 2019; Pennycook, & Rand, 2019, Salovich & Rapp, 2021). On a more aesthetic note, part of using and fostering *reflect and think metacognitively* is about building a shared language around critique and communication of opinions and suggestions about art in all forms.

Call for Future Research

Theatre and drama have been linked to language learning across a wide body of literature showing that involvement in theatre classes is linked to higher levels of vocabulary and better narrative skills in many different age groups (Brouillette, 2012; Greenfader & Brouillette, 2013; Nicolopoulou, 2019; Podlozny, 2000). What has not been well investigated is how these linguistic processes in acting classes are not just learning new vocabulary through plays or exercises, and not just gaining narrative understanding by working with the narratives inherent in creating performances, but also learning to think about a shared language of aesthetic reasoning and understanding what critique should and can sound like to get across a subjective and intersubjective opinion. Future work can look at how language and aesthetic metacognition and knowledge can work together through learning acting.

Now, let us turn our attention to what we found in our classes: How *reflect and think metacognitively* strategies are used, integrated, taught, and possibly fostered in acting classrooms themselves.

REFLECT AND THINK METACOGNITIVELY IN THE ACTING CLASSROOM

In Preparation activities, *reflect and think metacognitively* is integrated and used in any kind of warm-up where the students have to discuss or think about their lives in order to share about themselves as they begin their acting class. This is often done as a way to transition from the outside world into the world of the acting class. At Imagination Stage, to begin each class, for all eight classes that we observed, for 10 minutes each time, the teachers had the students go around the room and name the best and worst thing (hi/lo) that happened to them over the course of the week. This was used as a way to share a piece of news about themselves and think about their own emotional reactivity to the events of their week. This helps with class bonding (ensemble building, critical to performing together as a group onstage), but it is also meant as a quick warm-up for reflecting on themselves and their week, and separating their outside lives from their acting class exercises and putting on a character.

However, *reflect and think metacognitively* also can be used to prepare for productions as a whole. At McKinleyville in Humboldt County, we saw a different kind of reflection in their Preparation activities: a holistic Preparation for setting up acting and performance. Students in Class 39 spent the first 19 minutes of class discussing the possibilities for props and costumes for the Shakespearean play they were reading. Steve, the teacher, spent time showing the students art from previous productions, and then the students discussed what they knew about the play and how that would inform costume, art, and prop choices. This involves taking a step back from any individual line, movement, or character choice, and into thinking about what the students wanted to say as part of the play as a whole.

In Generation activities, students must *reflect and think metacognitively* about what they are creating in the moment, and whether it is adequately reflective of what they were trying to show their classmates and teacher. At Eureka High in Class 32, students were assigned a pantomime of attempting to replicate their morning routine as exactly as possible. They did not have to script it or try to perform as a character, but instead they were tasked with taking each definable step of their morning routine and recreating it in an improvised way for the class. They had to think about every single step—what were all the elements of an activity such as brushing your teeth? (Take toothbrush out of holder, turn on water, wet brush, get toothpaste, open toothpaste, adjust in hand, squeeze onto toothbrush, run toothbrush under water, etc.). The students had to adjust and try this pantomime improv in several different ways, including with each element taking the same amount of time in rhythm and tempo, then moving the rhythm and tempo faster. Then, the students had to pick a moment in the improvisation where they had to pause and pretend to react to a parent yelling at them.

After each change and new idea (so, three times), Justin paused and asked the students, "How did that feel? Why? What is something you observed about that?" He also asked whether each type of change caused an emotional shift from the performance of the routine before. The students had to think about what they had just done, how it was different than the moments they had done before with the same routine, and how the adjustments they made in reaction to the prompt changes made a difference. This invitation to *reflect and think metacognitively* on their own action allowed them to see the range and variation in the same activity. Though pantomiming through a morning routine is simple on the surface, and at first glance may only have one or two ways to try, the point of doing a different mode, then reflecting on it, then changing the mode, then reflecting, and back and forth, served the students to see how things could change so quickly and easily, and to see which elements within the changes could work for future performances, and which could not. Similarly taking a pause to *reflect and think metacognitively* in the moment of the changes also solidified all the variations that could be available to students, rather than trying to remember after the fact all the different activities the students had just completed. Importantly, though, in this class Justin also provided a formalized period of Reflection on the morning pantomime activity as a whole, so the students could back out of the momentary reactions to the smaller levels of changes, and think more about how the group of changes and the process of *reflect and think metacognitively* on those changes as a whole could inform their later performances.

We saw this mode of teaching a lot across many classes, where the teacher would give a small instruction, the students would complete that instruction, and then do a quick *reflect and think metacognitively* moment on the instruction. Then the teacher would give a different instruction, the students would perform and then reflect, and again multiple times, ending with a longer and larger period of formalized meta Reflection on the whole activity. This ties in well to more formalized rehearsal and scene study processes (see Chapter 11), where students are asked to perform characters, *reflect and think metacognitively* on the line they just said, make adjustments, and move forward.

Importantly, after they finished with the different ways of playing with tempo, Justin led the class through a discussion of how this activity linked to a later assignment of doing karaoke with character performance, and how it was based in the broader theory of Viewpoints in acting—that "tempo" is one of the Viewpoints. This pause shows how in an acting classroom, the teachers are constantly working to connect activities up to performance, and back to theory. As mentioned before, while from the outside, class activities may look like games or play, those games and that play always has a broader meaning and purpose.

In Interpretation activities, *reflect and think metacognitively* is central to performance, as students must make adjustments and different choices based on whether they think their performance was successful in communicating the ideas, characters and emotions of the script. For example, in our class of seniors at Boston Arts Academy, the central section of Class 14—1 hour and 15 minutes—was spent discussing scenes the students had performed and filmed. The entire group sat in front of the television screen and replayed the filmed scene, discussing it moment by moment. Teacher Maura and the students gave feedback on what they saw, what it meant, and how it worked. This feedback ranged from the physical location of the students on the screen (as in screen acting, the students need to stand much closer to one another than people stand in real life) to the impulses and intentions of the characters coming through the acting. Maura noted that understanding the space difference is a technical skill, while engaging in moments of *reflect and think metacognitively* on the character's subtext and intention was an acting skill. The reflection here was on specific moments of the performance, but it was on every aspect, and every moment of the performance, over and over again. This was showing students that they should be engaging in *reflect and think metacognitively* moments about every element of their work and every element of their interpretative engagement. Not just their voice, or their emotional expression, but that every aspect of the day is important. Maura noted in her interview that "individualized feedback in front of the class" was important for the day as a whole. Students needed to engage not only with *reflect and think metacognitively* on their own actions and acting, but also to think carefully about how others' actions and acting could be improved. To give and take *reflect and think metacognitively* on full scenes is a relatively advanced skill, because it is not just one line of Interpretation the students need to think about, but how the Interpretation of the character is seen and understood across multiple minutes and units of time. Eventually, of course, the Interpretation of a character will be over an entire film, television series, or play, and to be able to *reflect and think metacognitively* not only on the momentary performance in the moment to moment of a single scene but also how the character is being portrayed and seen from the audience's perspective as a whole will be critically important. When the students are more junior, or as they are first beginning to be trained, *reflect and think metacognitively* about interpretation of characters may span just a moment, a line, or a facial expression of a character. As students advance, the amount of material they are asked to *reflect and think metacognitively* on becomes larger and larger.

Finally, it may be obvious that the Reflection period of class is where students are asked to use the Acting Habit of Mind of *reflect and think metacognitively*. But it is important to note that students are not just being asked to *reflect and think metacognitively* on one moment of class, or the particularly behavior and activity that they just completed (as we see in the other types of activities in class, integrated into those activities). In many classes, a period of Reflection is formalized, in which students have to stop and think not just about what just happened, but the themes, connections, and emergent properties of a class as a whole. They are asked to take a metacognitive stance for a longer period of time than has just occurred and summarize everything that has just happened. This form of *reflect and think metacognitively* requires broader thinking and more awareness than discussing the activity that occurred a moment ago and thinking about what worked and what did not work. Instead, this time of Reflection requires higher-order meaning making and summary thinking.

For example, at The Madeira School in Class 24, with 1 minute left before the bell rang, after a day of warm-up, blocking exercises, improv games about tactics and objectives, and feedback from peers and scene work, the students were asked to circle up and give one word/one phrase to state overall how they were feeling about all of the exercises and work they had done that day for their scenes, and the next steps that they had practiced and were assigned as homework. The students said things like "good foundation," "confused," "ready to build on it." Kelsey closed out the moment by stating that she was excited about the playful week to come . . . she ended class as the bell rings with, "Good work today. Be proud." Rarely do more traditional academic classes end with an overarching check-in about how students are doing and feeling about the work and time to *reflect and think metacognitively* on the work they had done that day; rarely would a traditional academic class begin with a personal check-in about how the students are feeling about their lives and the kinds of highs and lows they may have experienced before entering the classroom.

Across these four sections of class, then, the students are consistently asked to *reflect and think metacognitively* about their thinking about their acting. They are reflecting on their daily lives to separate into class time and on class as a whole to transition back out to the rest of their days. They are reflecting on plays as a whole and how they are structured. They are metacognating about their morning routines and habitual behaviors and about their performances. We see all of these possibilities in our two focal exercises for *reflect and think metacognitively*.

Focal Exercise 1: Getting to the World Series, and Breaking Down a Script

Connecting goals, objectives, and tactics across levels of focus.

In Class 16 at Boston Arts Academy, teacher Maura's goal for the day with the sophomores is to understand the framework of objectives, goals, and tactics as a way to break down and to think about a scene. She begins with a complex but accessible metaphor for this relatively intricate concept in acting—how to get to the World Series. She has a few students actually pretend to act out a baseball game, with the class "crowd" cheering and going wild for the players hitting home runs. Then, she asks them to list goals for baseball players, from the highest level (wining the World Series) through winning individual games, and ending with individual at-bats. She pushes them to think about the multitude of different objectives for each moment of the baseball game. "When you're the pitcher, you want to get the batter out. How many different objectives can you do to get the batter out?" she asks. This ends with the idea that there are tons of ways to win the World Series.

(This school, by the way, is next to Fenway Park, home of the Boston Red Sox, so baseball is always present.)

She asks the class to *reflect and think metacognitively*: "How many different things in that goal of getting to the World Series are active choices about what to do?" She leads the group to connect active choices in baseball to active choices in acting. This goes from the ultimate goal of any particular scene or idea, down through the huge numbers of steps along the way. From here begins approximately 30 minutes on how to break down and begin to interpret a script for elements that will enable active choices, based on the truth of the script.

Maura notes: "Each play is a baseball game. Each scene is an inning. And in each inning, there are beats. This is what I want you to learn today. Beats. If you're in this inning, and the batter hits the ball, that's a beat. It changes everything."

As she discusses the definition of objective (the actor's tool for action), she asks the students to *reflect and think metacognitively* on their current assigned scenes, and what their characters want in their lives. The students answer questions about what they as actors will be doing to show their characters' objectives and tactics are. Not just the wants of the characters (e.g., "to be the cool kid"), but the actual behaviors an actor can do to show that desire. When students are not quite sure or do not give a definitive answer, Maura pushes, "Think bigger than that. This is where your imagination can come in . . . . That keeps you in the game. And it's high stakes; you make that really important. Now we see you working your angles and your objectives in that scene."

This exercise involves thinking about the play as a whole, and their characters as a whole, while also connecting that whole back to individual moments and lines the students can see and discover deeper meaning to. Students have to be able to think at a broader level about their overarching goals and objectives within the play, while also thinking at the finer level about their actions and behaviors minute by minute while performing.

Maura then goes into how to score the scene to mark where beats and tactics are changing, and discusses with students what causes the beat to change, noting differences in emotions and objectives. She gives a handout of how to score a script and find active verbs. The class discusses how beats changed throughout the class the day before, when Maura had staged the fake fight for the class to react to. The assignment for the rest of the week is to score out their own scripts with these ideas in mind. She has them repeat "I am doing, not being" as a rule for deciding about tactics for beats in scripts.

To be able to engage in this *reflect and think metacognitively* exercise on how the broader ideas of beats and objectives link to their own scripts, a number of other Acting Habits of Mind have to be pulled in, including *commit to choices, be flexible, consider others, imagine and envision,* and *release inhibitions*. But for now, the most important thing Maura is trying to get the students to do is to *reflect and think metacognitively* on the level and the structure of what they are doing with their scripts, to have a sense of what their characters want overall. This will enable the students to have a structure that will apply across scenes and plays; it will enable them to engage with any work of theatre regardless of what the actual actions are. This is *reflect and think metacognitively* structural teaching for the approach to the character and play.

Focal Exercise 2: Reflecting on Reflections

Engaging with metacognitive thinking across activities at a high level.

One class in which we saw high levels of *reflect and think metacognitively* was at Eureka High in Humboldt County, in which the entire class period was devoted to formalized Reflection periods on different elements of the classroom and the students' lives. This then led the students into metacognition about their reflection style and how metacognition about their activities could be helpful or not. Important to note, this class was filmed on March 12, 2020, just as COVID-19 closures and restrictions were beginning across the entire United States. The opening of the class was the students' moment to *reflect and think metacognitively* on and discuss how they felt about COVID-19 and what they thought might happen.

Nannette invited the students to engage in a "things you need to share, things you need to ask about" moment, giving the students a chance to *reflect and think metacognitively* about how they were thinking about COVID-19 and the uncertainty that was constant in the early days of the pandemic. She went around the circle, so that everyone was given a chance to talk, and the most extraverted or confident students were not the only ones who had a chance to share. The students shared fears about their friends, graduating online, their show being cancelled, or getting sick. A time capsule just before everything changed, for sure. Nanette reminded the students to be respectful of each other's opinions and feelings, critical for students to know and be able to engage with each other with less self-awareness, as discussed in Chapter 4.

What is interesting about this moment in the classroom is that even though it has nothing to do with performance or acting, Nanette is still getting the students to engage, *reflect and think metacognitively* and she is still scaffolding and training them in the Acting Habit of Mind of reflection. The students are still being guided into reflecting on their lives and thinking about their lives not just in the living of them, but in the feedback on them. This use of *reflect and think metacognitively* is useful and transferable throughout students' daily experiences across multiple contexts.

Nannette then split the students into small groups and paired them for performance and discussion. They were tasked with discussing and giving feedback to each other on how the scene and group performances had gone over the past week. Some of the groups still needed to perform, while the other groups of students sat and watched. This was a continuation of the *reflect and think metacognitively* exercise of the day before—the students had already begun performing for each other and giving each other feedback. Importantly, the students in groups and scenes were paired with each other in different formations, so they could get feedback from multiple groups of peers. The students engaged with both reflection about their classmates, formalized and written down, but also metacognition in discussing with each other how they could best give feedback (an exercise in *consider others* as well).

The feedback was a formalized assignment in this class, making it very obvious that the students were supposed to approach watching each other's performance to reflect back how they were doing. The assignment also made clear that as they created their own performances, they were supposed to be thinking about how it would be reflected back to them from their classmates. Nanette had forms for the students to complete to reinforce their reflection—on what they saw, what worked and did not work, and how the performance was successful or needed improvement and editing. Nanette laying out the *reflect and think metacognitively* exercise for the students worked to scaffold their own abilities (as we saw in multiple classrooms). The students could not just passively watch. They had to actively observe so they could write and discuss later. The expectation was a conscientious and purposeful watching. The students had to turn their papers in to for grading, raising *reflect and think metacognitively* to the level of a formal assignment. Being prepared for critique as both an audience member and as a performer is critical for moving forward into rehearsals and performance in the professional world (outside of classes), as this is how rehearsals work—with constant reflective feedback from directors and producers. See Chapter 11 for a longer discussion of how a rehearsal-style activity of scene study integrates all of the activities.

For the last 8 minutes of class, Nannette brought the groups all back together. She began by asking the students to again go around in a circle to share feedback they gave or feedback they received or thought was particularly helpful. So, in this moment, she was asking them to *reflect and think metacognitively* about the reflections that they gave others and the ways that others gave them reflection. Reflection inception! Nannette kept it brief, again, so that every student, even those who were not particularly extraverted or who felt inhibited had a moment to discuss their feedback and experiences of *reflect and think metacognitively*. The students shared comments about being more specific about actions, moving more or being more stationary, better memorization of lines, having more energy, and liking facial expressions and vocal choices. Together the class was 15 minutes of COVID *reflect and think metacognitively*, 34 minutes of student-to-student peer reflection and feedback, and 9 minutes of teacher guided large group *reflect and think metacognitively* on how the reflection and feedback went. The students had to use this Acting Habit of Mind practically the entire time. The mindset for the day was a metacognitive one.

Critical to note is that an acting class, where students are used to feedback, critique, and reflections may be one of the few spaces in the students' lives in which they can engage in this kind of activity. They are ready and prepped to engage in *reflect and think metacognitively* on all sorts of experiences. In other classrooms, they may engage in a range of activities but are not asked to reflect on them in any real way. In our last day of filming pre-COVID, in March 2020, the students in Humboldt County spent a whole day of watching each other's scenes and reflecting back to each other what they had seen. The students took it in stride and dove in, fully engaged in focusing on the critique and feedback for each other.

REFLECT AND THINK METACOGNITIVELY, IN SUMMARY

- *Reflect and think metacognitively* is about building connections and metaphors, forming a web of knowledge across different activities, building your knowledge and understanding to levels of depth and breadth.
- Students are constantly asked to *reflect and think metacognitively* and critique performances, as well as discuss their own performance with the teachers. Teachers ask students, "What did you see?" "What did you think?" "Why did you make the choice you made?"
- *Reflect and think metacognitively* on others' work and performances allow students to think broadly and meta-analytically about what works and does not work onstage.
- *Reflect and think metacognitively* is built informally into exercises and improvisational games and is also a formal period of class time, often taking place at the beginning or end of the class period, to frame the classwork in terms of what students should be thinking about as they perform.
- *Reflect and think metacognitively* is similar to the type of formal discussion inherent in many types of educational settings and is critical to be able to bring skills learned in one domain (such as imagining) into other unrelated domains (Diamond & Ling, 2016).
- Beyond the acting classroom, being able to engage *reflect and think metacognitively* is critical to any kind of learning and growth and will serve students well across their lives to continue to learn and be creative, flexible, and accomplish their goals.

Part III

CONNECTIONS

In these last eight chapters, I have focused on each Acting Habit of Mind individually. However, the truth is that acting classes are whole, complex, integrated experiences for students that take place over time. I take on this complexity in singular exercises, moments, and in the ways acting classes work in total, in Part III, Connections.

CHAPTER 11

The Scene Study Cycle

Where the Acting Habits of Mind Come Together, Integrating and Connecting in an Iterative, Scaffolding, Complete Way to Create Performance

We have now seen how each individual Acting Habit of Mind is integrated and used in individual segments in acting class exercises, and how each is expressed throughout the different activities of class. Now, let us investigate and show how they can be used in conjunction with one another. While in previous chapters I delineated exercises in which individual Acting Habits of Mind were at the forefront, or moments where a teacher was pointing out the use of a particular strategy or framework for the task at hand, in the real-world context of an acting classroom, the Acting Habits of Mind work in concert. This is one of the strengths of acting classes, and how they foster a variety of skills; students are not just being taught one psychological perspective or mindset at a time—they can use and choose which will work best for them in any particular moment for any particular task.

As discussed in the Part II Habits of Mind Introduction, the Acting Habits of Mind are not singular psychological constructs and mindsets that are orthogonal (i.e., unrelated) to one another. Rather they are dynamic and interactive. And nowhere in an acting class is that seen more clearly than in scene study.

Scene study is the segment of class in which students take a piece of script and work on making it performance ready. This is not just about understanding character or interpreting script, but taking on a scene as a whole with a goal of performance. Every acting class we observed used scene analysis and performance as an ultimate goal, if not for the year, then for each unit. We saw this sometimes called "jury" or "final" performances. While not every class we filmed had a scene study, every class was working toward one. There have been some scene study exemplars already discussed in previous chapters (e.g., in many Interpretation sections throughout Chapters 3–10), but now we take scene study as its own separated activity in class.

Sometimes these performances were fully scripted from the beginning, taken from the classic American theatre canon, Shakespeare, films, or modern plays written for students. Other times, the scenes were devised by the students in class. The classics of scene study in the United States theatre curriculum include Shakespeare, Tennessee Williams, Thornton Wilder, and Arthur Miller. However, newer works also have come into the curriculum, particularly focused (finally) on playwrights who are women or writers of color. In most cases, scenes are typically pulled from full plays, and teachers have a wealth of knowledge about the scenes as well as the broader context of the play and the world the play was written in and about. Teachers use the same scenes over many classes and years so they can guide students through difficult moments or pitfalls of a character.

Scene study as seen in our acting classes is also not just a full scene from a play or movie, with a pair or trio of actors having an argument that would be shown in an Oscar clip at an awards show. Scene study is also a monologue the student is preparing for themselves, a dialogue taken from a classical work of theatre, a small and quiet scene with low tension from a movie, or an over-the-top Greek tragedy that involves 20 people onstage and interplays of dialogue from the chorus with discussions and monologues. These are not rehearsals like one would engage in when hired to perform in a play—the students are not necessarily moving toward a full performance with lights, sets, and an audience in a theatre space. But, all five of our school districts had performance in their classes over the course of the year.

From an Acting Habits of Mind perspective, what can scene study include? The Acting Habits of Mind are used from the first time the students read the script, when they are just defining the words for themselves and thinking about what the characters are saying and why they are saying it, to giving performances to class and teacher as audience and taking feedback and reflection to integrate into their performance for future presentations.

Scene study in an acting classroom is a kind of lab, a preparation for the activities that occur during rehearsal for professional performances. Much like in a chemistry or biology class where students will perform experiments guided by a teacher where all of the intermediate steps and the outcome are well known, the student is recreating what has been done before, scene study is experimentation. As they build performance, they build their own knowledge.

In fact, Lin-Manuel Miranda, one of theatre's most public-facing stars, has made a joke on social media multiple times and noted in an interview that in the lead up to his blockbuster and record-breaking Broadway musical *Hamilton*, the excitement of being in the student play working on scenes and the excitement of being in a Broadway musical are the same. The excitement of signing in to the cast sheet, of seeing your friends be brilliant in rehearsal, and the job of memorizing your lines are all similar, and the excitement around acting never goes away (Miranda, 2015; Sherman, 2016). Scene study in the classroom is the first step students take to how a professional paid performance will go.

The goal of scene study is therefore often to prepare students for the professional world of theatre, film, and television, where they could use their acting skills for professional performance. In professional settings, actors engage in warm-up and character development at home, analyzing and often memorizing the script before rehearsals begin. Prepping scene study in class means students have the foundation of how to work a script, how to prepare for performance, and how to take reflection, critique, and feedback of their performance into the next iteration of the preparation. When and if students ever join a production (professional, community, or academic), the rehearsal process is generally connected to this scene study cycle, although occasionally sped up, where actors may only have a few tries at a scene in rehearsal before they are expected to perform for the director and designers.

As a result of all of these elements, I anticipated that scene study exercises would use every Acting Habit of Mind. What was surprising as it emerged from our data was that the Acting Habits of Mind emerged as a *cycle,* with each one following and building on the one before. Below I outline what an exemplar of a scene study cycle might look like when students are in active rehearsal, where they prepare to perform for feedback, make changes, and then perform again (about 50% of scene study exercises in our data). Earlier in the process, when the scene study is in its table-read phase, blocking phase, or group-work phase (see sections below), the cycle is slightly different and individualized to the level and abilities of the performers.

THE SCENE STUDY ACTING HABITS OF MIND CYCLE

1. Briefly, a scene study typically begins with a discussion of what is happening in the scene, and the feelings, thoughts, and emotions of the characters, using the Acting Habit of Mind *consider others*.
2. Students are then instructed to think about the inner states of the characters and how those emotions, beliefs, desires, and thoughts are expressed through words and actions onstage, using *imagine and envision.*
3. Once they have envisioned possibilities, students must make a choice of how they will portray a character, keeping in mind that muddled or weak choices do not come across onstage, the Acting Habit of Mind of *commit to choices*.

4. Teachers often talk of brave choices, meaning the student must *release inhibitions* to portray their choice freely.
5. They must then think about whether that choice will work with the other characters and onstage, or for the lighting or directing, therefore they must *think collaboratively*.
6. Then, finally, students perform the moment of the scene. This involves the Acting Habit of Mind of *body awareness and control* in which the student moves their face, voice, and body in a way to portray inner states.
7. Once the performance is over, whether it was a 3-second line reading or a full 10-minute scene, the teacher, other students, and performers will be asked to *reflect and think metacognitively* about what just happened in the scene, whether it works or not, and how.
8. For moments that need teaching, change, or adaptation, the performer will need to *be flexible* to come up with new ideas about how they could portray that moment.

Students may need to dip back into the thoughts, feelings, intentions, and behaviors of their characters, once again *consider others* and beginning the cycle over again. This cycle does not always happen in just this order, for example, someone could *think collaboratively*, realize the choice does not work, and have to go back to *be flexible*, but this is generally what emerged from scene study exercises in our data set. The amount of time it takes to get through the cycle may vary by student and level, with some students spending longer amounts of time in particular Acting Habits of Mind. Some habits of mind may not even fully consciously expressed, but rather inherent and implicit in the work the student is doing to get from idea to performance. See Figure 11.1 for an example of how this cycle might work.

If a student is struggling with a scene in class or in performance, it may be helpful to think about where in the scene-study cycle the student seems to be stuck. Are they not *being flexible* about the other choices they could make with the character? Have they not *considered others* and all of the possibilities of what the character is thinking or feeling? Are they struggling to *be aware of and control their body* in a particular way? Do they hold *inhibitions* in their performance, or are they not thinking about how their actions connect with the actions of the other students around them in a *collaborative* way?

It is important not to think about the scene-study cycle as unidirectional, or to assume every step must necessarily be taken before moving on to the next step. Instead, the scene-study cycle can be taken in stages, or moved through backwards and forwards as needed for each student at each time. Moving through and around the circle, however, is likely necessary for a successful performance.

Figure 11.1. The Basic Scene Study Cycle.

CALL FOR FUTURE RESEARCH

Without fully going through each Acting Habit of Mind when approaching a scene, I hypothesize something in the performance will be "off" or "missing." The question of how much time students must spend on each stage, how they interact with one another, and the ways in which synchrony in Acting Habits of Mind stage must happen across areas is still open for investigation. Another area for future research!

In multiple different examples in our data set (although we saw a cycle every time we saw a scene study), teachers gave instructions to students on how to use and integrate all of the Acting Habits of Mind iteratively, jumping across and back and forth across them and cycling through over the time of the scene study. Scene study was a major part of classes, altogether taking up 32.7% of the class minutes (with a range of 2–55% of any one class) in our sample.

SCENE STUDY ACROSS DIFFERENT LEVELS AND STAGES

Below, I give examples of each of the different types of scene study we saw in our classes. The scene-study cycle can happen in a variety of ways, depending on the class level, time in the academic year, and where the group itself was in the timeline to performance. These stages included

- literary read throughs (i.e., table reads), where students read through the script, just getting used to the words and the characters;
- analytical sit-downs, with thorough discussion and script work, where students delve into who the characters are, what they want, why they say the words they do, and what it means for movement and reactions;
- blocking or "getting on your feet," where students stand up and walk through the scene, figuring out where and how they will be moving with each other;
- rehearsal, once the movement is set and the analyses of the characters mostly completed, to get ready to show to the teacher (i.e., early rehearsal); and
- performing in front of the teacher and students, which always incorporates moments of reflection, reworking, and feedback (i.e., later rehearsal).

None of these moments are mutually exclusive—students often perform for teachers while still actively analyzing and blocking a scene, to get feedback. Teachers send students off to rehearse and analyze on their own, to get them to actively learn and be engaged in the work. One note: there was one school where we saw practically no scene study—in St. Louis at Eureka High. Here, teacher Justin was more focused on improvised scenes and devised work during the week where we filmed. We saw a few "final performances" for grades, but no active scene study. The majority of the class time in the 5 days filmed was focused on improvised exercises and games. However, scene study was still a major part of the classes' curriculums (just at a different time than when we filmed at Eureka).

As one can see from even a brief discussion of each of these types of scene study, they include Preparation work, Interpretation work, Generation work, and even Reflection, and they incorporate all Acting Habits of Mind. I detail each of these types of scene study in the following sections.

Reading and Analyzing

Before any performance can begin, or even before any rehearsals with movement and full characterization can start, actors must read through their scripts for a sense of understanding of the characters and the play as a whole, and then must engage in some analysis of their character, how they understand the role in context of the play, and why the character talks and acts the way they do. We saw this first step of reading and analyzing in a variety of ways in our data set. This can include "translating" Shakespeare into modern language, thinking about the context and background of why a character says certain lines, and working through how the atmosphere and energy in a scene changes as it progresses.

For example, at Imagination Stage in Class 3, the group was given a new script and had to make decisions about who would play which part in which scene. They spent 99 minutes of class just reading through the pages, and then talking about which scenes and lines they would each take. There was no real analysis or discussion here, just hearing the lines out loud and becoming familiar with the play's themes and arc.

In another class, at The Madeira School in Class 23, teacher Kelsey had her students sit with their Shakespearean scripts and analyze the words for specific action verbs they could play as they figured out how to put their assigned scenes into performance, as noted in the Interpretation example in Chapter 9.

In a more thorough analysis before reading, in two classes, 35 and 39, on two consecutive days at McKinleyville High School in Humboldt County, the students spent the whole class in scene study. In these classes, it was a seated reading, not a blocked out, memorized, or even performed experience. Here, the class was reading *Taming of the Shrew*, and dealing with the difficulties of Shakespearean language (as we saw in many of our high school classrooms), names, and complex situations. Students were assigned roles by Steve, the teacher, picking names out of a deck of cards, not for any assigned or auditioned reason. Steve began with a discussion and reminder of all the major characters in the show, and then noted on a worksheet, handed out to the class, that they needed to be thinking about and filling out the "motivation, objective, obstacle, and action" for the characters.

This language of motivations and objectives is where the students can engage with the text as a document to engage in close reading and discover what is happening. In other classrooms, we also saw "motivations and objectives" work discussed in concert with movement and blocking. In each type of class, *consider others* is central, but in Steve's classes, where the students are reading through, they did not use the Acting Habit of Mind *body awareness and control*. However, all the other Acting Habits of Mind were used, and in cycle. Steve noted that knowing a character's job, function in life, and perhaps, too, their social status would also be helpful in knowing how to portray them and what their motivations (or as he put it "their deal") were—starting with *consider others*. He also noted that the characters in Shakespeare were all coming to the moments of the plays with previous experiences and knowledge that would set them up for the current moments in the play itself. As the students changed roles each day, students who had read the roles in previous days were asked to talk about what they thought about the characters in preparation for that next day. As the students read through the script while analyzing it, they stopped for clarification. For example, students noted that Katarina's conflict over wanting to get married had evidence in both directions, and it would be up to the players and the class to figure out which side they wanted to argue for.

The set up and intro for reading out loud took almost 20 minutes, while the reading out loud itself, not just discussion of characters, but the lines and what they meant, took 15 minutes. In this class, analysis > reading time. When it was time for reading out loud, the students who were assigned the day's roles moved to the stage, separated from the rest of the class. This turned the class into the audience, making this activity beyond how literary analysis would work in an English class. The reading itself was slow and full of pauses, as the students had very little to no experience with the words out loud (they had only read it themselves the night before). However, the students were still asked to think about *release inhibitions and be playful* to read out loud, *consider others'* mental and psychological states, and pay attention to the ways in which their classmates were speaking, to *think collaboratively*, onstage.

One critical note is that the literary prep of understand the character is not the same thing as having to personalize it and act it out. In fact, I hypothesize this is the major difference between why findings from the scientific study of literature cannot necessarily be applied to acting. Steve noted his primary interest in the scene study and for the day was to get the students past the language and cultural differences for Shakespeare. However, as discussed in Chapter 3 on *body awareness and control,* there are cognitive effects to embodiment. The literary analysis and engagement with a work of theatre is necessary, but only a first step, and actors always read through shows and scenes before they do any other work of acting at all. Shakespeare is complicated, with unfamiliar names, difficult to parse language (compared to everyday American speech) and situations and locations (though not emotions) that are foreign to the modern American high school student. This kind of prereading almost runs parallel to a form of warm-up, to prepare for the act and actions of acting. This may be why in all of his interviews, Steve mentioned empathy and thinking about others. Before any acting takes place in a scene study, students must spend a lot of time thinking and talking about the characters. A lot of character analysis must be put into the background when students actually start acting because the embodied nature of it means you cannot simultaneously be deeply thinking about the character and performing it at the same time.

Blocking and Building

After the students are familiar with the script and the characters, it is time to start putting movement and staging to the lines. This is a long part of the rehearsal process, where the student actors must bring the Acting Habits of Mind of *body control* and *think collaboratively* together with each other (if they are blocking themselves) or with the director (if they are being blocked). This can happen line by line, with working on each moment in the script before moving into the next one, or as a whole, trying to get the arc of the full scene set in a general way to refine later. We saw this second step of putting a scene on its feet in a few different ways in our data, but not as often as anticipated. This is possibly because of our filming timeline. At the beginning of the year (September and October), students do not yet have full scenes that they will stage with movement, and late in the year (March) they are already in full rehearsals. However, we did have a few distinct instances of blocking rehearsals for scene study in our sample. At The Madeira School in Class 24, Kelsey had the students work on their own to figure out how they might want to block the scene with just their own understanding and engagement with the material. She gave only minimal instruction about figuring it out and then let them work independently for much of the class.

In Class 10, as noted in the *imagine and envision* chapter, with the Boston Arts Academy sophomores, teacher Maura gave the class a short lesson in "as if" thinking, again while working with Shakespeare, to think about how to act out their various scenes "as if" they had experienced a similar emotion or situation before (asking them to both *imagine* the connection to their own experiences and *release inhibitions* to really go for and *commit to choices*). Then, she also released them to work through the scripts on their own, giving them 45 minutes to figure out how their "as if" moments translated into *body control,* movement for performance.

In our most in-depth example of full blocking, at Imagination Stage in Class 8, Nikki spent 41 minutes with the group as a whole, figuring out the movement for their ensemble performance of *Antigone*. Here, she worked as a director would, helping the students figure out the best way to perform under her guidance and vision for the play.

The scene begins with all of the players walking, as a Greek chorus, and speaking jointly. She started the group in a circle, telling them, "It's not important that you sound the same, only that you speak at the same time," an exercise in *think collaboratively*. She noted that rehearsals have to be consistent, and in particular the students need to "make choices and stick with them," obviously pointing to *commit to choices.*

The students were a bit distracted and talkative, but when one student really got into their performance, Nikki actually stopped the rehearsal to get excited about the commitment to the performance, giving positive *reflection* and feedback about it. The students then said only one more line before Nikki stopped them again. She gave two body movement options, one that was heavy and slow, and the other more energetic, asking them to perform with a *body awareness* of energy and aliveness.

"I'm giving you the staging but your job is to layer on the intention. . . . You can play with an intention to the me, the audience. So, what do you want me [the audience] to do? Or what do you want to do to me?" asking the students to *consider others* and inner states for their performance, keeping the audience in mind. She says the action is "to excite" the audience by giving a specific action with their *body*. After seeing each of the students choose a different action (showing *be flexible* in interpretation), she chose one of the students to use for the next go round.

"Give me something interesting to look at!" Nikki says, asking the students to *release inhibitions* and give her full engagement to a body position.

They then moved on to the next step in the scene, a fight. They have to make some decisions, and begin to list off the possibilities, *imagine and envision* what each one would look like. But first, after some student distractions, Nikki says, "My job is not to tell you what to do. We are working as an ensemble, so everyone needs to be fully, fully, fully, fully focused on me," reminding the students to *think collaboratively* through the process.

She spent some time reviewing where everyone is standing, but then decided to change something. She says, "I'm making a change, and you are going to say 'and change is good.'" Then, she pronounces: "I'm making a change." And the class dutifully repeats back: "and change is good." A moment to *be flexible!* "Working on something like this, we're going to erase, and cross out, and re-do, until we find something that works." She corrects two students who are not on the same "plane" in the space, activating their *body awareness*. She keeps with *body awareness*, giving the students physical movements to do during the next moment of the scene.

As the scene progresses, Nikki lets students put forward their ideas for movements and engagement, asking them to explain and then show what it might look like, with additional "what if" *envision* questions. She chastises some of the students who are not as engaged, saying, "The rest of you need to start taking ownership and start *making choices*," pairing flexibility and choices that are so active in this kind of work. She does note the need for paying close attention and not goofing off. "This is not the place to be on break," she says. Goofing off is a way of protecting the students from fully engaging, and allows them to inhibit looking silly, making this a comment in line with *release inhibitions*. This works, and the students rush to keep sharing ideas, continuing to build the scene together, *think collaboratively*. "Listen to each other!" Nikki says.

The students are then released to a break, and when they return, they run through everything they had worked on that night so far, to make sure that the next time they had class, they remembered the changes and the building. As can be seen from this scene work with the students, all the Acting Habits of Mind are being activated and used, built on each other, and looped back, to create the scene in real time as students learn what they will be doing in their eventual performances.

A Quick Note on Memorization

Memorization of lines is obviously critically important for performing a show (while staged readings with scripts are a valid form of performance, but basically every other kind of theatrical performance is memorized). A good amount of research from the 1990s shows that actors actually report their memorization occurring naturally as they work through the intentions, analyses, and blocking of a scene—and that memorization of lines is strongly connected to the psychological intentions and emotional engagement they put into the words (Noice, 1992). That being said, it is a task to learn how to memorize lines and scripts, and a challenge students need to undertake until they know what methods work best for them.

In our classes, there were just a few distinct exercises that were focused on teaching the students a way to memorize their lines. At Boston Arts Academy, in Classes 9 (freshman) and 13 (juniors), teacher Juanita had the students try two techniques. First, she had the freshman pass a ball back and forth rapidly while saying their lines out loud. This is the idea of providing some distraction from just saying lines, to make it more automatic and connect to the fact that when acting you also need to be moving and keep the pace up. She also asked the juniors to record the lines they did *not* say, with breaks for their own lines, so they could rehearse on their own. In Class 8, just before Nikki started blocking and building the scene above, she had the students walk around together in a circle for 6 minutes, saying the lines over and over until they had it right. Most of the time, however, memorization was a task for homework, and students were chastised for not having their lines fully memorized before coming in to do the psychologically more complex blocking, analyses, rehearsals, and workshop performances in class.

Rehearsal

Another way scene study is used is when students are sent off on their own to rehearse through a scene that was already blocked and analyzed, to fine-tune it and prepare for performance. Teachers often would release their students to work in small groups or pairs, and would visit each group to give momentary feedback and check in on how they were doing. This occurred in about 24% of our scene-study time in classes. This is active learning and experimentation for the students (see Chapter 13) where they could practice and figure out their scripts, characters, and performance on their own, from their own perspectives. Students would rehearse not only in the classroom itself, but would often move to the hallway or other classrooms to work on their own. The teachers would walk around the classroom and other spaces to work individually with groups, checking in and giving short feedback, but mostly leaving the students to work on their own. An exercise, of course, in *think collaboratively* with peers.

In Class 9 at Boston Arts Academy, Juanita spent 31 minutes working with a few pairs of students on a ball-passing improvisation (after they had completed the ball-passing memorization exercise), in which they had to say the subtext and underlying meaning of the words for their script (see Chapter 12 for a discussion of this exercise in its Acting Habits of Mind complexity). Then, using instructions to *consider others* and *imagine and envision* what was going on in the scripts, she released the students to workshop their scenes by themselves in pairs. She noted, too, they needed to be listening actively and *be flexible* to what they were given by their partners, and not just "set and forget" the ways in which they were performing and working with their lines. "When you guys are rehearsing today, I want y'all to change it up. I don't care what you've worked on, I want you to say different things." For this rehearsal, Juanita asked the students to set up their physical environments "really quickly and really shallowly" so they could rehearse the whole scene, and keep what they had explored and discovered through the ball-passing improv where they had been focusing in on subtext. During this time, she interacted with one pair for 12 minutes while the other students worked on their own, and then brought everyone back together for a 9-minute Reflection on how the group work went.

In Class 16 at Boston Arts Academy, teacher Maura broke the students into groups about an hour into class, after having gone through one scene with the whole class giving feedback, so the students could work their smaller scenes on their own. She kept working with the main scene, but asked the other students to rehearse together in other rooms. She gave very little instruction to the students, trusting them to work on their own, and visiting them to see their progress after about 30 minutes. As she visited each group, she asked the students to show what they had worked on, and asked them in particular to show how they had made sense of the scene for themselves. She asked them to explain how they had broken down the subtext of the script (*consider others*), the physical environment they were in (*imagine and envision*), and how they were embodying (*body control*) what they meant to show. Even in just a few minutes with one group, Maura activated all of the Acting Habits of Mind to then take for themselves and keep rehearsing.

Performance for Feedback

Finally, much of what we saw in scene study in our classrooms was an active performance–feedback–performance–feedback loop (approximately 54% of the scene-study minutes in our classrooms, almost 18% of total class time). Here, teachers had individuals, pairs, or small groups of students perform the scene they were working on, pausing the performance throughout to give feedback and corrections, push the students to go father, gather critique and ideas from the class, and put all of it into practice for another performance moment. This is the closest we get in the classroom to how a professional rehearsal proceeds, where the actors perform what they will be showing to the audience and then the collaborative group of director and actors discuss and critique what worked and what did not from the perspective of audience members. Here, too, the students who were not performing took an active role as audience and active learners. Teachers often would bring a critique of the specific scene they had just watched back out into a broader lesson on acting, and often on a Acting Habit of Mind students needed to use and integrate more to better perform the scene.

There were a variety of ways in which performance for feedback occurred. In Nanette's classes at Eureka High in Humboldt County, where Classes 36 and 37 took place in the school's theater, the students worked in the lobby, in the aisles of the audience, and onstage, wherever they could find space to be separated from each other. Students were paired in their groups (with two groups of students performing scenes for each other). Nanette gave all students a worksheet and discussed giving feedback to each other in stages. First, they were instructed that they should consider their initial thoughts and reactions to watching the full scene without previous knowledge. Then, they should give feedback on whether the actors were clearly *committed to the choices* they made about their characters, whether they show the intentions of the characters (did they *consider others*), and whether the movement and blocking makes sense in terms of the underlying emotions and intentions (*body awareness*). She notes she wanted the students to give feedback to help each other, not just note "this was awesome!" She previewed the hardest part for everyone likely would be to just listen to the feedback without giving explanation or reasons for the choices, or push back on why the feedback might not be correct. This activity took up 35 minutes in one class, and 33 in the other, 57% and 70% of class time, respectively!

At Boston Arts Academy, in Class 18, the students spent 63 minutes in a performance-and-feedback loop for scene study. As mentioned in Chapter 6, this class was a small group of six seniors who were performing scenes from the movie *500 Days of Summer*. The focus here was on the intensity of acting for camera, which is smaller, more subtle, and in many ways harder than acting on a stage. Maura began the class with a discussion on listening and how to carefully *consider others* while listening in a performance. She then had the students set up the stage and camera, recording their performance so she could play it back while giving feedback. The other students watched the screen and engaged in the feedback as well. She noted that having the students work without their scripts in hand is better than with the scripts, which prevents active listening. She wanted the students to think about pushing through pretend listening or fake listening (because they know what is coming next) to really listening and reacting to the faces of their fellow actors. She wants them to think about *release inhibitions* and *think collaboratively*, as well as *be flexible* to react as if they are in the moment, not with preconceived notions. She says watching themselves later and each other on film will allow them to just listen while performing. The other stuff they have worked on should all be in the background: "What does my character want, the intentions, all the other stuff."

Because the focus of the day is on active listening, Maura asks the class to reflect on what they saw about the listening in the performance. "Was he? What is the challenge of listening when you're doing most of the talking?" "What are you doing"? After the first performance, Maura reflects that she did not see enough listening, paying attention, and reacting. She has the students do the scene again, asking them to focus on whether their scene partners are really listening to them. She tells them to build the stakes, keep their characters in mind, and actively think about the lines as they say them. As the students perform again, Maura stops them line by line, asking them to repeat each line, pushing further into their listening, understanding, and reacting, rather than running through each line to the next one they know is coming. She wants to see the *body control* of listening, the activity of *consider others*. She comments on pushing them to *imagine* how to listen deeper, and *be flexible* in response to the feedback and *reflection* of their fellow students.

Feedback on full performance scene study also came through in more formal academic ways. At Six Rivers School in Humboldt County, two students gave a performance of mask work, with the rest of the group giving feedback and reflection. The performing students paired music and wore a mask for performance. The other students were given score sheets and asked to observe carefully and prepare critique. The mask performance (to *Smooth Criminal* by Michael Jackson) had the class and teacher Melanie smiling. The second performance, to a more abstract piece of music, was also funny and captured attention. Melanie wrote notes to give formal feedback later in the class for more study and improvement. The class then met as a group to discuss the mask work as a whole, first noting the *body control and awareness* necessary. They *reflected and thought metacognitively* on their own process, and how they saw that process in the scenes they watched, noting how much they needed to *release inhibitions, commit to choices*, and *be flexible* when they felt something was not working. With this, they noted what they would change next time.

SCENE STUDY, IN SUMMARY

- Scene study may be closest to the popular notion of what an acting class is. It is thinking about, preparing, rehearsing, and critiquing a performance. This includes figuring out what the character wants and needs (*consider others*), determining how an actor wants to say lines (*imagine and envision*; *commit to choices*) and physicalize them (*body awareness*) how they might use alternatives (*be flexible*), and be fully present (*release inhibitions*), given what the director and other actors want (*think collaboratively*; *reflect and think metacognitively*).

- Scene study is also the closest to professional theatre experiences, and is often leading to the final exam, presentation, or juried experience for students. This ultimate professional goal is echoed throughout classrooms.
- We had 57 separate instances of scene study across our 40 classes, broken out into 4 instances of reading, 8 instances of analyses, 2 instances of blocking, 3 instances of memorization exercises, 11 instances of rehearsal without feedback, and, finally, 29 instances of performance for feedback from the teachers and class.
- In some of the lower-level classes, we never saw scene study at all (although all levels got there eventually over the course of a year), while in some of our upper-level classes, the entire day was devoted to a single 3-minute scene study (see Chapter 13 for a discussion of leveling of classes).
- While scene study occurs in every school where acting classes are offered, it is not the only element of acting class that is complex, layered, and requires individualized applications based on the level of the students. There are many other pieces of acting classes where all of the Acting Habits of Mind are present together.

CHAPTER 12

The Complexity of Acting Classes

How Acting Classes Are Leveled and Use Multiple Interacting Acting Habits of Mind

In previous chapters, I focused on and highlighted individual instances of teaching and single exercises in which a teacher enables and prompts students to engage with one focal Acting Habit of Mind. While scene study is a notable activity in class where all of the Acting Habits of Mind can be seen in rapid succession, it is not the only one. In fact, most exercises in acting classes use multiple Acting Habits of Mind, even those that center on one in particular. In this chapter, I highlight additional exercises and activities that engaged multiple Acting Habits of Mind simultaneously. While *all* of the Acting Habits of Mind were being used constantly and in tandem, in some moments, it is more obvious.

Remember our quote from Justin, back in the *body awareness* chapter: "Today I will be mindful of my body, my voice, my imagination, as I focus and collaborate."

While in Chapter 3 I used this quote as an example of *body awareness*, if we dig a bit deeper, we see it exemplifies the complexity of both whole acting classes and individual exercises. This simple quote incorporates at least four Acting Habits of Mind: *body awareness*; *imagine and envision*; *think collaboratively*; and *think metacognitively* about the body, the voice, the imagination, and others. This could also incorporate *consider others* in the focus, and *release inhibitions* around practicing today, but it is not explicitly said. And this is just one sentence that Justin asks his students to say at the beginning of each class he teaches at Eureka High!

In addition to the use of multiple Acting Habits of Mind, different exercises were often leveled out for different classrooms and applied differently for the students in different contexts—showing individual application of foundational concepts, leveling of the use of Acting Habits of Mind, and allowing the data to illuminate how acting class is flexibly used given the needs of the teachers, students, and school. It is from this complexity that theatre gains its power, and can be translated into other goals and contexts, as explained in Chapter 13.

Below, I go through a few exemplar exercises, showing how they integrate the use of multiple Acting Habits of Mind. I then turn to cases where we saw the same exercise in different schools or with different groups of students, showing how they are individuated by the teachers given the needs and levels of the class. I conclude with some general developmental and leveling trends observed in our data, which emerge naturally from a combination of the expertise of the teachers, and the curricular requirements set by federal, state, and local regulations.

MULTIPLE HABITS OF MIND IN COMPLEX EXERCISES

It is not just in formal scene study (as seen in Chapter 11) where students are engaging and integrating and using multiple Acting Habits of Mind in one moment, or iteratively and quickly in several moments. Often, a seemingly simple behavior or goal actually contained quite number of complex usages of multiple Acting Habits of Mind. The use of these exercises and Acting Habits of Mind was never just about the moment itself, although students were always encouraged to engage in the moment. Instead, these exercises were always about building into the next moment and the acting goals for the students, as reflected in teacher statements and interviews.

Space Walking

At Eureka High in Class 30, Justin engaged the students in a Viewpoints exercise called Space Walking to prepare them for the improvised scenes of the day. Justin used Space Walking a few times in the week we filmed in his classes, but each time it had a different focus. This day, it took place after the typical warm-up for the class, where the students had already had discussions about the agenda for the day, had completed a few tongue twisters and physical movements, including shaking out, and had said the daily mantra (noted previously). These students already knew what Justin was asking them to do at a basic level, and began moving around the room.

Justin then had them freeze a few times to focus on different aspects of the walking. He began with a focus on breath, engaging in some meditative breathing. They then continued to walk, be aware of what was happening perceptually, and noticing of new things they had not seen before in the space or in a person. This engaged *consider others, reflect, and think metacognitively* about their perspectives. If they were drawn to take more time to investigate an object, Justin gave them permission to engage in that way as well. Then they added more mental load to the task—to keep the breadth and noticing going, but also to notice when they named things in their mind and stopped investigating the object because they could just know it as a whole. (To note, this is exactly how categorization develops in humans—once babies have a vocabulary and knowledge and word for a specific object, they understand it as belonging to categories of objects, and therefore pay less attention to it; Booth & Waxman, 2002; Mandler et al., 1987).

Justin noted the students did not need to think about this concept of naming philosophically or intellectually. But he encouraged them to let names and terms for things to just soften—instead of just saying "there's the floor," to think about what does it really mean to notice and know something is the floor. He gave them an example: The floor is actually many different things, it is wood, it used to be seeds, it has experienced many different students rehearsing and performing plays. He said, "Don't worry about trying to understand it, give it a softer edge and flow."

Finally, the students were asked to bring awareness of the other people in the space into their own personal engagement. Justin noted the students already knew each other quite well, since they had already spent most of the year together in this class (and this was the advanced class). "See if you can allow more awareness and experiencing of one another that is not tied to the name, what you know about how they want to crystalize their personality or identity." He asked the students to not think about the labels around themselves and each other, and to allow for more beyond those identifiers. He encouraged students to "just see them."

This exercise involved complex and intellectual ideas around conceptual awareness and naming, physical presence and movement, and built over 9 minutes. The students had to use *body awareness* of their own movement and thoughts. They had to *release inhibitions* that they might look strange just walking and noticing, and *be playful* in noticing objects and each other without thinking of words. They had to *imagine* what it would be like to not know the name of something and *envision* all the alternative forms the object or person could take—also an exercise in *be flexible*. And, they had to *think metacognitively* about what they were doing in the moment—keeping the rules in mind. Altogether, a very complex exercise that from the outside just looked like walking around!

In the interview after the class, Justin noted the exercise was getting them primed and calibrated for present moment awareness. It is important to note that Justin started this from the physical, and it even comes after the beginning mantra and physical movement. This mindful walking was something he used in most of his classes, with various levels of complexity depending on the level of the students and how many times previously they had encountered these ideas. Sometimes the students walked as made-up characters they generated in the moment, and sometimes they walked in characters from a scripted work. Other times, as he did here, Justin used this mindful walking as a way to build up the Acting Habits of Mind he felt the students would need for the days' class.

Machine

At The Madeira School in Class 26, we saw the Machine game as an example of multiple Acting Habits of Mind pulled in to one timeless acting exercise. This Generation game is classically used across age groups, from young children to college students, for amateurs in team-building exercises at professional business retreats to first-year conservatory students. It is a true foundational exercise for beginners and for groups just beginning to come together. As described by Viola Spolin (1986; 1999), the founder of improvisational games for the theatre, she notes that it requires spontaneity and energy. She notes too that teachers can and should prompt use of the body, joining in, and taking a risk while coaching (so, *body awareness, think collaboratively, release inhibitions,* and *commit to choices*).

The basic format of the game is that one student steps to the front of the classroom and begins to make a repeating sound and movement: simple, but obvious and easy to maintain for a long time. Then, a second student steps to the front and also begins a repeating noise and movement that is related to the first student, while also adding to the overall picture, verbally and physically. Teacher Kelsey warned students they will have to keep making the movement and sound for a long time until someone else wants to add on. Then a third student, then a fourth, and so on until the entire class is standing at the front, integrated with each other in one large beeping, booping, whirring, and whooshing picture.

Each student has their own small part in the machine scene, repeated over and over, but when they all come together, it makes something larger than any individual part. As it was used at The Madeira School, this game required multiple Acting Habits of Mind, including *body awareness and control*, so the students can physicalize their idea of how to integrate into the whole, *release inhibitions*, as making machine noises and movements is quite silly, *imagine* to create a movement that will work with what they are already seeing onstage, *think collaboratively* to work towards the group goal of a whole machine, and *commit to choices* of a single moment and not trying to do too much. Once the students had all added themselves to the machine and created the whole picture, Kelsey asked them to speed up the functioning of the machine, then to slow it down, requiring the students to work with each other *collaboratively* without speaking about what was going to come next. The game also included Kelsey asking the students as a group to come up with the name of the machine and its function, requiring some *metacognition* about how the whole picture looks and sounds to an audience.

This took 7 minutes of time, during what Kelsey called the "Imagination Game" section of the class—a series of different activities all involving the Generation of new material and the improvisation of words and movements.

The 7 minutes of playing the Machine game was followed up with 3 minutes of Reflection on the game itself and its purpose. Kelsey introduced it as occurring "whenever someone was ready," meaning the students had agency and control over how the game progressed. Critically, Kelsey did not say ahead of time that this was an exercise for *body awareness* or *think collaboratively*. She just introduced the idea of movement and sound, repeatability, and that the students' choices would have to integrate with one another to make a whole machine. The students had fun while doing this, as seen through the smiles on their faces, and volunteered quite quickly to make the machine. The formation of the first machine itself took less than 60 seconds. As Kelsey slowed down and sped up the entire machine, the students began laughing outright (see "A Note on Joy," Chapter 14).

Once they were stopped, Kelsey noted: "So usually I have to try to get people to play with the idea of space. We end up with a machine that's kind of a straight conveyor belt, but you all naturally started to incorporate spatial relationship into yours, which is wonderful." She then had them create a second machine focused not just on space, but also on level. This brought some students to the floor, and some students moving upward with their arms. She asked them to name and discuss the machine's purpose, giving them a moment to *think metacognitively* about what had just happened. In a third iteration, Kelsey had the students come up with the idea of the purpose of the machine before they started—and they chose a time-travel machine. This led to choices with more global movement (a student had to spin in place for several minutes!) and it took longer to put the machine together with all students. After this, she had the students *reflect* purposefully. "Why do 'machine'?" she asked them. The students discussed that the machine required relying on each other, building off each other and teamwork, finding the balance with each other.

She also noted: "The thing that I don't think you realize that you're doing innately, in order to be successful with a machine to find a rhythm and to keep going even when I sped it up and slowed it down . . . you had to do what? Yeah . . . you have to really, truly listen to each other. And I as a scene partner can only react authentically. I'm doing what? . . . Listening to my other [i.e., partner onstage], absolutely." If the students cannot listen to each other, Kelsey noted, the scenes may not match in energy, intensity, relationship, and world between the players onstage. She noted that the Meisner technique, which the students had learned the past week, could be applied here. Breaking of imaginary circumstances happens when actors are not at the same energy levels or intensity, and living truthfully in imaginary circumstances is critical to the performance of the scene. In this way, Kelsey related this supposedly simple game of just movement and sound back to the more complex exercise of understanding interpretation and performance of complex human characters.

This is important to note throughout our classes—even when the students were being asked to do something simple on the surface that did not particularly look like acting per se—the teachers often pointed out explicitly to the students, and sometimes implicitly to us in interviews, that each of the activities was for a purpose. Sometimes that purpose was the integration and practice of a particular Acting Habit of Mind (e.g., a silly game for the express purpose of getting the students to *release inhibitions*, or a trust exercise to get them to *think collaboratively*) that would then be useful for performance of the character. Sometimes that purpose was to get the students warmed up and ready for the work of script analysis that was to come ahead. But no activity in the classroom was wasted. It was all a curriculum to engage the students' attainment of acting skills.

On this day, Kelsey said her goals were achieved by actually doing the activity, and not just talking about it or thinking about it. She noted that the physicalization of the machine and the way in which it forced the students to work together made all the difference for their learning.

Script Ball Toss

Beyond simply reading or performing a script for feedback (as described in Chapter 11), there are other Interpretive exercises teachers used to get students to really understand their characters that involved multiple and iterative Acting Habits of Mind. For example, Juanita in Class 9 at Boston Arts Academy asked her freshman students to practice their lines from a scene while tossing a ball back and forth. At first, this seems to be a very straightforward exercise in memorization. To be able to perform a scene, these students have to know the lines and be able to say them, in order, to each other at the right speed. But it starts to go far deeper as Juanita adds more elements and ideas to the exercise. She asks for *body awareness* when the students are throwing the ball back and forth to each other—that they do so with intention and energy. She tells them to *release inhibitions* and "allow whatever to come out. Because you know what situation you're in and you know why you're in that situation," which also requires them to *consider others*. She corrects several students to push farther and deeper into their understanding of the lines, and to try and *imagine* other ways to say the lines, not to just get stuck in one reading, but to *be flexible* and try their line readings a few different ways.

In the interview for this class, Juanita spoke about giving the students agency and understanding of their own processes and abilities in order to understand their materials and rehearse themselves through the work. She gave them the choice to start over if they needed to start over. This is a combination of *release inhibitions* so they were acting of their own accord, and not just responding to what the teacher was telling them to do, and *commit to choices* so the students would engage with material as they thought it was a good idea to do so.

In a feedback session with a pair, she asked pointedly what the situation and intentions were behind a student's choices, specifically around pauses: "What's happening for you at those times and in those moments? Just allow whatever to come out . . .'cause you know what your situation is, and you know why you're in that situation. Is it you don't want to be disrespectful, or you didn't feel like saying something?" In this way, she is setting up the students to *consider others* in their actions—what is the character thinking and feeling and how can that come out in this exercise? She did not want the students to get stuck in their head or in playwriting mode, presupposing what they were going to react as or what they were thinking in any particular moment. Instead, she wanted them to start acting on impulse. In this exercise, she is actually downplaying a need to *think metacognitively* and preplan, but instead promoting *flexibility* and initiative as they move through a scripted moment. She wants them to be "honestly and actively listening" spontaneously—"stop thinking about should I say this now." Happily, in the second time they did this, they just went forward and did it, and it was much faster. Juanita then came back to *reflect and think metacognitively,* asking students, "What was it like for you the second time around?" They said it was better and freer.

For a second pair, she gave feedback: "Take in what the person is saying, let it land on you and respond to it." This is about careful listening, *consider others*, and *commit to choices*, in that students have to listen, to think and to respond clearly. "Not to what it is to have in your brain to say. Respond first to what is being said to you. You have to 'breathe in' what the other person is saying to you in order to connect your response. You won't look like you're talking to each other, but rather past each other. You have to really listen and respond to what is being said. When you're listening and . . . you're on your voice, it's going to affect your body and your body is going to affect your emotions"—an example of *body awareness*.

She also noted that one actor needed to temper her sass in the scene, because she should not forget to *imagine* that she was in a scene where she could go to prison. So, all the behaviors shown in the scene needed to be in adjustment with the fact that she should not forget she is in a police station and could go to prison. With a fourth pair, she asked about underlying motivations and beliefs from the characters, asking them to *imagine* and *consider others*. She pointed out the difference between hearing something "physically" (as in, the end of the line) versus hearing something and taking it in, listening, and reacting.

This exercise (where, by the way, the ball continued to get tossed around through all of this discussion) also included technical instruction on how quickly lines should be said back and forth. Once she gave that correction, she asked for responses from the group and noted that when they *reflect,* they should think about what happened between the students' connection. "They were responding to each other and they had crazy energy," the students said. Juanita responded, "If you're really listening and really having an exchange and really allowing your attention on the other person . . . then you can receive stuff back, because it's not about you and how you're saying something, your attention is on that person and whatever is happening over there is going to cause something to happen here." Definitionally *consider others.*

She ended with, "Don't be so self-conscious." Let it go—*release inhibitions.* These are freshmen, importantly, so they are new to this combination of script, improvisation, and physical movement, even during this class in March. This means Juanita was still working on eye contact and being on voice with the students, the more physical and technical skills of acting. This exercise was about Interpretation, and perhaps even a form of scene study, but given the additional requirement of passing the ball back and forth, Juanita was able to move it to a sense of fun and playfulness and keep it away from feeling too formal.

DEVELOPMENTAL AND LEVELING TRENDS

Another way in which acting classes are complex is that they are both implicitly and explicitly leveled to the population of the classroom. This includes teacher expectations for the class as a whole, and for individual student levels. For example, there is a necessary difference between a conservatory, where students had to audition to get in and are perhaps preprofessional, and a general education school, in which this is but one of seven classes in the students' days and may be the only acting class they ever take. Where the class is in the academic year's trajectory also matters, as do the inputs of the students themselves, which serve as a feedback loop to prompt more teacher engagement on various aspects of the class and skill development.

In general, we saw differences between schools based on the type of school, and we saw leveling within schools based on the level of the students in the classroom (that is, age and years in the school). We also saw differences based on the part of the year we filmed in. We both filmed in the fall, the beginning of the academic year, when students were just coming together and getting to know each other, and in the spring when students had been together for a long time and knew each other and the requirements of the tasks at hand quite well. We filmed freshman and students in their first year of conservatory, where they were just getting to various acting techniques and learning about theory and practice of those techniques, and we filmed juniors and seniors, where students had enough experience in improvisation and interpretation of characters that they were performing full scenes with only minimal instruction and prompting. We also saw differences between our conservatory schools where the students were majoring in theatre, our public general education school, where theatre was one of many classes they took in their day, and our private school, where they were not necessarily majoring in theatre, but they were spending a significant block of time in a very small (six-person) theatre class every day.

However, the differences were significantly smaller than the similarities. We saw the eight Acting Habits of Mind across four types of activities in every single school. We saw similar exercises, teaching techniques, and student engagement. To make sure, my research assistants took notes on every class filmed, specifically on student receptiveness to teachers and general comments on the overall scope of class. Despite class levels and type, we saw the teachers as warm, caring, open, and friendly. The students were relaxed and had a good rapport with the teacher. In general, when the teacher asked for quiet, attention, respect, and calm, they got it, and quickly.

Students were observed to be "on task" even when the teacher was focused on other students; research assistants noted the students were "really into performances" and "willing to respond" to teacher questions. There was mutual respect between teacher and students, where even a look from the teacher could get the students to calm down and come back to task. Students called the teacher by their first name, talking to them about the problems in their lives. Most of the teachers had a call-and-response system with the class, often with a silly movement, so that the students knew when it was time to come back to group.

There was group cohesion, particularly in the classes filmed later in academic years (e.g., March) than earlier in school years (e.g., early October). The students knew the group activities and the group warms-ups, even early in the year, and both enjoyed doing those warm-ups (as evidenced by smiles and full engagement) and often asked to lead the warm-ups (particularly in our advanced conservatory students). We saw strong bonds between the teachers and students, where they were modeling silliness, joking, emotional honesty, and closeness.

For within school leveling, in the Boston Arts Academy classrooms, there were distinct differences between warm-up in the freshman class (e.g., Class 9) where Juanita walked around and corrected a preset physical set of movements, and the seniors, who were able to do this for themselves. Similarly, the younger group filmed at Imagination Stage had Nikki leading warm-up, while the older group was able to lead themselves.

The students' abilities to give feedback, critique, and engage with the Acting Habit of Mind of *reflect and think metacognitively* also became more automatic, more trained, and more complex over time. At Imagination Stage, for example, we filmed a few classes in October and November of 2017, and then one class of the same group in March 2018. In that March 2018 class, as described in the animal envisioning example in both Chapter 8 and Chapter 12, when Nikki asked for feedback, she did not need to explain or describe the kind of feedback she wanted. Instead, the students began automatically with what they observed, perceptually saw, whether it worked, and how they thought about it. This was not the same in the earlier classes for this school (such as Class 1), where Nikki had to prompt the students to focus first and only on what they observed and what they saw. Then, she would prompt on what they liked.

Similarly, in our four levels of class at Boston Arts Academy, there was a true distinction among the levels for the complexity of their feedback. We filmed in March 2018 and May 2018. Particularly for the seniors, the classes we filmed in May 2018 were only 2 weeks before they finished high school and moved on to college or the professional world. Their classes in these days were focused on full-scene performance, and Reflection on their performance, as can be seen in the notes on *reflect and think metacognitively* in the Interpretation section of the class. In earlier levels, the students were hesitant and vague in their feedback. In later levels, they had specifics and notes about themselves when they watched their videos.

We saw different approaches to classical work, particularly Shakespeare, across our different schools and levels. Yet even for Shakespeare, these were not as different as one might think, given the wide variety of classrooms. At The Madeira School, the students were working on Shakespearean monologues and dialogues, with Kelsey focusing on both the actual scansion of the words and how to say the poetry, and how to define and use the poetry to understand the intentions and desires of the characters. At Boston Arts Academy, the students focused on how to connect Shakespearean language and lines to their own lives, to create magic "as if" emotional scenarios for themselves to play out using words that felt foreign. In Humboldt County, Steve led his classes through discussions and worksheets about the contexts for their Shakespearean characters, including social status, jobs, and cultural and community context to set up why and how the characters said their particular lines. Across all of these schools, the focus was on getting into and under the lines to why the characters were saying what they were saying, putting those intentions, beliefs, desires, and emotions into the context of the play, and then connecting them to the realities of the students. You could have, with relative ease, put each student into a different classroom and they would likely be able to pick up on the teacher's questions and exercises quickly!

While Shakespeare was unsurprisingly seen across multiple districts and schools (both because he is considered the central figure to the canon of Western theatre and because his work is free of copyright and licensing requirements), teachers were not beholden to one kind of playwright. This is where the individual contexts and populations of the schools seemed to make a real difference. At Boston Arts Academy, where the majority of the students are Black and Hispanic and the free and reduced lunch rate (a measure of student poverty levels) is 47%, the works they performed dealt with issues such as racism, moving out of public housing, and dealing with the police. At Imagination Stage, which pulls from a relatively affluent area and has only a few students of color in their conservatory program, they had a range of works across modern plays set in high school, Ancient Greek work, and classic American theatre. In one of the performances we saw at Eureka High School, Justin had asked students to put together almost 30 minutes of material based in their favorite quotes and lyrics from books and songs, relating them back to their own lives as adolescents in middle America. In this way, teachers were able to be responsible and flexible in what they asked of their students and what kinds of materials they wanted their students to work on and think about. The scaffolding of class was the same, but the content they filled it in with was individualized.

Call for Future Research

Because we went to many different types of high schools with many different types of students across the United States, I feel confident that the Acting Habits of Mind are evident in almost every theatrical context, and can be combined to accomplish acting different goals for many different perspectives. However, expanding into pre-K or K–8 school experiences, as well as into acting classes for adults, to see how the Acting Habits of Mind occur in classrooms and theaters is an area for future research.

ACTING CLASS COMPLEXITY, IN SUMMARY

- What does it mean that acting classes are so complex? It means educators and policymakers must be aware and careful when making claims, when thinking about research, and when developing curriculum.
- While the psychological foundations of acting classes are cross-cutting, application and content can, and should, vary widely.
- Acting classes are not just collections of individual exercises where an Acting Habit of Mind is taught and used, then another, and then another. Students are dealing with many different components of an acting class simultaneously. They are working with multiple skills iteratively over time in the class itself.
- While the teachers had ideas of leveling, and we saw clear progression over the course of the year, it is in the holistic complexity that acting classes make their space.

CHAPTER 13

Goals and Contexts

Where the Acting Habits of Mind Can Be Applied Outside of a Traditional Acting Classroom

In the previous chapters, I have shown how the Acting Habits of Mind are connected to a number of different scientific findings from developmental psychology, social psychology, and neuroscience. The question that follows is when and how the Acting Habits of Mind move from use *inside* the acting classroom to abilities *outside* the acting classroom? That is, how might the Acting Habits of Mind transfer?

In this chapter, I will focus on what makes theater spaces conducive for transferrable learning, how the Acting Habits of Mind combine to serve and foster larger psychological needs and skills such as creativity and emotional intelligence, and how the Acting Habits of Mind can be used outside of the acting classroom for active learning, cultural competency, and joy.

Importantly, acting for acting's sake is a valuable and highly important goal itself. The aesthetic performance of theatre is itself inherently worthy of time, attention, funding, and promotion. Theatre teachers are not segmenting their class or focusing on a particular Acting Habit of Mind for transfer to any other kind of activity or Habit of Mind outside of acting class. Teachers are teaching to make the best actors they possibly can, and to see how far they can take their students into the world of theatre.

This focus on acting first, and outcome later (if at all), can be seen pretty clearly when we actually ask a large sample ($N = 173$) of acting teachers what they think is happening in acting classes, psychologically, and what external skills they think are being trained. In a previously published survey, we gave teachers a list of 28 possible outcomes of acting classes, and 27 possible classroom activities that could be causing change. We found universally high endorsement of activities as disparate as "speed-through," "role play games," and "relaxation/breathing" as positively affecting outcomes of "collaboration," "self-esteem," and "paying attention" (Goldstein et al., 2020). Teachers believe their art form to be important broadly, and holistically.

Thus, not to undercut acting for acting's sake, but to best understand theatre's potential and purpose, knowing where and how the Acting Habits of Mind learned and practiced in acting classes can serve students outside of acting classes can add value. This understanding and possibility for transfer can be a cornerstone for advocacy, and provide a deeper understanding into the intrinsic value of engagement in theatre as a teenager. I am not necessarily claiming a causal role of acting classes right now (i.e., taking an acting class will cause you to become more creative or have higher empathy), although there is evidence to suggest that such relationships exist. Instead, I am interested in building theories of connection between the Acting Habits of Mind, which are actually taught in acting classes, and psychological skills closely related in type, underlying neurological structure, and relevance. The beginning of these connections is built out in Chapters 3–10. For this chapter, I will start theorizing how the Acting Habits of Mind might be connected to more complex psychological skills and abilities, and then how acting classes and exercises could be used as interventions and training.

CONTAINMENT AND EMBODIMENT

What the acting classroom brings that makes it a particularly conducive place for building targeted interventions and psychological skills, regardless of how explicit that goal is, is the fact that at its core, acting is an *embodied* and *contained* activity (Goldstein & Hayes, 2022). It is this combination of frames for the acting classroom that can make it a place for the practice and ultimately the transfer from Acting Habits of Mind to other psychological skills.

Containment

The theatre space in our data was always set up to be unique and separated from the rest of the academic environment. This meant the students got to work with each other outside of the ways the rest of the school day required them to behave. This, I believe, is one of the functions of the Preparation warm-up and Reflection periods for the students. Starting each class with either a moment of warm-up or a moment of contemplation (39 out of 40 classes started with either Reflection or Preparation) separated acting class time from the rest of the activities of the day. Warm-up periods served dual purpose: they both allowed the students to prepare their bodies and minds for the work ahead, and allowed them to separate out, physically, the way they had been engaging with their day from the way they were about to be asked to engage with their day.

Reflection periods did this too for the students—it enabled them to separate out what they had just gone through during the work of the acting classroom from what they were returning to in the rest of their lives. As we saw in several classes and classrooms, the teachers often asked for Reflection about something that had happened in the past week that went well or poorly, or what they thought about the coming of COVID-19. This put a bit of separation between the student in regular moments of their lives, and the student in their acting class. Similarly, having a moment of Reflection at the end of the class for the students served to cap the experience of the classroom (25 of 40 classes ended with formal Reflection, even if just a closing ritual sentence said together). Instead of rushing into the next time period while still discussing the active experience of the last moments of the last class, students could take the whole experience, put a final *reflective* note on it, and then move on, separated from what just happened.

These small rituals allow the students to separate what is part of theatre class, and what is not part of theatre class, and engage fully in the present moment. Similarly, many practices that require full, mindful attention such as religious ceremonies and meditation contain moments to separate them from the everyday (Salamone, 2004). This can create a contained space for the theatre classroom, where students can take risks, express themselves fully, and join into the groups' goals and activities.

Call for Future Research

A contained space can be thought of as both physical and psychological in theatre (Lutterbie, 2001), and has been theorized by theatre scholars as a place to make meaning and engage in risky creativity (Hunter, 2008; Sloan, 2018). This is similar to how written fiction has been conceptualized as a safe space for practicing negative emotions in readers (Harris, 2000; Mar & Oatley, 2008), and how a therapy room is conceptualized as a safe container for patients to express themselves (Maliphant & Horner, 2016; Reynolds et al., 2006). How students and teachers see this idea of containment, however, is yet to be discovered (so many ideas for future research).

Embodiment

In addition to this contained separateness of acting class from the rest of the world, theatre is embodied in multiple ways. This is central to the Acting Habit of Mind of *body awareness* (Chapter 3), of course, because acting is a physical act, but more importantly, all of the elements students are learning in acting classes lead them back to physicalization in their own bodies. The students throughout the classes had a chance to try on different words, different roles, different emotions and backgrounds, personalities and temperaments, and see how each of these felt, physically, in their bodies. It was not just a theoretical exercise or academic study the students were engaging in. Instead, it was a physicalized, embodied form of interacting with the materials, both scripted and improvised. Some classes had a chunk of sitting, and some had no sitting, but not a single class in our sample had students sitting passively and listening to a teacher lecturing for the full class time. The sitting was always temporary, and always related back to a part of the class that was embodied.

This embodiment allows for a type of understanding students may not get as much of in other areas of their academic experiences. Traditional academic classes involve some amount of reading while sitting, or listening to and watching a teacher while sitting. There are notable exceptions of course—physical education classes are about the education of form and abilities in movement and sports. Many science classes such as chemistry, physics, and biology involve lab components, where the students get to engage physically with the chemicals or materials of the science and try their own preset experiments. As a note, this is both a positive and a negative of many science classrooms moving into virtual and computerized experiments. Students get to have individualized and singular experiences with experiments, and particularly in rural or impoverished schools they get to have experiences they might not otherwise get to have. However, as a negative, when everything happens virtually on the computer, the students might be missing out on important deeper embodied cognition focused ways of learning in the classroom.

In the acting classroom, the actual act of acting onstage is embodied, and therefore the learning and practice of acting is also embodied. The safety of the contained classroom that we saw over and over again, combined with the embodied practice of new experiences over and over again, where the Acting Habits of Mind are called upon, used, and integrated, means students' learning may be more sticky and deeper than nonactive learning. We know that active learning is best for all humans, child and adult (see below). Acting classes are definitionally active learning, in the safety of an ensemble space. Therefore, particularly as the task of acting classes is often engaging with emotions, creating something new, physicalizing inner experiences, and engaging with cultures and contexts that are not part of the students' everyday lives, it may be a particularly potent learning environment that reaches out into other areas.

Taken together, providing students with spaces that are contained, away from the rigors and pressures of their "normal" lives, and that are embodied and physicalized, allowing for practice and safe enactment of a variety of emotions and mental states, is likely critical for any learning in one space to transfer to learning in another space. Consistent across our classrooms was that teachers also enabled the spaces to be ones of community and trust.

The Acting Habits of Mind of *think collaboratively* and *consider others* encouraged the students to engage with each other from a place of care and safety. The Acting Habit of Mind *release inhibitions* encouraged students to engage authentically and without blocks.

EMOTIONAL INTELLIGENCE

As discussed in Chapter 3, *body awareness and control* are linked to emotional knowledge and understanding in the self. And as discussed in Chapters 6 and 7, *consider others* and *think collaboratively* are connected to psychological constructs of understanding others such as theory of mind, empathy, and communication. When you put these psychological skills and abilities together, you get something broader, what has often been deemed emotional intelligence (EI).

EI has been a source of much public (Goleman, 1995) and scholarly (Pool & Qualter, 2018) work, and has been tied to such disparate areas as academic performance (MacCann et al., 2020), health (Martins et al., 2010), work attitudes (Miao et al., 2017), job performance (O'Boyle et al., 2011), and romantic satisfaction (Jardine et al., 2022). In adolescents, regardless of how it is measured, emotional intelligence is highly correlated with feelings of well-being (Llamas-Díaz et al., 2022). Popular articles have discussed connections between emotional intelligence and acting, but as far as I know, no systematic research has actually found a connection between emotional intelligence and acting training. When teachers are interviewed about what they think acting does for their students, they are often quick to point out emotional control, awareness, regulation, all general aspects of emotional intelligence (Goldstein et al., 2020). And, as mentioned across a few chapters, emotions as a psychological area of study are where many of the scientific studies on acting have focused. We have found emotional outcomes—it is not that they never pop up in research. However, the findings are relatively inconsistent, and depend a lot of on the population being studied, the method of the study itself, and the ways in which the emotional outcome under study is actually measured (looking back at Table I.1 in the Introduction shows this range even just within high schools and adolescent acting populations).

Surprisingly, one thing we did not see a lot of in our classes was direct and purposeful discussions of emotions themselves! There was one exercise in one classroom at Eureka High School in St. Louis where Justin had the students enact different emotions through the word "Jabberwocky," where they had to express the emotions given to them in an improv. Across other classrooms, there were many pointed questions about what characters wanted and needed and were trying to do in scenes that sometimes led to discussions about the emotions of the characters, but often focused more on the mental states and social dynamics of the character.

Occasionally, there was also discussion of tension in scenes as an emotional state to induce in the audience to get them to pay attention. But rare was the discussion with the students that talked about the character being "happy" or "furious," or the way to act being "fearful" or "depressed." This is particularly interesting given the lore of Method acting in the United States. Often maligned but also the point of much fascination, "The Method" proposes that the way to true acting is to use the emotions of your life, the highs and lows, to learn about and then recreate the emotions of your character to therefore ring true to the audience. Our teachers were not focused on tapping into difficult emotions in students and then forcing them to relive those outwardly (a source of possible trauma and harm in acting training; Gross, 1982; Seton, 2010). Instead, our teachers asked students to deal with their own emotions and the emotions of characters cognitively through thinking about reasons, situations, and contexts, through being purposeful about their own body's role in the performance of such states, and through mindfully imagining possibilities, trying out options, and thoughtfully making choices.

In other types of classrooms, higher levels of emotional intelligence in teachers are predictive of better discipline and management of classrooms (Valente et al., 2019) and lower levels of burnout (Mérida-López & Extremera, 2017). In preschool populations, we know teachers are incredibly important when it comes to the emotion socialization of their students (Denham et al., 2012). Teachers set the emotional tone for a classroom, and by modeling the healthy regulation of emotions through naming them, talking about them, and physical techniques such as breathing, students can pick up and learn positive emotion-regulation strategies (Fatahi et al., 2022). Our acting teachers modeled meditation techniques, active listening of the students, careful reaction to their performances, and open, friendly teaching. This kind of emotion modeling, separate even from the teaching of acting, could serve as a model for other kinds of classrooms.

While instances of a harsher tone did occur, they were extremely rare, and mostly teachers used call-and-response classroom management. At Boston Arts Academy, the teachers would call "T2" and the students would respond "T-Unit" and then be quiet. At Imagination Stage, the call-and-response was "and a hush falls over the crowd." And the students responded, "HUSH." In fact, in several classrooms, we never saw the teacher have to call for attention more than once—the students were attuned and emotionally responsive to teachers in a way that mimicked the teacher's emotional responsiveness to them. This connection, not just the actual behaviors of the students in an acting class, could also lead to a variety of positive outcomes in the domain of emotional intelligence.

CALL FOR FUTURE RESEARCH ON EI

Going forward, teachers and researchers interested in how emotional knowledge, understanding, and control are related to acting training would do well to think carefully about acting exercises under study, the kind of outcomes of interest within emotional intelligence, and the ways that the acting classroom and teachers work. Different kinds of acting training and activities are likely to affect the different elements of emotional intelligence under certain conditions and contexts. Emotions are necessary for learning across domain (Meyer & Turner, 2006), but in the performance of human contexts and situations onstage, they are particularly central. While not discussed centrally in acting classes, they are cognitized, physicalized, and inherent in teaching acting.

The combination of cognitizing, embodiment, and teacher modeling that occurs in acting classes is something to study in the future. This is especially true for the kind of modeling and reacting teachers are doing implicitly. It is my hope that with the specificities of Acting Habits of Mind, research moving forward will be able to isolate acting experiences as a whole, and emotional intelligence as a whole, from individual exercises and the underlying skills of EI. This could lead to advances in interventions based on acting, as well as using elements from acting classes such as containment to advance other types of integrated interdisciplinary work.

THE CREATIVE PROCESS

While creativity is often thought of as just coming up with a lot of ideas in a short amount of time, it is actually more complex and active than a single brainstorming session. From western philosophy to modern business psychology, a long history of scientific research shows there is a fairly standard creative process involving a number of steps that lead to creative outputs. While these stages often iterate and improvise on one another (Sawyer, 2021), there is a general path one can point to when thinking about the creative process (Sawyer, 2011). Unsurprisingly, the Acting Habits of Mind and activities of acting class are well-suited to the creative process as a whole. As delineated by Keith Sawyer, and with my commentary on connections to acting classes, there are eight steps of the creative process:

1. First, and often considered most important, a person who wants to be creative needs to figure out exactly what the prompt or problem is that they want to solve. By *defining/finding the problem* in a firm way, the person knows exactly what kind of creativity they need to

engage in. In acting, this can be given by the script, the director, or the rules of an improvisation game.

2. Next, the creative person needs to *acquire the knowledge* they need to solve the problem. Teachers are consistently relating the Acting Habits of Mind to connections across areas of class. They are explicitly teaching students how to move from warm-ups and workouts to exercises and games to script analyses and performance, modeling the transfer of knowledge into a creative process. Any activity that is not the performance of scene study or Reflection can be seen as acquiring the knowledge.
3. The next step in the creative process is to *gather related information,* bringing in information that may not be directly related to the creative problem at hand, but is related to other versions of other problems. Again, in acting classes, students are engaged in wide varieties of ideas, exercises, and tasks, all requiring a set of Acting Habits of Mind that can be broadly applied. This allows for students to transfer and understand that a broad set of ideas can be brought to bear on one task.
4. Next is *incubation*—also sometimes called rest, or fun, or distraction! Here, the connection to the playfulness of acting, perhaps in silly warm-ups to meditative rest moments, can be seen.
5. Next, *generating ideas* is exactly what we see in the acting exercises that call upon and integrate the Acting Habit of Mind of *be flexible*, and almost every activity in the Generation section of class. This involves the creative person coming up with as many different responses to the question or prompt (from step 1) as they can.
6. After generating ideas comes *combining ideas* that are creative, and coming up with metaphors and new iterations of original ideas. This still involves *be flexible* in releasing any sense of fixedness or rigidity to original choices.
7. Next, *selecting an idea* is exactly what students are learning to do when they *commit to choices.* Students have to make a singular choice, as we see our teachers tell them repeatedly. Even if the choice does not work or is missing an element, making a choice and trying it out is a critical component of allowing the creative process to continue. This is also where many of the activities seen in the Interpretation section of class can be useful.
8. Last, *externalizing the ideas* is where we might see *body awareness* and expression in performance, but is definitely reliant on the skills built by *reflect and think metacognitively* and the activities in the Reflection period of class. Once a choice is externalized and a creative solution proposed and implemented, then the creative person can begin to make decisions about whether it works, how it works, and what might need to be changed.

CALL FOR FUTURE RESEARCH ON CREATIVITY

Teaching students the creative process while engaging in acting classes could provide a strong and transferrable model to the creative process in other domains, as it is theorized as the same process regardless of domain. While this transfer of knowledge would need to be made explicit and purposeful for students to best see its wide applicability (Perkins & Salomon, 1992; Sala & Gobet, 2017; Woodworth & Thorndike, 1901), making knowledge generalizable about the creative process could see broad and positive effects, as for these students, "Fundamental to living in the conceptual age will be the use of creativity" (Warner & Myers, 2009, p. 29).

In addition to the characteristics of containment and embodiment, and the complex psychological outcomes of emotional intelligence and creativity, acting classrooms and the Acting Habits of Mind hold two other potentially generalizable applications: active learning and cultural competencies.

ACTIVE LEARNING

Its inherent physicalized and engaged manner allows the theatre classroom to be a model for how to structure classrooms in non-arts subject areas. A significant portion of the acting classroom is active, meaning the students are not just sitting and listening to a teacher lecture, or filing out responsive worksheets. Scene study, of course, is a fully active engagement with material, and so are all the warm-ups and Generative activities. Students are only passive in moments of theoretical Preparation (e.g., when learning about the concept of an "objective" or when watching a film to get an example of physical change), and in moments of Reflection, when they are discussing and critiquing their own and others' performances. Otherwise, acting classes are very experiential.

While many classrooms and schools have begun to move toward a flipped classroom model, where students spend classroom time in discussion and practice problems, and then homework is to watch a lecture or read, theatre can still be held up as an exemplar and model classroom for active engagement with material. In the same way a chemistry lab requires students to replicate experiments with known endings in set stages, our theatre teachers assigned students to perform known roles and a classical canon of plays so they can explore, under constrained and known outcomes, how to figure out the inner lives of characters, turn that into personal choices, and perform the embodied actions.

Case-based learning, project-based learning, and other forms of direct engagement with material is proposed to lead to higher levels of transfer of knowledge—that is, higher levels of the information learned through the active engagement being applied to other scenarios and in other contexts (Kolodner et al., 2003; Perkins & Salomon, 1992). This can include students engaging in designing their own scientific experiments, working in groups on a question in history class by designing a museum exhibition, or building physical models of the rotations of the solar system by choreographing a dance. Theoretically, these experiences should lead to more productive reasoning, better interpretation and encoding of the necessary material and thus better access and learning in other contexts, and the ability to use feedback to apply information in other domains and across problems. By both doing and reflecting, active learning promotes deeper engagement. However, this is not automatic (Hodges, 2020). Teachers have to be trained in active learning experiences (Beatty et al., 2006), understand group dynamic in their classrooms (Johnson & Johnson, 1999), and enhancing cognitive engagement (Chi & Wylie, 2014). In adolescents, promoting collaborative goals in particular can help with academic and peer achievement (Roseth et al., 2008).

Our classes were full of active learning that promoted student autonomy and engagement. In Class 2, Jewel at one point says, "She's got to find it, not you," and tells the audience of other students they have to let the student currently performing her monologue discover stuff on her own. She also notes to another student who is embarrassed by her performance of someone with a mega crush that losing their minds over another person is something "everybody feels . . . at some point, they just express it differently. And it came out of you, so somewhere in you is a person who can feel this way." She notes to the audience of students that even though the performer had their back to the audience (bad form as an actor), it was about getting to the physicalized emotional reality first and then setting it for the audience. "If you do not have embodied emotional reality first, it will not work." This type of autonomy has been shown in theatre classrooms and visual arts classes, informed by teacher practices (Sheridan et al., 2022), as allowing students to own their learning process.

Using theatrical exercises and techniques in other types of academic classrooms is already a well-established form of integrated teaching, called "drama-based pedagogies" (DBP). DBP is a well-researched and well-developed form of arts integration that has taken elements of theatre experiences (such as taking on roles or determining a singular pose or *tableau* to represent a complex idea) and integrated them into other types of classrooms (Dawson & Lee, 2018). Meta-analyses (i.e., statistical studies of studies) have shown that drama-based pedagogies have significant positive effects on children's creative thinking (Lee et al., 2015), particularly when the DBP is led by a classroom teacher. This means that a teacher can use the techniques of drama in their classroom as effectively as a trained actor! The key to

DBP is that they get students physically active and engaging with their tasks actively, whether they are engaging with drama content or topics as varied as social studies, geometry, or social–emotional learning. Integrating purposeful thinking about the Acting Habits of Mind while engaging with the well-established exercises of drama-based pedagogy may be an additional productive way to look for certain outcomes (such as creative thinking or emotion regulation) going forward.

CULTURAL COMPETENCIES AND GIVING VOICE

Another area where the Acting Habits of Mind can be used across domains is wherever teachers and students need to purposefully give voice to those who may not have a voice, and work toward cultural competency when engaging with students. In the clinical therapy literature, having a culturally responsive therapeutic practice means being able to perform the tasks of therapeutic interventions in such a way that cultural mechanisms and sources of distress and healing are handled with appreciation, understanding respect for cultural differences, as well as adaptation of therapy for culturally unique needs (Rober & De Haene, 2014; Sue, 2003). In education, cultural competence is not just the purview of individual teachers, but also of schools, school districts, and curriculum plans (Bazron et al., 2005; Khalifa et al., 2016). Teachers need to keep in mind their communication norms with students and be purposeful about knowing how students' backgrounds may affect their understanding and engagement with material, as well as their own cultural blind spots and assumptions based on their own backgrounds (le Roux, 2002).

From a theatre perspective, much like with drama-based pedagogies and active learning, there is a wealth of knowledge from previous theatre-adjacent practices. In this case, Theatre of the Oppressed (Boal & McBride, 2015) is a form of community-based, improvisational theatre experience that helps people find their voices and act out issues in their community that need attention and time. The goal is to help the actor/community members to try and find solutions for themselves. These experiences center people who may not otherwise have a chance to speak about their lives, and provide a formal format for groups to give everyone an equal say on an issue.

One way in which the Acting Habits of Mind could have a real impact outside of theaters' walls is to both use the tools of Theatre of the Oppressed and keep in mind the goals of the Acting Habits of Mind when creating experiences for students across classrooms. Here, thinking about creating a space where students can trust themselves, *release inhibitions, be playful,* and *be flexible*, where they can make mistakes and *reflect* without suffering negative consequences, will allow for space to engage, perhaps, with difficult topics. Similarly, thinking about giving that space and voice will allow teachers and others with power over students to take a step back and allow students to show their own cultural perspectives. This requires care and careful training to ensure that teachers are knowledgeable enough to allow students to try on topics and characters that may provide discomfort. A teacher in these situations can cause harm in the same way a parent can, if they cut a student off, or deny their reality. But a positive influence can change a student's life.

A NOTE ON JOY

In this chapter, I have focused on a variety of purposeful goals and contexts that bring in the real-world applications of theatre classes: the sense of embodiment and containment that allows for learning, possible gains in emotional intelligence and creativity through the combination of multiple Acting Habits of Mind, and the ability of theatre classrooms to model applied learning and cultural competencies. But I want to end on a much simpler note:

Theatre is fun.

It is! The students are laughing, being silly. (Sometimes the teacher has to work at bringing back focus). The students are volunteering to be first in line. They are focusing in on the problems and materials of the class. Joy is not to be underestimated. In psychological discussions of well-being and thriving that fill workplaces, schools, college campuses, clinical psychology, and social media, there is often discussion of how moments of pleasure and joy should be sought and savored to lead to higher overall levels of well-being (Bryant & Veroff, 2007; Jose et al., 2012). Well-being and thriving are not just the absence of fear or negative emotions—negative emotions are unavoidable and may be necessary for a full and complete life. But the theatre space allows students to think about fear or negativity in their lives with a sense of separateness. And theatre allows for joy and play, both of which are critically important for development, fullness, and well-being. In addition, the sense of being in the moment and fully engaged in performance is a flow experience, which is both intrinsically motivating and related to both better cognitive processing and positive emotions (Csikszentmihalyi, 2013). Moving forward, I encourage all teachers, students, actors, scholars, and advocates to never forget the importance of fun and joy that can come through in the theatre.

* * *

Now that we have undertaken the Acting Habits of Mind in science, the Acting Habits of Mind in the acting classroom, and the Acting Habits of Mind outside of the classroom, where should the future of acting classes and research on such classes look? How can we be responsive to both the realities of our students and the standards of our curriculum? How can we be culturally relevant and sensitive, inclusive, and celebratory of differences? I offer suggestions in our final chapter.

CHAPTER 14

The Future of Acting Classes and Research

Knowing the Acting Habits of Mind, Where Should Research, Advocacy, and Curriculum Go?

Over the last 13 chapters, we have learned about the Acting Habits of Mind, how they connect to basic (and complex) scientific understanding of human psychology, and how they can combine, interact, be used, fostered, and integrated into the very real world of acting classes in all their complexity and requirements. In this chapter, I ask the questions: What did we learn, and what do we still need to know?

We learned that even though many think acting classes are about empathy and emotional understanding, the reality is both more complex and more fundamental than that. Acting classes are about bodies and their movements, thinking about your own flexibility, and thinking about others' mental states, emotional states, and needs. And acting classes are about thinking about thinking (*metacognitively*). What did you do, what did you mean to do, how did it go, and what can you do differently?

As we see throughout the Acting Habits of Mind chapters and their scientific connections, much of the work in drama and theatre education outcomes has focused on language and social and emotional outcomes. Without direct measurement, there are another large set of scientific constructs that are readily apparent in their connections to theatre. Taking our acting classes from the ground up and focusing in on what psychological skills and frameworks and mindsets are being used in the classes themselves, we saw almost no explicit or implicit language lessons, and very little engagement directly with emotional states. Students were instead asked often to think and think deeply about the reasons why characters did what they did and what their behaviors meant. In this way, it is explicit training for thinking about the mental and emotional states of others. Students then have to use these skills implicitly in their collaboration with others, and think about how they fit into the group and into the classroom. Students have to use language of course, constantly in acting classes. They have to use the scripts and deep analyses of the scripts to determine what is happening in scenes. They have to be able to talk about and discuss characters, and they have to think through multiple options and choices and choose the best one. Yet much of acting class is also nonverbal, about the movement and projection of the body, and in particular about getting comfortable and knowing your own body well. This leaves open the door for a new direction for theatre education research and the effects of acting training, tied to the Acting Habits of Mind integrated and used in the classes.

THE CONTRADICTIONS OF LEARNING TO ACT

One element that has come up repeatedly is the complexity of learning how to act and the repeated psychological contradictions that acting asks of its students. There is a contradiction in *commit to choices* and *be flexible*. There is a contradiction in *release inhibitions* for the self and *consider others'* thoughts and opinions. There is a contradiction in *think collaboratively* and *envision* for yourself. Yet in those contradictions is how an actor learns to find different balances for each character. An actor cannot portray each character and each action they go through in the same way. Actors need to have a flexible tool kit to apply these thoughts and ways of performing and reacting regardless of where, when, and how they are doing their work.

Acting classes involve all of the Acting Habits of Mind used together and separately, to build more than each of their component parts. For each level of an acting class, it is possible to go into more depth and more complexity. For each run-through of a script, more analyses can be done, and the student can be pushed farther in their thinking about intentions, bodily movements, expressions, and alternative possibilities.

Critically, both theatrical plays and acting exercises deal with difficult emotions and situations that have to be processed in the self and simultaneously with others. This requires the care of teachers to set up an environment that is safe and respectful. The students must learn how to not do harm to each other, and the teachers must take care not to do harm to the actors. There are discussions and stories in the theatre literature of actors being harmed by teachers that did not take care with the emotions and the *release of inhibitions* that occur in acting classes and are central to performing. Avoiding harm is necessary in the contradiction that actors are both dealing with sensitivity and performing it for others.

This includes harm around multiple vulnerabilities. Racism and historically white and misogynistic practices, the canon of white male authors, trauma and abuse, consent and the physical nature of many scenes, and awareness of mental health are all areas for care. Being purposeful and conscientious about best practices, modeling safety, bringing in outside experts when possible, and maintaining open and autonomy promoting lines of communication with students will begin to heal previous harms. The academic and professional training standards put forward as demands by We See You White American Theatre (https://www.weseeyouwat.com/demands) are a strong place to start, and include centering antiracism as a core value, mentoring from an ethnocultural perspective, diversifying adjudication panels, creating space for the hiring of guest artists of color, and not just for plays that deal with racial and social justice issues, but across the canon, and transparency around hiring and retention practices for faculty to ensure equity. Theatre education cannot move forward into wellbeing and health without attention paid to healing and reconciliation with the past.

ACTING CLASSES AS HOLISTIC LEARNING EXPERIENCES

While holding contradictions and best practices in mind, taking acting classes as holistic and flexible leaning experiences will provide the best possibilities for research and advocacy on behalf of theatre moving forward. Once again, the flexible toolbox is the key here.

As noted in Chapter 12, it is the complexity and the richness in the holistic nature of acting classes that makes them so unique. Yet it also makes it particularly difficult for researchers who are looking to isolate the mechanistic, causal moments in acting classes that lead to outcomes. Similarly, it makes it particularly difficult for educational or psychological interventionists who want to cause change for people using theatre in general. The specificity of the goal is key, but so is the flexibility within the acting class itself to be specific to who you are working with, and what backgrounds, experiences, and social identities they hold.

Inherent in the idea of full learning experiences is that "holistic" is key to theatre. Although the theatre classroom has not suffered the same fate as other classrooms, with the idea of a standardized test taking over and giving minimum competencies for theatre experiences, the Acting Habits of Mind are not set psychological skills that can be pigeonholed into singular testable skills. While there are requisite psychological abilities inherent in each one, acting classes are a whole, with all the component parts. Breaking those component parts may be helpful in thinking about outcomes, but at some point, such an activity will stop being theatre. The way in which theatre allows for the fullness of experience is critical to its importance in so many students' lives.

THEATRE AS A FLEXIBLE TOOL KIT

As discussed in Chapter 13, the combination of Acting Habits of Mind and activity type takes a different form in each classroom even for the very same exercise. While acting teachers all use a similar kind of broad scaffolding, the specific exercises, ideas, psychological perspectives, and aspirations are highly flexible—differing by context, teacher, and population (keeping in mind curricular standards, of course). This can also be seen in Chapter 12, in the discussion of how theatrical thinking and the Acting Habits of Mind can be combined for various psychological skills, but also used across other types of classrooms and in various environments with many different kinds of students and people.

This flexibility is why theatre holds the potential to change the lives of so many different kinds of people and why no two theatrical productions—even of the same show and with similar casts—can be the same. Teachers can create and change exercises depending on how and when they think they will be most appropriate for use. Noting how each of the Acting Habits of Mind appears in each of the content areas of classes shows us just how broad the world of theatre education can and should be considered!

THE FUTURE (RESEARCH AND OTHERWISE)

Many questions remain, including:

1. What kinds of activities within theatre classrooms are associated with what kinds of outcomes?
2. Where within outcomes of interest such as social skills or empathy is acting class most effective at opening the door for growth or change?
3. When in development are acting classes most effective, and how do the effects of acting classes change across development?
4. How do the different contexts of acting classes matter for psychological changes?

Where does the discovery of the Acting Habits of Mind and related concepts leave us going forward? I am optimistic. So many different kinds of studies may prove most useful for acting teachers, scholars, and researchers in the future.

First, we can think about the Acting Habits of Mind both as specific habits in themselves, and as combinations that can lead to psychological skills and abilities or that can transfer out of the acting classroom and into students' larger lives. We can then begin to test for the gains in those skills and abilities and the learning trajectories of those skills and abilities for students in and across acting classrooms.

Second, we can think about how the acting techniques and exercises used here, the specific ones, can be shifted and flexibly changed to focus on the habits of mind that a teacher might want use to help groups of students with their flexibility, their collaboration, or their body awareness.

Third, we can think about how the skills and exercises can be built into other types of classrooms when a particular Acting Habit of Mind is called for. Scientific habits of mind such as curiosity and rigor, for example, could be built through engaging with *be flexible* and *commit to choices*.

Lastly, we can make room for students to engage in expression, exploration, and joy. There is no rule that says that students must take acting classes to increase their imagining and therefore apply that imagining to their biology class. Exploration, expression, and joy are key elements of the human experience and are important unto themselves.

Every student, in every classroom, under all circumstances, deserves a chance to discover who they are and what they want, to express themselves safely, with collaboration and scaffolding. And everyone deserves joy.

May the future of acting classes everywhere be full of all the qualities of theatre that our students deserve. Go forth! Make art!

Technical Research Information

In this appendix, I offer additional details about the schools, classes, coding techniques, and analyses that led to the eight Acting Habits of Mind.

SCHOOL DETAILS

1) *Imagination Stage* is an afterschool conservatory program for high school students, located in Bethesda, Maryland, a relatively high SES suburb on the East Coast of the United States. Students must audition to be accepted into the program, and spend between 3–6 hours each week after school taking classes in acting, dance, musical theatre, and performance. The program lasts 2 years and is part of a larger, professional theatre that produces multiple in-house and touring productions each year, specifically for young people. Students have a chance to audition and perform for a final showcase at the end of the year. The students enrolled in this program are also typically full-time students at local high schools, where they may receive additional acting classes or theatre experiences. In fact, students in this program did discuss their auditions and casting in roles at their academic schools. Most students would be classified as middle or upper-middle class. Class size for our data collection ranged from 13–15 students, and were called "Acting Conservatory" classes. Each class was between 2 and 2½ hours long. We filmed eight different classes, of two different types, for a total of 16 hours and 32 minutes. These were numbered as Classes 1–8. Our teachers at this school were Jewel and Nikki.

2) *Boston Arts Academy* is a public magnet school for the arts located in the middle of Boston, Massachusetts, in the United States. Students must audition to gain entry to the school and study their specific art form (acting, dance, art, or music) but admission does not take academic record into account. Students study theatre 10–15 hours per week in addition to an academic curriculum. Students follow a relatively strict theatre curriculum throughout their 4 years at the school, and many students enroll in top conservatory arts programs after graduation. The school has produced many notable professional actors. The majority of students are Black and Hispanic, and 47% receive free or reduced-price lunch. Class size ranged

from 6 students (seniors) to 25 (sophomores), and each class is approximately 1 hour and 45 minutes long. Class titles were simply "Acting." We filmed 10 different classes, of four different types, for a total of 16 hours and 34 minutes. These were numbered as Classes 9–18. Our teachers here were Juanita (the freshman and junior classes) and Maura (the sophomore and senior classes).

3) *The Madeira School* is an all-girls independent boarding school located in McLean, Virginia, another relatively high SES suburb on the East Coast of the United States. Students can take theatre and acting classes as one of many elective choices, and are in a "mod" system, a 5-week period in which classes are 80 minutes each, 5 days per week. There are three levels of acting classes and a larger, more fully realized theatre program at the school including devised theatre, directing, and stage craft. There are also several plays and musicals per year that students can audition for separately from classes. Approximately one-third of the student body receives some kind of financial aid, and there is a strong international presence on campus (>10%). Importantly, these students take acting and theatre as part of a general education program, not as a "major." Class size was only six students, and each class was approximately 80 minutes long, and was called "Acting 1." We filmed eight different classes, of just one type, for a total of 10 hours and 6 minutes. These were numbered as Classes 19–26. Our teacher was Kelsey for all classes at this school.

4) *Eureka High School* is a suburban public school in a midwestern suburb of St. Louis, Missouri, in the United States, with a student body of several thousand students. Students take acting classes as a general elective along with their traditional academic subjects. Students who show interest in acting, theatre, and performance can take higher-level courses over the course of their high school career. There are separate performance and audition opportunities in the school. The students who enroll in acting classes may be taking their first class in theatre, or may be heavily invested in their theatre and performance education. The majority of students are White (86%), with a smaller population of Black (4%), and Latiné (2%) students. At this school, 11% of the students receive free or reduced-price lunch. Classes filmed here included Acting and Directing (which the teacher asked we include because it was acting-focused). Classes lasted from 41 minutes to 1½ hours, and 10–24 students. We filmed seven different classes of two different types, for a total of 6 hours and 37 minutes. These were numbered as Classes 27–33. Our teacher here was Justin.

5) *Humboldt County* is a relatively small public school district in a rural area in California, on the West Coast of the United states. There were four schools, sharing two buildings, located within this district: McKinleyville, Arcata, Six Rivers, and Eureka High (which is totally separate from the school in St. Louis, but it did make data analyses confusing sometimes). Students

take acting classes as a general elective along with their traditional academic subjects. Students who show interest in acting, theatre, and performance can take higher-level courses over the course of their high school career, and there are separate audition and performance opportunities across multiple schools in the district. The different schools share buildings due to their size (i.e., the entire school district, K–12, is fewer than 4,000 students), even though they pull from various local areas. These students take acting and theatre as a general education program, not as a "major." Class size ranged from 12 (International Baccalaureate–level Theatre) to 27 (Theatre Arts), and lasted 40 minutes to 1½ hours. The overall student body is 44% White, 2% Black, 12% Asian/Pacific Islander, 24% Latiné, 6% Native American, and 10% two or more races. Between 28 and 52% of students receive free or reduced-price lunch, depending on school. We filmed seven different classes of five different types, for a total of 6 hours and 37 minutes. These were numbered as Classes 34–40. Teachers here were Melanie, Steve, Nanette, and Jean.

In Table A.1, I list all 40 classes filmed for this study, when they were filmed, and the individual length, teacher, number of students, and location for each.

Table A.1. Details of Each Class by Number Noted in Book

Class Number	School Name	Length of Class	Class Type	Date Filmed (m/d/yr)	Teacher	Class Size
1	Imagination Stage	1 hr, 53 min	Conservatory freshman	10/2/17	Nikki	16
2	Imagination Stage	2 hr, 3 min	Conservatory juniors	10/3/17	Jewel	13
3	Imagination Stage	2 hr, 23 min	Conservatory juniors	10/17/17	Jewel	16
4	Imagination Stage	2 hr, 9 min	Conservatory freshman	10/23/17	Nikki	16
5	Imagination Stage	1 hr, 59 min	Conservatory juniors	11/7/17	Jewel	13
6	Imagination Stage	2 hr, 3 min	Conservatory freshman	11/13/17	Nikki	15
7	Imagination Stage	2 hr, 1 min	Conservatory juniors	11/28/17	Jewel	14
8	Imagination Stage	2 hr, 11 min	Conservatory freshman	3/19/18	Nikki	13

(*continued*)

Table A.1. Details of Each Class by Number Noted in Book (*continued*)

Class Number	School Name	Length of Class	Class Type	Date Filmed (m/d/yr)	Teacher	Class Size
9	Boston Arts Academy	1 hr, 45 min	Freshmen acting	3/15/18	Juanita	18
10	Boston Arts Academy	1 hr, 42 min	Sophomore acting	3/15/18	Maura	23
11	Boston Arts Academy	1 hr, 30 min	Freshmen acting	5/8/18	Juanita	18
12	Boston Arts Academy	1 hr, 42 min	Sophomore acting	5/8/18	Maura	25
13	Boston Arts Academy	1 hr, 20 min	Junior acting	5/8/18	Juanita	18
14	Boston Arts Academy	1 hr, 42 min	Senior acting	5/8/18	Maura	6
15	Boston Arts Academy	1 hr, 32 min	Freshmen acting	5/9/18	Juanita	19
16	Boston Arts Academy	1 hr, 57 min	Sophomore acting	5/9/18	Maura	26
17	Boston Arts Academy	1 hr, 50 min	Junior acting	5/9/18	Juanita	16
18	Boston Arts Academy	1 hr, 34 min	Senior acting	5/9/18	Maura	5
19	The Madeira School	1 hr, 15 min	Acting 1	12/5/19	Kelsey	6
20	The Madeira School	1 hr, 19 min	Acting 1	12/9/19	Kelsey	6
21	The Madeira School	1 hr, 19 min	Acting 1	12/10/19	Kelsey	6
22	The Madeira School	1 hr, 10 min	Acting 1	12/11/19	Kelsey	6
23	The Madeira School	1 hr, 17 min	Acting 1	12/16/19	Kelsey	6
24	The Madeira School	1 hr, 11 min	Acting 1	12/17/19	Kelsey	6
25	The Madeira School	1 hr, 17 min	Acting 1	12/18/19	Kelsey	6

(*continued*)

Class Number	School Name	Length of Class	Class Type	Date Filmed (m/d/yr)	Teacher	Class Size
26	The Madeira School	1 hr, 18 min	Acting 1	12/19/19	Kelsey	6
27	Eureka High	41 min	Acting 1	3/2/20	Justin	21
28	Eureka High	45 min	Directing	3/2/20	Justin	10
29	Eureka High	41 min	Acting 1	3/3/20	Justin	24
30	Eureka High	46 min	Directing	3/3/20	Justin	10
31	Eureka High	1hr, 25 min	Directing	3/4/20	Justin	11
32	Eureka High	1 hr, 1 min	Acting 1	3/5/20	Justin	24
33	Eureka High	44 min	Acting 1	3/6/20	Justin	24
34	Arcata	42 min	Drama 1	3/9/20	Melanie	20
35	McKinleyville	40 min	Drama 1 & 2	3/10/20	Steve	20
36	Eureka-Humboldt	49 min	Theater arts	3/11/20	Nanette	27
37	Eureka-Humboldt	57 min	Theater arts	3/12/20	Nanette	24
38	Northcoast Prep	1 hr, 35 min	IB theater	3/12/20	Jean	12
39	McKinleyville	45 min	Drama 1 & 2	3/13/20	Steve	24
40	Six Rivers	1 hr, 9 min	Drama 1–4	3/13/20	Melanie	14

CURRICULUM

While not explicitly discussed in our data, the schools and teachers (particularly Humboldt County, Eureka High, and Boston Arts Academy) are informed by The National Core Arts Theatre standards. These consist of 11 different standards that can be applied across K–12 theatrical contexts. These standards give a long and comprehensive list, but briefly propose that by high school, students should be able to:

- construct ideas about the visual composition of a theatre work,
- critically understand influences of ideas applied to a theatrical work,
- question belief systems through theatrical work,

- understand how character relationships work in a play,
- practice various acting techniques,
- rehearse theatre works,
- respond to and critique theatre works,
- compare artistic choices across works,
- understand what criteria to use to evaluate theatrical choices,
- collaborate across artistic ideas and on theatrical works, and
- justify their own theatrical choices (taken from https://www.nationalartsstandards.org/sites/default/files/Theater_resources/Theatre%20at%20a%20Glance.pdf).

There are fairly clear lines from several of these standards to our Acting Habits of Mind (e.g., from "understand how character relationships work in a play" to *consider others,* or "respond to and critique theatre works" to *reflect and think metacognitively*). However, because we approached these classrooms with a grounded theory analytical plan, we did not consider theatrical standards when uncovering our Acting Habits of Mind.

While there may be debates about what kinds of acting theories are most appropriate for the best acting outcomes, and there are publicity campaigns for actors that center around the Method acting theory and its rigors (Bastién 2016), the truth is that we saw only a few explicitly named and discussed small notes about theories in our classes. The first was Stanford Meisner and his proposal of "living truthfully under imaginary circumstances." The second was Mary Overlie (although we never heard her name) and the Viewpoints. The third was Kristen Linklater's voice work. And finally, when Stanislavski was mentioned, the lesson was very focused on the idea of objectives, super objectives, beats, and tactics, and never on deep emotional memory. Outside of these specific acting theories, the teachers primarily presented exercises and work for the students to do without a strong perspective from a particular kind of acting technique. Teachers gave students multiple options, ideas, and tools to begin to build their own repertoire.

FILMING DETAILS

We filmed, as unobtrusively and naturalistically as possible, by setting up a camera in a corner of a classroom, focusing in on the teacher, and otherwise not engaging in the class in any way. Occasionally a teacher would divide the class into small groups and walk around giving feedback. On those occasions, we would follow the teacher with the camera to ensure we captured the teacher's voice and movement. We prepared a standard post-class interview protocol to ask follow-up questions after each class and gain more contextual information and framing about class activities. We interviewed teachers about their pedagogical goals for the class, whether they felt they had achieved those goals, and what they thought about certain aspects of the classroom that day. We transcribed those interviews for analyses and paired them with the filmed classes.

Altogether, we filmed 40 different classes of 14 different types, for a total of 56 hours and 26 minutes of film. Class sizes ranged from 5 students to 27 students (average = 15 students), from freshman in high school to seniors. Classes ranged in time from 40 minutes to 2 hours and 23 minutes, with an average of 84 minutes.

ANALYSES DETAILS

Once we filmed a class, we uploaded it to an academic server called Databrary (databrary.org), backed it up on our external hard drives in the lab, and typed up the interviews to pair with the classes. We then began the painstaking process of transcribing the classes and watching the videos multiple times, focused entirely on what the teachers were saying. If the students were speaking, we allowed for some contextualization of what they said that may have caused the teacher to respond, but we focused almost entirely on what teachers were saying. We then rewatched each class multiple times to ensure the transcript and the description of what was happening in each moment of the class was categorized correctly.

ACTIVITY CODING

To divide the classes into activity sections, we noted each time a teacher introduced a new activity and the students then engaged in this activity. Some classrooms moved quickly from activity to activity: For example, in one class at Eureka High in St. Louis, the 40-minute class period was divided into nine sections, with students moving from an introductory discussion to physical warm-up, then an improv game, discussion of that game, another introduction to another activity including a teacher demonstration from Justin, then a discussion of Justin's demonstration, then students trying the new activity, and then discussing their experiences, and finally closing with a quick improv game again. Students here had to change tactics, ideas, and quickly engage with reflection and ideas.

However, other classrooms spent the entire time in just one or two activities. For example, in one class at McKinleyville High school in Humboldt County, the students spent 20 minutes in discussion of costuming and production plots for their scenes, and then 24 minutes engaged in a class read throughs of the scripts. In this class, students went deep into a single topic and practiced building their reflections into further practice. Both fast-switching and single-activity classes recruited and used similar Acting Habits of Mind from their students.

By breaking the classes into the short activity-by-activity segments first, I was able to look at the types of activities across segments. This allowed me to investigate the structure of an acting class and the main actions taken by the teachers and students. What were the deeper activity types and goals that structure the class? How did different activities share properties of instruction and time to create meta-goals from the teachers? This analysis is reported in Chapter 2, The Content and Structure of Acting Classes. These distinctions allowed me to see, too, how the types of activities in acting classes are actually independent of the kinds of Acting Habits of Mind used and integrated into the classes—the scaffolding on which classes are built. Similarly, it allowed me to think clearly about how the Acting Habits of Mind are used and engaged with in classes in a variety of ways across activity type.

HABITS OF MIND CODING

The primary type of analysis for the discourse was qualitative coding, using grounded theory analyses, applied to the films, transcripts, and interviews to uncover the Habits of Mind used in acting classes (Braun & Clarke, 2013; Chun Tie et al., 2019; Glaser & Strauss, 1967; Saldaña, 2016). Grounded theory means we first conducted systematic collection of the data (films and interviews), and then built the theory of activities and Acting Habits of Mind through multiple rounds of iterative coding of the data, revisiting our category codes until we felt the scheme of codes was fully established, engaging in note taking (i.e., memoing), and comparative analyses across classes. While the COVID-19 pandemic did stop us from collecting more data, we felt that after March 2020, we did not need any additional data (i.e., data saturation had been achieved).

From memoing and multiple revisits of our categories and data, I developed a preliminary list of the possible Habits of Mind used in acting classes. This list was compared with the list of Habits of Mind in visual arts classes (Sheridan et al., 2023), and a similar list that has been developed for music ensemble playing (Hogan & Winner, 2019). I also consulted the extensive work on Habits of Mind created outside of the arts, which has listed up to 16 or more individual Habits of Mind students need to use in education (Costa & Kallick, 2000; Perkins, 1995; see the Part II intro for more discussion). After I had created a long list, I sent it, with explanations, to professors of theatre at a few universities, high school acting teachers (both those who participated in the study and a few who did not), and professional actors, to look for elements that were missing or unnecessary. I wanted to make sure that my psychological analysis made sense to the people in the classroom and on the ground with student actors. For the most part, I am happy to report, it did! From there, the Eight Acting Habits of Mind were identified and codified. Then I watched the films again, with an eye toward the set Acting Habits of Mind, to identify moments and exercises where they were brought to the forefront and could be used as examples throughout this book.

References

Adolph, K. E., Hoch, J. E., & Cole, W. G. (2018). Development (of walking): 15 suggestions. *Trends in Cognitive Sciences*, *22*(8), 699–711. https://doi.org/10.1016/j.tics.2018.05.010

Agnoli, S., Vanucci, M., Pelagatti, C., & Corazza, G. E. (2018). Exploring the link between mind wandering, mindfulness, and creativity: A multidimensional approach. *Creativity Research Journal*, *30*(1), 41–53.

Alfonso-Benlliure, V., Teruel, T. M., & Fields, D. L. (2021). Is it true that young drama practitioners are more creative and have a higher emotional intelligence? *Thinking Skills and Creativity, 39*, 100788.

Allen, J. P., & Loeb, E. L. (2015). The autonomy-connection challenge in adolescent–peer relationships. *Child Development Perspectives*, *9*(2), 101–105.

Allen, J. P., Narr, R. K., Kansky, J., & Szwedo, D. E. (2020). Adolescent peer relationship qualities as predictors of long-term romantic life satisfaction. *Child Development*, *91*(1), 327–340.

American Psychiatric Association. (2022). *Diagnostic and statistical manual of mental disorders* (5th ed.). https://doi.org/10.1176/appi.books.9780890425787

Andersen, P. N., Klausen, M. E., & Skogli, E. W. (2019). Art of learning—An art-based intervention aimed at improving children's executive functions. *Frontiers in psychology*, *10*, 1769.

Baas, M., Nevicka, B., & Ten Velden, F. S. (2020). When paying attention pays off: The mindfulness skill act with awareness promotes creative idea generation in groups. *European Journal of Work and Organizational Psychology*, *29*(4), 619–632.

Ballard, P. J., Hoyt, L. T., & Pachucki, M. C. (2019). Impacts of adolescent and young adult civic engagement on health and socioeconomic status in adulthood. *Child Development*, *90*(4), 1138–1154.

Barone, P., Corradi, G., & Gomila, A. (2019). Infants' performance in spontaneous-response false belief tasks: A review and meta-analysis. *Infant Behavior and Development*, *57*, 101350.

Barrett, L. F. (2017). *How emotions are made: The secret life of the brain.* Pan Macmillan.

Barrett, L. F., Gross, J., Christensen, T. C., & Benvenuto, M. (2001). Knowing what you're feeling and knowing what to do about it: Mapping the relation between emotion differentiation and emotion regulation. *Cognition & Emotion*, *15*(6), 713–724.

Bastién, A. J. (2016, August 11). Hollywood has ruined method acting. *The Atlantic*. http://www.theatlantic.com/entertainment/archive/2016/08/hollywood-has-ruined-method-acting/494777/

Bazron, B., Osher, D., & Fleischman, S. (2005). Creating culturally responsive schools. *American Educator*, *11*(1), 38–47.

Beatty, I. D., Gerace, W. J., Leonard, W. J., & Dufresne, R. J. (2006). Designing effective questions for classroom response system teaching. *American Journal of Physics*, *74*(1), 31–39.

Berry, M., & Brown, S. (2019). Acting in action: Prosodic analysis of character portrayal during acting. *Journal of Experimental Psychology: General*, *148*(8), 1407.

Blakemore, S. J. (2008). The social brain in adolescence. *Nature Reviews Neuroscience*, *9*(4), 267–277.

Blakemore, S. J., & Mills, K. L. (2014). Is adolescence a sensitive period for sociocultural processing? *Annual Review of Psychology*, *65*, 187–207.

Boal, A. (2013). *Theatre of the Oppressed*. Theatre Communications Group.

Boal, A., & McBride, C. A. (2015). Theatre of the Oppressed. In R. Caines & A. Heble (Eds.), *The improvisation studies reader* (pp. 79–86). Routledge.

Booth, A. E., & Waxman, S. (2002). Object names and object functions serve as cues to categories for infants. *Developmental Psychology, 38*(6), 948.

Branje, S., De Moor, E. L., Spitzer, J., & Becht, A. I. (2021). Dynamics of identity development in adolescence: A decade in review. *Journal of Research on Adolescence*, *31*(4), 908–927.

Braun, V., & Clarke, V. (2013). *Successful qualitative research: A practical guide for beginners*. Sage.

Broomhall, A. G., Phillips, W. J., Hine, D. W., & Loi, N. M. (2017). Upward counterfactual thinking and depression: A meta-analysis. *Clinical Psychology Review*, *55*, 56–73.

Brouillette, L. (2012). Advancing the speaking and listening skills of K–2 English language learners through creative drama. *TESOL Journal*, *3*(1), 138–145.

Brown, A. L. (1997). Transforming schools into communities of thinking and learning about serious matters. *American Psychologist*, *52*(4), 399.

Brown, B. B. (2004). Adolescents' relationships with peers. *Handbook of adolescent psychology*, 363–394.

Brown, S., Cockett, P., & Yuan, Y. (2019). The neuroscience of Romeo and Juliet: An fMRI study of acting. *Royal Society Open Science*, *6*(3), 181908.

Bryant, F. B., & Veroff, J. 2007. *Savoring: A new model of positive experience*. Lawrence Erlbaum Associates.

Burnett, S., Bird, G., Moll, J., Frith, C., & Blakemore, S. J. (2009). Development during adolescence of the neural processing of social emotion. *Journal of Cognitive Neuroscience*, *21*(9), 1736–1750.

Burnette, J. L., Billingsley, J., Banks, G. C., Knouse, L. E., Hoyt, C. L., Pollack, J. M., & Simon, S. (2022). A systematic review and meta-analysis of growth mindset interventions: For whom, how, and why might such interventions work? *Psychological Bulletin, 149*(3–4).

Butler, L. P. (2020). The empirical child? A framework for investigating the development of scientific habits of mind. *Child Development Perspectives*, *14*(1), 34–40.

Byrne, R. M. (2016). Counterfactual thought. *Annual Review of Psychology, 67*, 135–157.

Caine, M. (2000). *Acting in film: An actor's take on movie making*. Hal Leonard Corporation.

Carlson Jones, D. (2004). Body image among adolescent girls and boys: A longitudinal study. *Developmental Psychology, 40*(5), 823–835. https://doi.org/10.1037/0012-1649.40.5.823

Chalkiadaki, A. (2018). A systematic literature review of 21st century skills and competencies in primary education. *International Journal of Instruction, 11*(3), 1–16.

Charleroy, A., Gentry, C., Greco, A., Rubino, N., & Schatz, M. (2011). *Arts education standards and 21st century skills: An analysis of the national standards for education (1994) as compared to the 21st Century skills map for the arts*. The College Board Office of Academic Initiatives, 45, 10023–16992.

Chi, M. T. H., & Wylie, R. (2014). The ICAP framework: Linking cognitive engagement to active learning outcomes. *Educational Psychologist, 49*(4), 219–243.

Chun Tie, Y., Birks, M., & Francis, K. (2019). Grounded theory research: A design framework for novice researchers. *SAGE Open Medicine, 7*. https://doi.org/10.1177/2050312118822927

Clark, R. C., & Mayer, R. E. (2008). Learning by viewing versus learning by doing: Evidence-based guidelines for principled learning environments. *Performance Improvement*, *47*(9), 5–13.

Cole, P. M., Martin, S. E., & Dennis, T. A. (2004). Emotion regulation as a scientific construct: Methodological challenges and directions for child development research. *Child Development*, *75*(2), 317–333.

Corbett, B. A., Ioannou, S., Key, A. P., Coke, C., Muscatello, R., Vandekar, S., & Muse, I. (2019). Treatment effects in social cognition and behavior following a theater-based intervention for youth with autism. *Developmental Neuropsychology*, *44*(7), 481–494.

Corbett, B. A., Swain, D. M., Coke, C., Simon, D., Newsom, C., Houchins-Juarez, N., . . . & Song, Y. (2014). Improvement in social deficits in autism spectrum disorders using a theatre-based, peer-mediated intervention. *Autism Research, 7*(1), 4–16.

Corbett, B. A., White, S., Lerner, M., Preacher, K. J., Klemencic, M. E., Simmons, G. L., Pilkington, J., Gable, P., Gioia, A., & Key, A. P. (2023). Peers, play, and performance to build social salience in autistic youth: A multisite randomized clinical trial. *Journal of Consulting and Clinical Psychology, 91*(7), 411–425. https://doi.org/10.1037/ccp0000821

Costa, A. L., & Kallick, B. (2000). Discovering and exploring habits of mind. *Explorations in Teacher Education*, *36*, 36–38.

Craig, A. D. (2002). How do you feel? Interoception: The sense of the physiological condition of the body. *Nature Reviews Neuroscience, 3*(8), 655–666.

Crocetti, E. (2017). Identity formation in adolescence: The dynamic of forming and consolidating identity commitments. *Child Development Perspectives*, *11*(2), 145–150.

Crone, E. A., & Dahl, R. E. (2012). Understanding adolescence as a period of social–affective engagement and goal flexibility. *Nature Reviews Neuroscience, 13*(9), 636–650.

Crone, E. A., & Fuligni, A. J. (2020). Self and others in adolescence. *Annual Review of Psychology, 71*, 447–469.

Csikszentmihalyi, M. (2013). *Flow: The psychology of happiness*. Random House.

Cuoco, A., Goldenberg, E. P., & Mark, J. (1996). Habits of mind: An organizing principle for mathematics curricula. *The Journal of Mathematical Behavior, 15*(4), 375–402.

Dahl, R. E., Allen, N. B., Wilbrecht, L., & Suleiman, A. B. (2018). Importance of investing in adolescence from a developmental science perspective. *Nature, 554*(7693), 441–450.

Danovitch, J. H., Mills, C. M., Sands, K. R., & Williams, A. J. (2021). Mind the gap: How incomplete explanations influence children's interest and learning behaviors. *Cognitive Psychology, 130*, 101421.

Davidson, R. J., & Kaszniak, A. W. (2015). Conceptual and methodological issues in research on mindfulness and meditation. *American Psychologist, 70*(7), 581.

Davis, J. H. (2008). *Why our schools need the arts*. Teachers College Press.

Dawson, K., & Lee, B. K. (2018). *Drama-based pedagogy: Activating learning across the curriculum*. Intellect.

DeBettignies, B. H., & Goldstein, T. R. (2020). Improvisational theater classes improve self-concept. *Psychology of Aesthetics, Creativity, and the Arts, 14*(4), 451.

Denham, S. A., Bassett, H. H., & Zinsser, K. (2012). Early childhood teachers as socializers of young children's emotional competence. *Early Childhood Education Journal, 40*, 137–143.

Diamond, A., & Ling, D. S. (2016). Conclusions about interventions, programs, and approaches for improving executive functions that appear justified and those that, despite much hype, do not. *Developmental Cognitive Neuroscience, 18*, 34–48.

Ding, X., Tang, Y. Y., Deng, Y., Tang, R., & Posner, M. I. (2015). Mood and personality predict improvement in creativity due to meditation training. *Learning and Individual Differences, 37*, 217–221.

Dudeck, T. R., & McClure, C. (2018). *Applied improvisation: leading, collaborating, and creating beyond the theatre*. Bloomsbury Publishing.

Duell, N., & Steinberg, L. (2019). Positive risk taking in adolescence. *Child Development Perspectives, 13*(1), 48–52.

Duell, N., & Steinberg, L. (2021). Adolescents take positive risks, too. *Developmental Review, 62*, 100984.

Dumontheil, I., Apperly, I. A., & Blakemore, S. J. (2010). Online usage of theory of mind continues to develop in late adolescence. *Developmental Science, 13*(2), 331–338.

Dunn, B. D., Galton, H. C., Morgan, R., Evans, D., Oliver, C., Meyer, M., Cusack, R., Lawrence, A. D., & Dalgleish, T. (2010). Listening to your heart: How interoception shapes emotion experience and intuitive decision making. *Psychological Science, 21*(12), 1835–1844.

Edwards, W. (1954). The theory of decision making. *Psychological Bulletin, 51*(4), 380.

Emler, N. (2001). *Self-esteem: The costs and causes of low self-worth*. York Publishing Services Ltd.

Erikson, E. H. (1994). *Identity and the life cycle*. W. W. Norton.

Fatahi, N., Park, C., Curby, T. W., Zinsser, K. M., Denham, S. A., Moberg, S., & Gordon, R. A. (2022). Promoting preschoolers' social and emotional competencies through emotion-focused teaching. *Early Education and Development*, 1–20.

Feist, G. J. (2019). Creativity and the Big Two model of personality: Plasticity and stability. *Current Opinion in Behavioral Sciences*, *27*, 31–35.

Felsman, P., Gunawardena, S., & Seifert, C. M. (2020). Improv experience promotes divergent thinking, uncertainty tolerance, and affective well-being. *Thinking Skills and Creativity*, *35*, 100632.

Fincham, G. W., Strauss, C., Montero-Marin, J., & Cavanagh, K. (2023). Effect of breathwork on stress and mental health: A meta-analysis of randomized-controlled trials. *Scientific Reports*, *13*(1), 432.

Foglia, L., & Wilson, R. A. (2013). Embodied cognition. *Wiley Interdisciplinary Reviews: Cognitive Science*, *4*(3), 319–325.

Fox, K. C., & Beaty, R. E. (2019). Mind-wandering as creative thinking: Neural, psychological, and theoretical considerations. *Current Opinion in Behavioral Sciences*, *27*, 123–130.

Freeman, G. D., Sullivan, K., & Fulton, C. R. (2003). Effects of creative drama on self-concept, social skills, and problem behavior. *The Journal of Educational Research*, *96*(3), 131–138. doi:10.1080/00220670309598801

Freeman, S., Eddy, S. L., McDonough, M., Smith, M. K., Okoroafor, N., Jordt, H., & Wenderoth, M. P. (2014). Active learning increases student performance in science, engineering, and mathematics. *Proceedings of the National Academy of Sciences*, *111*(23), 8410–8415.

Galla, B. M., O'Reilly, G. A., Kitil, M. J., Smalley, S. L., & Black, D. S. (2015). Community-based mindfulness program for disease prevention and health promotion: Targeting stress reduction. *American Journal of Health Promotion*, *30*(1), 36–41.

Ganesan, S., Beyer, E., Moffat, B., Van Dam, N. T., Lorenzetti, V., & Zalesky, A. (2022). Focused attention meditation in healthy adults: A systematic review and meta-analysis of cross-sectional functional MRI studies. *Neuroscience & Biobehavioral Reviews*, *141*(2), 104846.

Geisinger, K. F. (2016). 21st century skills: What are they and how do we assess them? *Applied Measurement in Education*, *29*(4), 245–249.

Gil, K., Rhim, J., Ha, T., Doh, Y. Y., & Woo, W. (2014, September). AR Petite Theater: Augmented reality storybook for supporting children's empathy behavior. In *2014 IEEE International Symposium on Mixed and Augmented Reality-Media, Art, Social Science, Humanities and Design (ISMAR-MASH'D)* (pp. 13–20). IEEE.

Gilbert, P. (2019). Explorations into the nature and function of compassion. *Current Opinion in Psychology*, *28*, 108–114.

Ginwright, S., & James, T. (2002). From assets to agents of change: Social justice, organizing, and youth development. *New Directions for Youth Development*, *2002*(96), 27–46.

Glaser, B. G., & Strauss, A. L. (1967). *The Discovery of Grounded Theory: Strategies for Qualitative Research*. Transaction Publishers.

Goldenberg, E. P., Shteingold, N., & Feurzeig, N. (2003). Mathematical habits of mind for young children. *Mathematics, Education, 6*, 51–61.

Goldstein, T. R., & Hayes, K. (2022). Embodiment and containment: Flexible pathways to flourishing in theatre. In L. Tay & J. O. Pawelski (Eds.), *The Oxford Handbook of the Positive Humanities*. https://doi.org/10.1093/oxfordhb/9780190064570.013.10

Goldstein, T. R., & Lerner, M. D. (2018). Dramatic pretend play games uniquely improve emotional control in young children. *Developmental Science, 21*(4), e12603.

Goldstein, T. R., Tamir, M., & Winner, E. (2013). Expressive suppression and acting classes. *Psychology of Aesthetics, Creativity, and the Arts, 7*(2), 191.

Goldstein, T. R., & Winner, E. (2011). Engagement in role play, pretense, and acting classes predict advanced theory of mind skill in middle childhood. *Imagination, Cognition and Personality, 30*(3), 249–258.

Goldstein, T. R., & Winner, E. (2012). Enhancing empathy and theory of mind. *Journal of Cognition and Development, 13*(1), 19–37.

Goldstein, T. R., Wu, K., & Winner, E. (2009). Actors are skilled in theory of mind but not empathy. *Imagination, Cognition and Personality, 29*(2), 115–133.

Goldstein, T. R., Young, D. L., & Thompson, B. N. (2020). It's all critical: Acting teachers' beliefs about theater classes. *Frontiers in Psychology, 11*, 775.

Goleman, D. (1995). *Emotional intelligence*. Bantam Books.

Göncü, A., & Perone, A. (2005). Pretend play as a life-span activity. *Topoi, 24*(2), 137–147.

Good, C., Aronson, J., & Inzlicht, M. (2003). Improving adolescents' standardized test performance: An intervention to reduce the effects of stereotype threat. *Journal of Applied Developmental Psychology*, *24*(6), 645–662.

Greaves, D. A., Pinti, P., Din, S., Hickson, R., Diao, M., Lange, C., Khurana, P., Hunter, K., Tachtsidis, I., & Hamilton, A. F. D. C. (2022). Exploring theater neuroscience: Using wearable functional near-infrared spectroscopy to measure the sense of self and interpersonal coordination in professional actors. *Journal of Cognitive Neuroscience*, *34*(12), 2215–2236.

Greenfader, C. M., & Brouillette, L. (2013). Boosting language skills of English learners through dramatization and movement. *The Reading Teacher*, *67*(3), 171–180.

Gross, R. (1982). The promise of the new actor training—A professional challenge for teachers. *Theatre News*, *14*(9), 14–15.

Guli, L. A., Semrud-Clikeman, M., Lerner, M. D., & Britton, N. (2013). Social Competence Intervention Program (SCIP): A pilot study of a creative drama program for youth with social difficulties. *The Arts in Psychotherapy*, *40*(1), 37–44.

Gumley, A. (2011). Metacognition, affect regulation and symptom expression: A transdiagnostic perspective. *Psychiatry Research*, *190*(1), 72–78.

Guyotte, K. W., Sochacka, N. W., Costantino, T. E., Walther, J., & Kellam, N. N. (2014). STEAM as social practice: Cultivating creativity in transdisciplinary spaces. *Art Education*, *67*(6), 12–19.

Hainselin, M., Aubry, A., & Bourdin, B. (2018). Improving teenagers' divergent thinking with improvisational theater. *Frontiers in Psychology*, *9*(1759), 1–9. doi:10.3389/fpsyg.2018.01759

Harris, P. L. (2000). *The work of the imagination*. Blackwell Publishing.

Harris, P. L. (2021). Early constraints on the imagination: The realism of young children. *Child Development*, *92*(2), 466–483.

Harris, P. L. (2022). *Children's imagination*. Cambridge University Press.

Hartup, W. W., & Stevens, N. (1999). Friendships and adaptation across the life span. *Current Directions in Psychological Science*, *8*(3), 76–79

Heberle, A. E., Rapa, L. J., & Farago, F. (2020). Critical consciousness in children and adolescents: A systematic review, critical assessment, and recommendations for future research. *Psychological Bulletin*, *146*(6), 525.

Henriksen, D., Richardson, C., & Shack, K. (2020). Mindfulness and creativity: Implications for thinking and learning. *Thinking Skills and Creativity*, *37*, 100689.

Hetland, L., Winner, E., Veenema, S., Sheridan, K. (2007). *Studio thinking: The real benefits of visual arts education*. Teachers College Press.

Hetland, L., Winner, E., Veenema, S., & Sheridan, K. M. (2013). *Studio thinking 2: The real benefits of visual arts education*. Teachers College Press.

Hirsh-Pasek, K., Golinkoff, R. M., & Eyer, D. (2004). *Einstein never used flash cards: How our children really learn—and why they need to play more and memorize less*. Rodale Books.

Hodges, L. C. (2020). Student engagement in active learning classes. *Active Learning in College Science: The Case for Evidence-Based Practice*, 27–41.

Hogan, J., & Winner, E. (2019). Habits of mind as a framework for assessment in music education. *The Oxford Handbook of Philosophical and Qualitative Assessment in Music Education*, 202–227.

Holcomb, S. (2007). State of the arts: Despite mounting evidence of its role in student achievement, arts education is disappearing in the schools that need it most. *NEA Today*.

Hope, E. C., Keels, M., & Durkee, M. I. (2016). Participation in Black Lives Matter and deferred action for childhood arrivals: Modern activism among Black and Latino college students. *Journal of Diversity in Higher Education*, *9*(3), 203.

Hruschka, D. J. (2010). *Friendship: Development, ecology, and evolution of a relationship* (Vol. 5). University of California Press.

Hughes, C., & Devine, R. T. (2015). Individual differences in theory of mind from preschool to adolescence: Achievements and directions. *Child Development Perspectives*, *9*(3), 149–153.

Hughes, J., & Wilson, K. (2004). Playing a part: the impact of youth theatre on young people's personal and social development. *Research in Drama Education*, *9*(1), 57–72.

Hunter, M. A. (2008). Cultivating the art of safe space. *Research in Drama Education*, *13*(1), 5–21.

Imuta, K., Henry, J. D., Slaughter, V., Selcuk, B., & Ruffman, T. (2016). Theory of mind and prosocial behavior in childhood: A meta-analytic review. *Developmental Psychology*, *52*(8), 1192.

Ivcevic, Z., & Brackett, M. A. (2015). Predicting creativity: Interactive effects of openness to experience and emotion regulation ability. *Psychology of Aesthetics, Creativity, and the Arts*, *9*(4), 480.

Jaquish, G. A., & Ware, J. (1993). Adopting an educator habit of mind: Modifying what it means to "Think like a Lawyer." *Stanford Law Review*, 1713–1729.

Jardine, B. B., Vannier, S., & Voyer, D. (2022). Emotional intelligence and romantic relationship satisfaction: A systematic review and meta-analysis. *Personality and Individual Differences*, *196*, 111713

Johnson, D. W., & Johnson, R. T. (1999). *Learning together and alone: Cooperative, competitive, and individualistic learning* (5th ed.). Allyn and Bacon.

Jose, P. E., Lim, B. T., & Bryant, F. B. 2012. Does savoring increase happiness? A daily diary study. *The Journal of Positive Psychology, 7*(3),176–187. doi:10.1080/17439760.2012.671345

Kapitany, R., Hampejs, T., & Goldstein, T. R. (2022). Pretensive Shared Reality: From childhood pretense to adult imaginative play. *Frontiers in Psychology, 13*, 614.

Kardash, C. A. M., & Wright, L. (1987). Does creative drama benefit elementary school students? A meta-analysis. *Youth Theatre Journal*, *1*(3), 11–18.

Kever, A., Pollatos, O., Vermeulen, N., & Grynberg, D. (2015). Interoceptive sensitivity facilitates both antecedent-and response-focused emotion regulation strategies. *Personality and Individual Differences*, *87*, 20–23.

Khalifa, M. A., Gooden, M. A., & Davis, J. E. (2016). Culturally responsive school leadership: A synthesis of the literature. *Review of Educational Research*, *86*(4), 1272–1311. https://doi.org/10.3102/0034654316630383

Khalsa, S. S., Adolphs, R., Cameron, O. G., Critchley, H. D., Davenport, P. W., Feinstein, J. S., Feusner, J. D., Garfinkel, S. N., Lane, R. D., & Mehling, W. E. (2018). Interoception and mental health: A roadmap. *Biological Psychiatry: Cognitive Neuroscience and Neuroimaging*, *3*(6), 501–513.

Kolodner, J. L., Gray, J., & Fasse, B. B. (2003). Promoting transfer through case-based reasoning: Rituals and practices in learning by design classrooms. *Cognitive Science Quarterly*, *3*(2), 183–232.

Konijn, E. (2005). The actor's emotions reconsidered: A psychological task-based perspective. In *Acting (Re) Considered* (pp. 62–81). Routledge.

Koppett, K. (2013). *Training to imagine: Practical improvisational theatre techniques for trainers and managers to enhance creativity, teamwork, leadership, and learning*. Stylus Publishing.

Koriat, A., & Levy-Sadot, R. (2000). Conscious and unconscious metacognition: A rejoinder. *Consciousness and Cognition*, *9*(2), 193–202.

Kreplin, U., Farias, M., & Brazil, I. A. (2018). The limited prosocial effects of meditation: A systematic review and meta-analysis. *Scientific Reports*, *8*(1), 2403.

Ku, K. Y., Kong, Q., Song, Y., Deng, L., Kang, Y., & Hu, A. (2019). What predicts adolescents' critical thinking about real-life news? The roles of social media news consumption and news media literacy. *Thinking Skills and Creativity*, *33*, 100570.

Kuhn, D. (2000). Theory of mind, metacognition, and reasoning: A life-span perspective. In P. Mitchell & K. J. Riggs (Eds.), *Children's reasoning and the mind* (pp. 301–326). Psychology Press/Taylor & Francis.

Kuhn, D. (2022). Metacognition matters in many ways. *Educational Psychologist*, *57*(2), 73–86.

LaFontana, K. M., & Cillessen, A. H. (2010). Developmental changes in the priority of perceived status in childhood and adolescence. *Social Development*, *19*(1), 130–147.

Le Roux, J. (2002). Effective educators are culturally competent communicators. *Intercultural Education*, *13*(1), 37–48.

Larson, R. W., & Brown, J. R. (2007). Emotional development in adolescence: What can be learned from a high school theater program?. *Child Development, 78*(4), 1083–1099.

Lee, B., Patall, E., Cawthon, S., and Steingut, R. (2015). The effect of drama-based pedagogy on preK–16 outcomes: A meta-analysis of research from 1985 to 2012. *Review of Educational Research, 85*(1), 3–49. doi:10.3102/0034654314540477

Leslie, A. M. (1987). Pretense and representation: The origins of "theory of mind." *Psychological Review*, *94*(4), 412.

Lewandowska, K., & Węziak-Białowolska, D. (2020). The impact of theatre on empathy and self-esteem: A meta-analysis. *Creativity Research Journal*, *32*(3), 237–245.

Lewis, C., & Lovatt, P. J. (2013). Breaking away from set patterns of thinking: Improvisation and divergent thinking. *Thinking Skills and Creativity*, *9*, 46–58.

Liao, S. Y., & Szabó Gendler, T. (2011). Pretense and imagination. *Wiley Interdisciplinary Reviews: Cognitive Science*, *2*(1), 79–94.

Lillard, A. S., Lerner, M. D., Hopkins, E. J., Dore, R. A., Smith, E. D., & Palmquist, C. M. (2013). The impact of pretend play on children's development: A review of the evidence. *Psychological Bulletin*, *139*(1), 1.

Llamas-Díaz, D., Cabello, R., Megías-Robles, A., & Fernández-Berrocal, P. (2022). Systematic review and meta-analysis: The association between emotional intelligence and subjective well-being in adolescents. *Journal of Adolescence*, *94*(7), 925–938.

Lomas, T., Froh, J. J., Emmons, R. A., Mishra, A., & Bono, G. (2014). Gratitude interventions: A review and future agenda. In A. C. Parks & S. M. Schueller, *The Wiley Blackwell Handbook of Positive Psychological Interventions* (pp. 1–19). John Wiley & Sons.

Luna, B. (2009). Developmental changes in cognitive control through adolescence. *Advances in Child Development and Behavior*, *37*, 233–278.

Lutterbie, J. (2001). Phenomenology and the dramaturgy of space and place. *Journal of Dramatic Theory and Criticism*, *16*(1), 123–132.

MacCann, C., Jiang, Y., Brown, L. E., Double, K. S., Bucich, M., & Minbashian, A. (2020). Emotional intelligence predicts academic performance: A meta-analysis. *Psychological Bulletin*, *146*(2), 150

Macnamara, B. N., & Burgoyne, A. P. (2022). Do growth mindset interventions impact students' academic achievement? A systematic review and meta-analysis with recommendations for best practices. *Psychological Bulletin, 149*(3–4), 133–173. https://doi.org/10.1037/bul0000352

Maliphant, J., & Horner, T. (2016). Feeling at sea: The anchor of the therapeutic space. *Infant Observation*, *19*(1), 24–41.

Mandler, J. M., Fivush, R., & Reznick, J. S. (1987). The development of contextual categories. *Cognitive Development, 2(*4), 339–354.

Mar, R. A., & Oatley, K. (2008). The function of fiction is the abstraction and simulation of social experience. *Perspectives on Psychological Science*, *3*(3), 173–192.

Marcia, J. E. (1966). Development and validation of ego-identity status. *Journal of Personality and Social Psychology, 3*(5), 551.

Martin, E., Dourish, C. T., Rotshtein, P., Spetter, M. S., & Higgs, S. (2019). Interoception and disordered eating: A systematic review. *Neuroscience & Biobehavioral Reviews, 107*, 166–191.

Martins, A., Ramalho, N., & Morin, E. (2010). A comprehensive meta-analysis of the relationship between emotional intelligence and health. *Personality and Individual Differences, 49*(6), 554–564.

Marulis, L. M., Baker, S. T., & Whitebread, D. (2020). Integrating metacognition and executive function to enhance young children's perception of and agency in their learning. *Early Childhood Research Quarterly, 50*, 46–54.

McCammon, L. A., Saldaña, J., Hines, A., & Omasta, M. (2012). Lifelong impact: Adult perceptions of their high school speech and/or theatre participation. *Youth Theatre Journal, 26*(1), 2–25.

McLauchlan, D. (2010). Keeping the kids in school: What the drama class tells us. *Encounters in Theory and History of Education, 11*, 135–154.

Mehr, S. A. (2015). Miscommunication of science: Music cognition research in the popular press. *Frontiers in Psychology*, 6, 988. https://doi.org/10.3389/fpsyg.2015.00988

Mérida-López, S., & Extremera, N. (2017). Emotional intelligence and teacher burnout: A systematic review. *International Journal of Educational Research, 85*, 121–130.

Meyer, D. K., & Turner, J. C. (2006). Re-conceptualizing emotion and motivation to learn in classroom contexts. *Educational Psychology Review, 18*(4), 377–390.

Miao, C., Humphrey, R. H., & Qian, S. (2017). A meta-analysis of emotional intelligence and work attitudes. *Journal of Occupational and Organizational Psychology, 90*(2), 177–202.

Mills, C. M. (2013). Knowing when to doubt: Developing a critical stance when learning from others. *Developmental Psychology, 49*(3), 404.

Miranda, L.-M. [@Lin_Manuel]. (2015, June 18). *My texts w Groffsauce at the other school. We're in the play!* [Image attached]. [Tweet]. Twitter. https://twitter.com/Lin_Manuel/status/611586342129111041?lang=en

Montirosso, R., & McGlone, F. (2020). The body comes first. Embodied reparation and the co-creation of infant bodily-self. *Neuroscience & Biobehavioral Reviews, 113*, 77–87.

Moreau, D., Macnamara, B. N., & Hambrick, D. Z. (2019). Overstating the role of environmental factors in success: A cautionary note. *Current Directions in Psychological Science, 28*(1), 28–33.

Müller, B. C., Gerasimova, A., & Ritter, S. M. (2016). Concentrative meditation influences creativity by increasing cognitive flexibility. *Psychology of Aesthetics, Creativity, and the Arts, 10*(3), 278.

Murray, S., Liang, N., Brosowsky, N., & Seli, P. (2021). What are the benefits of mind wandering to creativity? *Psychology of Aesthetics, Creativity, and the Arts*. Advance online publication. https://doi.org/10.1037/aca0000420

Newcomb, A. F., Bukowski, W. M., & Pattee, L. (1993). Children's peer relations: a meta-analytic review of popular, rejected, neglected, controversial, and average sociometric status. *Psychological Bulletin, 113*(1), 99.

Nicolopoulou, A. (2019). Using a storytelling/story-acting practice to promote narrative and other decontextualized language skills in disadvantaged children. *Narrative, Literacy and Other Skills: Studies in Intervention*, 263–284.

Nicuţă, E. G., & Constantin, T. (2021). Take nothing for granted: Downward social comparison and counterfactual thinking increase adolescents' state gratitude for the little things in life. *Journal of Happiness Studies*, 1–28.

Noice, H. (1992). Elaborative memory strategies of professional actors. *Applied Cognitive Psychology*, *6*(5), 417–427.

Noice, H. (2013). *The nature of expertise in professional acting: A cognitive view*. Psychology Press.

Noice, H., & Noice, T. (2001). Learning dialogue with and without movement. *Memory & Cognition*, *29*(6), 820–827.

Noice, H., & Noice, T. (2006). What studies of actors and acting can tell us about memory and cognitive functioning. *Current Directions in Psychological Science*, *15*(1), 14–18.

Noice, H., Noice, T., & Staines, G. (2004). A short-term intervention to enhance cognitive and affective functioning in older adults. *Journal of Aging and Health*, *16*(4), 562–585.

O'Boyle Jr, E. H., Humphrey, R. H., Pollack, J. M., Hawver, T. H., & Story, P. A. (2011). The relation between emotional intelligence and job performance: A meta-analysis. *Journal of Organizational Behavior*, *32*(5), 788–818.

Oleynick, V. C., DeYoung, C. G., Hyde, E., Kaufman, S. B., Beaty, R. E., & Silvia, P. J. (2017). Openness/intellect: The core of the creative personality. In G. J. Feist, R. Reiter-Palmon, & J. C. Kaufman (Eds.), *The Cambridge handbook of creativity and personality research* (pp. 9–27). Cambridge University Press. https://doi.org/10.1017/9781316228036.002

Olson, J. M., Buhrmann, O., & Roese, N. J. (2000). Comparing comparisons. An integrative perspective on social comparison and counterfactual thinking. In J. Suls & L. Wheeler (Eds.), *Handbook of social comparison: Theory and research*. (pp. 379–398). Springer.

Onishi, K. H., & Baillargeon, R. (2005). Do 15-month-old infants understand false beliefs? *Science*, *308*(5719), 255–258.

Panero, M. E. (2019). A psychological exploration of the experience of acting. *Creativity Research Journal*, *31*(4), 428–442.

Panero, M. E., & Winner, E. (2021). Rating the acting moment: exploring characteristics for realistic portrayals of characters. *Frontiers in Psychology*, 11, 615311.

Panero, M. E., Goldstein, T. R., Rosenberg, R., Hughes, H., & Winner, E. (2016). Do actors possess traits associated with high hypnotizability?. *Psychology of Aesthetics, Creativity, and the Arts, 10*(2), 233.

Panero, M. E., Michaels, L., & Winner, E. (2020). Becoming a character: Dissociation in conservatory acting students. *Journal of Trauma & Dissociation*, *21*(1), 87–102.

Pasupathi, M., Mansour, E., & Brubaker, J. R. (2007). Developing a life story: Constructing relations between self and experience in autobiographical narratives. *Human Development*, *50*(2–3), 85–110.

Pearson, J., & Kosslyn, S. M. (2015). The heterogeneity of mental representation: Ending the imagery debate. *Proceedings of the National Academy of Sciences*, *112*(33), 10089–10092.

Pearson, J., Naselaris, T., Holmes, E. A., & Kosslyn, S. M. (2015). Mental imagery: functional mechanisms and clinical applications. *Trends in Cognitive Sciences, 19*(10), 590–602.

Pennycook, G., & Rand, D. G. (2019). Lazy, not biased: Susceptibility to partisan fake news is better explained by lack of reasoning than by motivated reasoning. *Cognition, 188*, 39–50.

Perkins, D. N. (1995). *Outsmarting IQ: The emerging science of learnable intelligence*. The Free Press.

Perkins, D. N., & Salomon, G. (1992). Transfer of learning. *International Encyclopedia of Education*, 2, 6452–6457.

Phinney, J. S. (1990). Ethnic identity in adolescents and adults: Review of research. *Psychological Bulletin, 108*(3), 499.

Podlozny, A. (2000). Strengthening verbal skills through the use of classroom drama: A clear link. *Journal of Aesthetic education, 34*(3/4), 239–275.

Pool, L. D., & Qualter, P. (Eds.). (2018). *An introduction to emotional intelligence*. John Wiley & Sons.

Poulin-Dubois, D., Goldman, E. J., Meltzer, A., & Psaradellis, E. (2023). Discontinuity from implicit to explicit theory of mind from infancy to preschool age. *Cognitive Development, 65*, 101273.

Preckel, K., Kanske, P., & Singer, T. (2018). On the interaction of social affect and cognition: Empathy, compassion and theory of mind. *Current Opinion in Behavioral Sciences, 19*, 1–6.

Preiss, D. D., Cosmelli, D., & Kaufman, J. C. (Eds.). (2020). *Creativity and the wandering mind: Spontaneous and controlled cognition*. Academic Press.

Reiter-Palmon, R., Forthmann, B., & Barbot, B. (2019). Scoring divergent thinking tests: A review and systematic framework. *Psychology of Aesthetics, Creativity, and the Arts, 13*(2), 144.

Reynolds Jr., D. A. J., Stiles, W. B., & Grohol, J. M. (2006). An investigation of session impact and alliance in internet based psychotherapy: Preliminary results. *Counselling and Psychotherapy Research*, 6(3), 164–168.

Rober, P., & De Haene, L. (2014). Intercultural therapy and the limitations of a cultural competency framework: About cultural differences, universalities and the unresolvable tensions between them. *Journal of Family Therapy, 36*, 3–20.

Roemer, L., Williston, S. K., & Rollins, L. G. (2015). Mindfulness and emotion regulation. *Current Opinion in Psychology, 3*, 52–57.

Romer, D., Reyna, V. F., & Satterthwaite, T. D. (2017). Beyond stereotypes of adolescent risk taking: Placing the adolescent brain in developmental context. *Developmental Cognitive Neuroscience,* 27, 19–34.

Roseth, C. J., Johnson, D. W., & Johnson, R. T. (2008). Promoting early adolescents' achievement and peer relationships: The effects of cooperative, competitive, and individualistic goal structures. *Psychological Bulletin, 134*(2), 223–46.

Sala, G., & Gobet, F. (2017). Does far transfer exist? Negative evidence from chess, music, and working memory training. *Current Directions in Psychological Science, 26*(6), 515–520.

Salamone, F. A. (2004). *Encyclopedia of religious rites, rituals, and festivals*. Routledge.

Saldaña, J. (2016). *The coding manual for qualitative researchers*. Sage.

Salovey, P., & Mayer, J. D. (1990). Emotional intelligence. *Imagination, Cognition and Personality*, *9*(3), 185–211.

Salovich, N. A., & Rapp, D. N. (2021). Misinformed and unaware? Metacognition and the influence of inaccurate information. *Journal of Experimental Psychology: Learning, Memory, and Cognition*, *47*(4), 608.

Sawyer, R. K. (2004). Creative teaching: Collaborative discussion as disciplined improvisation. *Educational Researcher*, *33*(2), 12–20.

Sawyer, R. K. (2011). *Explaining creativity: The science of human innovation*. Oxford University Press.

Sawyer, R. K. (2014). *Group creativity: Music, theater, collaboration*. Psychology Press.

Sawyer, R. K. (2021). The iterative and improvisational nature of the creative process. *Journal of Creativity*, *31*, 100002.

Schleider, J. L., & Weisz, J. R. (2016). Reducing risk for anxiety and depression in adolescents: Effects of a single-session intervention teaching that personality can change. *Behaviour Research and Therapy*, *87*, 170–181.

Schultz P. P., & Ryan, R. M. (2015). The "why," "what," and "how" of healthy self-regulation: Mindfulness and well-being from a self-determination theory perspective. In B. D. Ostafin, M. D. Robinson, & B. P. Meier (Eds.), *Handbook of mindfulness and self-regulation* (pp. 81–94). Springer.

Schuman-Olivier, Z., Trombka, M., Lovas, D. A., Brewer, J. A., Vago, D. R., Gawande, R., Dunn, J. P., Lazar, S. W., Loucks, E. B., & Fulwiler, C. (2020). Mindfulness and behavior change. *Harvard Review of Psychiatry*, *28*(6), 371.

Schurz, M., Radua, J., Tholen, M. G., Maliske, L., Margulies, D. S., Mars, R. B., Sallet, J., & Kanske, P. (2021). Toward a hierarchical model of social cognition: A neuroimaging meta-analysis and integrative review of empathy and theory of mind. *Psychological Bulletin, 147*(3), 293–327. https://doi.org/10.1037/bul0000303

Sedlmeier, P., Eberth, J., Schwarz, M., Zimmermann, D., Haarig, F., Jaeger, S., & Kunze, S. (2012). The psychological effects of meditation: a meta-analysis. *Psychological Bulletin*, *138*(6), 1139.

Seton, M. C. (2010). The ethics of embodiment: Actor training and habitual vulnerability. *Performing Ethos: International Journal of Ethics in Theatre & Performance*, *1*(1), 5–20.

Sheridan, K. M., Veenema, S., Winner, E., & Hetland, L. (2023). *Studio thinking 3: The real benefits of visual arts education*. Teachers College Press.

Sheridan, K. M., Zhang, X., & Konopasky, A. W. (2022). Strategic shifts: How studio teachers use direction and support to build learner agency in the figured world of visual art. *Journal of the Learning Sciences*, *31*(1), 14–42.

Sherman, H. (2016, March). *Lin-Manuel Miranda. Hamilton creator has worked toward this since sixth grade*. https://dramatics.org/lin-manuel-miranda/

Siegler, R. S. (1998). *Emerging minds: The process of change in children's thinking*. Oxford University Press.

Silvia, P. J., Nusbaum, E. C., Berg, C., Martin, C., & O'Connor, A. (2009). Openness to experience, plasticity, and creativity: Exploring lower-order, high-order, and interactive effects. *Journal of Research in Personality*, *43*(6), 1087–1090.

Sloan, C. (2018). Understanding spaces of potentiality in applied theatre. *Research in Drama Education: The Journal of Applied Theatre and Performance*, *23*(4), 582–597.

Smetana, J. G., Campione-Barr, N., & Metzger, A. (2006). Adolescent development in interpersonal and societal contexts. *Annual Review of Psychology*, *57*, 255–284.

Smith, E. D., & Lillard, A. S. (2012). Play on: Retrospective reports of the persistence of pretend play into middle childhood. *Journal of Cognition and Development*, *13*(4), 524–549.

Sokol-Hessner, P., Wing-Davey, M., Illingworth, S., Fleming, S. M., & Phelps, E. A. (2022). The actor's insight: Actors have comparable interoception but better metacognition than nonactors. *Emotion, 22*(7), 1544–1553. doi:10.1037/emo0001080

Somerville, L. H., Jones, R. M., Ruberry, E. J., Dyke, J. P., Glover, G., & Casey, B. J. (2013). The medial prefrontal cortex and the emergence of self-conscious emotion in adolescence. *Psychological Science, 24*(8), 1554–1562.

Spolin, V. (1986). *Theater games for the classroom: A teacher's handbook.* Northwestern University Press.

Spolin, V. (1999). *Improvisation for the theater: A handbook of teaching and directing techniques.* Northwestern University Press.

Stanislavski, C. (1989). *An actor prepares* (E. R. Hapgood, Trans.). Routledge. (Original work published 1950)

Stets, J. E., & Burke, P. J. (2000). Identity theory and social identity theory. *Social Psychology Quarterly*, 63, 224–237.

Stillman, B. C. (2002). Making sense of proprioception: The meaning of proprioception, kinesthesia and related terms. *Physiotherapy*, *88*(11), 667–676.

Stutesman, M. G., Havens, J., & Goldstein, T. R. (2022). Developing creativity and other 21st century skills through theater classes. *Translational Issues in Psychological Science*, *8*(1), 24.

Sue, S. (2003). In defense of cultural competency in psychotherapy and treatment. *American Psychologist*, *58*(11), 964.

Taggart, J., Becker, I., Rauen, J., Al Kallas, H., & Lillard, A. S. (2020). What shall we do: Pretend or real? Preschoolers' choices and parents' perceptions. *Journal of Cognition and Development*, *21*(2), 261–281.

Taggart, J., Heise, M. J., & Lillard, A. S. (2018). The real thing: Preschoolers prefer actual activities to pretend ones. *Developmental Science*, *21*(3), e12582.

Tangney, J. P., Baumeister, R. F., & Boone, A. L. (2004). High self-control predicts good adjustment, less pathology, better grades, and interpersonal success. *Journal of Personality, 72*(2), 271–324.

Telzer, E. H., Dai, J., Capella, J. J., Sobrino, M., & Garrett, S. L. (2022). Challenging stereotypes of teens: Reframing adolescence as window of opportunity. *American Psychologist*, *77*(9), 1067.

Terburg, D., & van Honk, J. (2013). Approach–avoidance versus dominance–submissiveness: A multilevel neural framework on how testosterone promotes social status. *Emotion Review*, *5*(3), 296–302.

Thibodeau-Nielsen, R. B., Gilpin, A. T., Nancarrow, A. F., Pierucci, J. M., & Brown, M. M. (2020). Fantastical pretense's effects on executive function in a diverse sample of preschoolers. *Journal of Applied Developmental Psychology*, *68*, 101137.

Thompson, B. N., & Goldstein, T. R. (2019). Disentangling pretend play measurement: Defining the essential elements and developmental progression of pretense. *Developmental Review*, *52*, 24–41.

Thompson, B. N., & Goldstein, T. R. (2022). Observing the developmental progression of pretend play across the preschool years. *Journal of Cognition and Development*, *23*(4), 482–502.

Thomson, P., & Jaque, S. (2011). Testimonial theatre-making: Establishing or dissociating the self. *Psychology of Aesthetics, Creativity, and the Arts*, *5*(3), 229.

Thomson, P., Keehn, E. B., & Gumpel, T. P. (2009). Generators and interpretors in a performing arts population: Dissociation, trauma, fantasy proneness, and affective states. *Creativity Research Journal*, *21*(1), 72–91.

Trayes, J., Harré, N., & Overall, N. C. (2012). A youth performing arts experience: Psychological experiences, recollections, and the desire to do it again. *Journal of Adolescent Research*, *27*(2), 155–182.

Tymula, A., Rosenberg Belmaker, L. A., Roy, A. K., Ruderman, L., Manson, K., Glimcher, P. W., & Levy, I. (2012). Adolescents' risk-taking behavior is driven by tolerance to ambiguity. *Proceedings of the National Academy of Sciences*, *109*(42), 17135–17140.

Vadeboncoeur, J., & Göncü, A. (2018). Playing and imagining across the life course: A sociocultural perspective. In P. Smith & J. Roopnarine (Eds.), *The Cambridge Handbook of Play: Developmental and Disciplinary Perspectives* (pp. 258–278). Cambridge University Press. doi:10.1017/9781108131384.015

Valente, S., Monteiro, A. P., & Lourenço, A. A. (2019). The relationship between teachers' emotional intelligence and classroom discipline management. *Psychology in the Schools*, *56*(5), 741–750.

Veenman, M. V., & Spaans, M. A. (2005). Relation between intellectual and metacognitive skills: Age and task differences. *Learning and Individual Differences*, *15*(2), 159–176.

Vogel, E. A., Rose, J. P., Okdie, B. M., Eckles, K., & Franz, B. (2015). Who compares and despairs? The effect of social comparison orientation on social media use and its outcomes. *Personality and Individual Differences*, *86*, 249–256.

Warner, S. A., & Myers, K. L. (2009). The creative classroom: The role of space and place toward facilitating creativity. *Technology Teacher*, *69*, 28–34.

Wedel, M., Pieters, R., & van der Lans, R. (2023). Modeling eye movements during decision making: A review. *Psychometrika*, *88*(2), 697–729.

Weil, L. G., Fleming, S. M., Dumontheil, I., Kilford, E. J., Weil, R. S., Rees, G., Dolan, R. J., & Blakemore, S.-J. (2013). The development of metacognitive ability in adolescence. *Consciousness and Cognition*, *22*(1), 264–271.

Weisberg, D. S., & Sobel, D. M. (2022). Imaginative processes in children are not particularly imaginative. *Behavioral & Brain Sciences*, *45*, 1.

Weisberg, D. S., Sobel, D. M., Goodstein, J., & Bloom, P. (2013). Young children are reality-prone when thinking about stories. *Journal of Cognition and Culture*, *13*(3–4), 383–407.

Wellman, H. M. (1978). Knowledge of the interaction of memory variables: A developmental study of metamemory. *Developmental Psychology*, *14*(1), 24.

Werner, N. S., Schweitzer, N., Meindl, T., Duschek, S., Kambeitz, J., & Schandry, R. (2013). Interoceptive awareness moderates neural activity during decision-making. *Biological Psychology*, *94*(3), 498–506.

Wilson, M. (2002). Six views of embodied cognition. *Psychonomic Bulletin & Review*, *9*(4), 625–636.

Winner, E. (2022). *An uneasy guest in the schoolhouse: Art education from colonial times to a promising future*. Oxford University Press.

Winner, E., & Hetland, L. (2000). The arts in education: Evaluating the evidence for a causal link. *Journal of Aesthetic Education*, 3–10.

Winner, E., Goldstein, T. R., & Vincent-Lancrin, S. (2013). *Art for art's sake? The impact of arts education*. Educational Research and Innovation, OECD Publishing.

Woodworth, R. S., & Thorndike, E. L. (1901). The influence of improvement in one mental function upon the efficiency of other functions. (I). *Psychological Review*, *8*(3), 247.

Wright, P. R. (2006). Drama education and development of self: Myth or reality? *Social Psychology of Education*, *9*(1), 43–65. doi:10.1007/s11218-005-4791

Yassa, N. A. (1999). High school involvement in creative drama. *Research in Drama Education*, *4*(1), 37–49.

Yeager, D. S., & Dweck, C. S. (2020). What can be learned from growth mindset controversies? *American Psychologist*, *75*(9), 1269.

Yeager, D. S., Dahl, R. E., & Dweck, C. S. (2018). Why interventions to influence adolescent behavior often fail but could succeed. *Perspectives on Psychological Science*, *13*(1), 101–122.

Yeager, D. S., Lee, H. Y., & Jamieson, J. P. (2016). How to improve adolescent stress responses: Insights from integrating implicit theories of personality and biopsychosocial models. *Psychological Science*, *27*(8), 1078–1091.

Zelazo, P. D. (2006). The Dimensional Change Card Sort (DCCS): A method of assessing executive function in children. *Nature Protocols*, *1*(1), 297–301.

Zelazo, P. D., & Carlson, S. M. (2012). Hot and cool executive function in childhood and adolescence: Development and plasticity. *Child Development Perspectives*, *6*(4), 354–360.

Zinsser, K. M., Denham, S. A., Curby, T. W., & Shewark, E. A. (2015). "Practice what you preach": Teachers' perceptions of emotional competence and emotionally supportive classroom practices. *Early Education and Development*, *26*(7), 899–919.

Names Index

Subjects Index

About the Author

Thalia R. Goldstein is a former professional actress, dancer, and lifelong theatre nerd. She is currently an associate professor and director of the Applied Developmental Psychology program in the Department of Psychology at George Mason University, where she directs the Play, Learning, Arts, and Youth Lab (PLAYlab), and codirects the National Endowment for the Arts Lab, the Mason Arts Research Center (MasonARC). Her work has been funded by the National Science Foundation, The John Templeton Foundation, Arts Connection, the National Endowment for the Arts, and the American Psychological Foundation among others. With her students and colleagues, she has published more than 70 academic papers on the effects of pretend play, imagination, theatre, and other art forms (dance, marching arts, video games, literature) on child and adolescent development. She earned her BA at Cornell University, her MA and PhD at Boston College, and completed a postdoctoral fellowship at Yale University. Since 2017 she has been the coeditor of the journal *Psychology of Aesthetics, Creativity, and the Arts,* the Division 10 journal for the American Psychological Association, where she has also won several awards and was recently named fellow. She lives outside Washington, DC with her family.

